SIMPLY MICK

ALSO BY ROBIN MCGIBBON AND ROB MCGIBBON:

New Kids on the Block

Gazza!

Phillip Schofield

SIMPLY MICK

MICK HUCKNALL OF SIMPLY RED

THE INSIDE STORY

Robin McGibbon
and Rob McGibbon

WEIDENFELD & NICOLSON · LONDON

To Katrina, Alison and Jayne

ILLUSTRATIONS

Between pp 54 and 55 (all from private collections)
Mick, aged three-and-a-half, pretending to be a pop star
Mick and Billy Grimshaw at Santa's grotto in Manchester in 1964
Mick, aged four, with childhood friend Billy Grimshaw
Mick at a young friend's birthday party
Mick, aged five, at St Lawrence's Primary School in Denton
Mick, aged six, at St Lawrence's Primary School
Mick, aged seven, at St Lawrence's Primary School
Reg and Mick, aged eight, with his pet rabbit
Mick's mother Maureen in 1967 with her two children, Lyndsay and
    Ricky
The West Park Avenue gang on Mick's eleventh birthday
Mick on holiday visiting relatives in Barrow-in-Furness
Mick aged thirteen at Audenshaw Grammar
Mick aged fifteen at Audenshaw Grammar
Mick aged sixteen as a waiter at the Broomstair Working Men's Club
Mick's mother Maureen in the 1980s

Between pp 86 and 87 (all photographs by Richard Watt)
Mick at the Palm Grove Club in Bradford in 1978
The Elevators at the Palm Grove in Bradford in 1978
The Frantic Elevators
Mick in his studio at the Polytechnic's art centre
Mick in the Poly art class of 1981
Mick with Brian Turner in Clynes Wine Bar
Mick and Kevin Williams at Adams Club, Liverpool
The Frantic Elevators at Adams Club, Liverpool
Mick and Moey at a UMIST gig
Mick performing with The Frantic Elevators at the Band on the Wall
The studio where Mick recorded 'Holding Back The Years' for the first
    time in 1982
Rehearsing in Brian Turner's flat

Mick with Brian Turner and another friend
Mick and Mog at Simply Red's first gig at the Poly in 1984
An early Simply Red gig

*Between pp 182 and 183 (all photographs by Richard Watt unless otherwise
    stated)*
The first Simply Red line-up
Simply Red posing as pop stars
Mick with guitarist Dave Fryman
Mick and Dave Fryman at one of the first Simply Red gigs in 1984
The Simply Red line-up soon after the release of *Men and Women* in
    1987 (All Action Pictures/D Raban)
Mick performing for the audience (All Action Pictures)
Mick with a friend's baby
Mick with his surrogate mum, June Shaw, and her daughter, Gaynor
Mick backstage in 1987
Dee, the beautiful Texan model who inspired *A New Flame*
Mick's house near Old Trafford in Manchester
Mick changing backstage on tour in 1987
Aziz Ibrahim and Sylvan Richardson
Mick on the *Stars* world tour in 1992 (All Action Pictures/Justin Thomas)

ACKNOWLEDGEMENTS

The response we received researching this book was overwhelming: hundreds of people gave us their time to talk about Mick, search for photographs, or simply think about who could provide additional information. It would be wonderful to mention everyone by name, but sadly that is impossible.

We would like to say a big thank you to everyone who gave an interview and is quoted in the book, and to many others who are not, but whose memories provided vital background material. Special thanks must go to those people who provided crucial information but who asked not to be named.

Certain people, however, do deserve a mention. In no particular order they are: Florence Gibbons and Imre Kozarits for their candour in reliving painful memories; Gary and Gaynor Shaw for always responding so well; Frank Ollerenshaw and Gary Hulston for their trust; their former headmaster, Ken Exley, and his colleagues for their memories; Julie Garcia for that early help; Steven Howarth, Paul Sutcliffe and Harry Bradbury for their humour; Ian Moss, Pete Dervin, Steve Tansley and Mark Reeder for their patience when we were going Frantic; and Dave Fryman, Mog, Sylvan and Aziz for their honesty.

Thanks also to: Oldham Chronicle journalist Paul Genty for turning detective; Terry Neilan for help in New York; Declan Allen at the National Discography; Christine Morey for helping so willingly, like a true fan; and, very sincerely, to Reg for always being so courteous in awkward circumstances.

On the personal side, thanks as ever to Micky Moynihan for still being there; to John and Vicky Scotchmer for the name-check; to Vanessa Perry for her support and helpful comments; also to Allegra and Elizabeth at Weidenfeld for their enthusiasm and invaluable help.

Above all, thanks to Sue, who suggested the book and worked tirelessly, at all hours, to try to meet the deadline.

PROLOGUE

Beneath the flaming red hair, her sparkling green eyes brightened a face of exquisite Irish beauty. But it was not the girl's face Reg Hucknall noticed first in the centre of Manchester that warm July evening; it was her legs, long and shapely under the hula-hoop skirt. The hula-hoop craze had Britain in a spin that long, hot summer of 1959, and the fashion for narrow-waisted, full skirts and stiff petticoats suited teenage girls with slim ankles and curvaceous calves. The tall girl walking towards him on stiletto heels was blessed with both, and Reg could not take his eyes off them. He had never been what he would call a 'leg man'; he preferred sensuous curves elsewhere. But he was impressed by the lovely legs heading towards him and, as the girl got nearer, he decided to tell her so. Complimenting a girl on her legs was hardly an original chat-up line. But the girl was young and flirtatious and, although aware of the impact her looks and stunning figure had on the opposite sex, she was susceptible to flattery, particularly from an older man. She agreed to have a drink with Reg in one of the city's bustling pubs.

The 24-year-old ginger-haired barber could not believe his luck. The landlady of his rented room in nearby Denton had gone on holiday to Spain with her two daughters, leaving him at a loose end, and he had gone into the city centre in search of company. To pick up such a stunner was more than he could have wished for.

They got on well. The girl liked Reg's direct, down-to-earth manner and sense of humour. And when he asked to see her again, she willingly said yes. On the bus back to Denton, Reg sat upstairs smoking a cigarette, feeling pleased with himself. He had struck lucky and made the most of it. The girl had been good fun. She was beautiful and clever and seemed to know what she wanted out of life. And she was sexy, too. Originally from Barrow-in-Furness, Reg had come to Manchester in 1957 after four years in the RAF, and had started work as a barber in Stockport. Since his arrival he had not made that many friends; maybe the girl would change his life for the better, he thought.

If Reg had been able to look into the future, however, he would have seen that the casual meeting he had enjoyed so much was the beginning of a relationship that, once the passion cooled, would bring nothing but heartache and misery.

If, in the ensuing months, the girl's parents had any idea that she was falling in love with an older man, they were powerless to do anything about it: they lived about twenty miles away, and rarely had anything but telephone contact with their daughter.

And anyway, Maureen Gibbons, even at eighteen, was a fiery, single-minded, headstrong young lady, who always did what suited her, not anyone else.

1

Maureen was a war baby, born on 9 January 1941, and was brought up in a village near Warrington in Lancashire called Penketh, nicknamed Little America because it was next to a US Air Force base. Her father, Michael, was an easy-going, unambitious Irish mechanic, but her mother, Florence, was a dominant, forceful personality with an iron will and fierce determination to get what she wanted out of life. She brought up Maureen and her four other daughters to be as strong and independent as she was, and to feel free to do as they pleased, when they pleased.

At fifteen Maureen abused that encouragement. She would go out in the evenings and deliberately disobey her parents' orders to be home at a certain time. Her despairing father would lock her out to teach her a lesson, but Florence would lie awake until she heard Maureen at the door, then sneak downstairs to let her in. The girl was, as her mother freely admits today, a 'terror, unable to be controlled'.

At sixteen, Maureen got a job with a firm of solicitors in Warrington and a few months later came home with a self-satisfied look. 'I have been talking to my boss,' she told her mother snootily, 'and he says that now I am sixteen, I can leave home if I want.'

About a year later she did leave. She went to Manchester and got herself another secretarial job, persuading an uncle to let her share his home just outside the city centre. Like her father, Maureen had no career ambitions, but she wanted the good things in life and knew she wouldn't find them in Warrington. She was only seventeen, but there was nothing her parents could do: Maureen was doing as she pleased – just as she had been taught.

Then, the following July, she met Reg Hucknall. As Britain basked in the unexpected warmth of an Indian summer, their relationship deepened, and she moved out of her uncle's home into her own rented flat. She and Reg started sleeping together, and two months later Maureen's fears were realized: she was pregnant.

There was no question of not having the baby and on 28 October 1960, just two months before Maureen's nineteenth birthday, the couple were married at Aspinal Methodist Church, Reddish. The bride wore white, but it was a quiet affair, followed by a modest and inexpensive reception in a nearby pub. Reg felt it unnecessary to invite members of the large Hucknall family to make the 100-mile trip from Barrow-in-Furness; and he settled for Brian Kennedy, a hairdressing colleague, to be best man.

Seven months later, on 8 June, Maureen gave birth to a chubby baby boy, with bright red hair like both his parents, in Manchester's St Mary's Hospital. Reg got on well with Maureen's father, Michael, and she was delighted when Reg suggested naming the baby after him. Choosing the middle name, James, after Reg's own father, the proud parents registered the baby at Denton Register office on 1 July.

*

The young Hucknalls' first home was the top half of a detached house, owned by a couple named Beezer, in the village of Bredbury, five miles from Denton. It was awful. The newly-weds had just a small lounge, an even smaller bedroom and a tiny box-room that served as a kitchen. But there was no plumbing in the box-room and they had to do their washing-up in the communal bathroom. What made matters worse was that the Beezers refused to allow Maureen to dry washing in the back garden, and she had to ask a young next-door neighbour, Joy Truett, if she could hang it in hers.

Joy lived up to her name as far as Maureen was concerned, particularly when the hyperactive Michael refused to go to sleep. In desperation, Maureen would carry him to the Truetts' front door and plead for help. Joy was heavily pregnant and put Michael on her swollen tummy. To her amazement, he cuddled up and dropped off to sleep within seconds.

'It was most peculiar, the first time it happened, and we never really understood it, but it was a great relief for Maureen,' Joy recalls today. 'After that she would pop in regularly, sometimes two or three times a week, at any time of the day or evening, whenever she had difficulty getting Michael to sleep. Once he was sound asleep, we would sit and have a chat over coffee and get to know each other.

'I felt desperately sorry for her and Reg, because the Beezers were an awkward couple and not the easiest people to live with. The husband used to repair vehicles and the driveway was always cluttered with spare parts. That, and the constant banging, got on our nerves. Goodness knows what it must have been like living in the same house. I know that if it had been me, I would have fought tooth and nail for somewhere else.'

4

Maureen, particularly, wanted a home of their own. Like her mother, she was a home-maker and was prepared to make sacrifices to get what she wanted. Being just nineteen, she naturally missed working and not being able to afford to go out in the evening, but she rarely complained, and seemed as keen as Reg to save what money they could to put down on a house.

Little Michael did not suffer in those tough, scrimp-and-save days. He was always beautifully dressed, either in smart woolly jumpers Maureen had knitted, or new clothes she had bought. 'Maureen didn't spoil Michael, but he had everything they could afford,' Joy Truett says. 'She was a friendly, down-to-earth person and a doting mother, who idolized her baby.'

Maureen could remember sitting – as a child herself – round the fire with her sisters on winter evenings, singing nursery rhymes at the tops of their voices. Maureen sang them so much that she knew all the words, even at the age of two. Now, in that shared house in Bredbury, waiting for Reg to come home from work, she would sing to baby Michael, and one of the popular songs of the day suited him perfectly: 'Michael Row The Boat Ashore'. That September – 1961 – Lonnie Donegan had taken the song into the Top Ten, and the chubby, red-haired toddler, who had heard his mother sing it to him so many times, seemed to be picking up the words.

By early 1962 Reg and Maureen had saved enough for a deposit on a house, and they found one they could just about afford. It was a small but smart semi-detached in West Park Avenue, a narrow cul-de-sac of about seventy houses, on a sprawling development of council and privately-owned properties back in Denton.

For someone barely twenty-one, Maureen showed surprisingly mature and good taste, and she quickly transformed that house into a home she and Reg were proud of. A side entrance opened on to the kitchen, and a front sitting room, about sixteen feet square, looked out on to a tiny garden. At the back, a coal bunker in a thirty-foot garden separated them from the adjoining semi, owned by Bernard and June Shaw and their three-year-old son, Gary, and newborn daughter, Gaynor. And when her seventeen-year-old sister, Marlene, started work in Manchester, Maureen was quick to suggest she moved in with them to save her the arduous, early-morning rush-hour crawl from Warrington. The house was nowhere near large enough for three adults and a growing baby, but it did not worry Maureen: she saw her sister as much-needed company for her, particularly on the evenings Reg went greyhound racing at Belle Vue Stadium.

Whether it was jealousy at seeing Marlene getting made up and trotting off to work every morning is not clear but, overnight it seemed, Maureen became restless and moody. Suddenly that summer the house was not enough for her; nor was her baby. She didn't want to be a housewife. She didn't want to be stuck at home all day, pottering around in the garden or chatting to neighbours she barely knew. She was young and happy-go-lucky and she wanted to be with young and happy-go-lucky people. She wanted to go back to work.

Reg did not like the idea. A mother's place was in the home, he felt. And when Maureen argued that they needed extra money, he reminded her that, with tips and commission, he was earning nearly £30 a week from hairdressing – enough to feed them all and his gambling habit. In any event, he pointed out, there would not be much left out of Maureen's wages after she had paid a nursery to care for Michael and forked out fares to and from work, not to mention lunch.

Nothing Reg could say, however, made any difference. Maureen's mind was made up, and it was not in her character to change it. She was going to do as she pleased. And that meant getting a bit more out of life than just sitting in a suburban backstreet, miles from the bustling excitement of the city centre.

It seems the thought of getting something part-time locally never occurred to Maureen. She was determined to get a full-time job – in the middle of Manchester, not dreary Denton – and she got one within a couple of weeks. It was only a typing job, with a salary less than a quarter of Reg's, but Maureen was overjoyed, and happily arranged for a woman living nearby to take Michael to and from the Russell Scott Nursery in Denton and to look after him until she got home in the evening.

The woman was Nellie Spike, who lived with her husband, Alfred, and four daughters in Manor Close, a cul-de-sac on the other side of Mill Lane, less than 400 yards from West Park Avenue. Nellie liked the look of Michael the first time she saw him and she was delighted to have the chance to look after him. He would be like the son she never had.

If Maureen had been happy enough to stay at home and accept her role as a mother, it is possible, if unlikely, that she and Reg would have stayed together; certainly, before she got itchy feet, the relationship was sound enough for them to consider having another child. But, at twenty-one, Maureen was basically a fun-loving girl, who revelled in compliments about her good looks and figure and who felt she was missing out through having married so young.

'She was a girl who wanted to do everything,' Reg recalls today. 'She wanted this, she wanted that – she was never satisfied.'

Even Maureen's mother, Florence, agrees on that point. 'It was her who laid the law down. We want this, we want that, we'll do this, we'll do that.'

Maureen wanted excitement in her life, and could not resist the temptation to be unfaithful. She secretly started seeing another man, but one night made the mistake of letting him drive her home.

If Reg had not run out of cigarettes that night, she might have got away with her infidelity. As it was, Reg decided to pop round the corner to a cigarette machine in Mill Lane, and found himself staring at his wife in a car with a man he had never seen before. Maureen obviously said something like, 'Oh, God, that's my husband,' because the driver accelerated away fast. In a stormy confrontation with her husband later, Maureen swore it was not her in the car. But Reg was in no doubt and there was a blazing row.

After that, the relationship went from bad to worse until, shortly before Michael's second birthday in June, Maureen could stand it no longer. She waited until Reg had left for Stockport one morning, then went out and phoned her mother at a sweet shop in Warrington, where she worked as a sales assistant.

'I'm leaving Reg,' Maureen said, without preamble.

Florence, who had no idea the marriage was troubled, was furious: she had always taught Maureen that if she did wrong she would pay for it. 'You will do nothing of the kind,' she fumed. 'No way do you leave that house and your baby. Get back there and stick it out.'

But Maureen had never been one to take anybody's advice – even her mother's. She was fed up with marriage and with Reg, and had made up her mind that she did not want any more of either. She had found a rented room in Manchester Road, at the other end of Denton, and happily moved in there, taking two-year-old Michael with her.

She was leaving behind a house into which she had poured an enormous amount of effort, but it did not bother her. The grass looked greener on the other side. And she wanted to lie on it.

*

For the next six months Maureen lived her own life, working during the day and enjoying herself as much as she could in the evenings. The only time Reg saw his son was on Friday evenings when he called at Maureen's rented room to give her money. He supported her from the moment she walked out, giving her more than he was obliged to legally. But he reduced the allowance when he discovered that Maureen was spending a lot of what he gave her on babysitters – one as young as thirteen – so that she could go out on the town.

Two weeks before Christmas that year, Maureen's sister Marlene went to the nursery to pick up Michael and look after him until Maureen got home from work.

Marlene got a shock. The little boy was in a terrible state: he was coughing from a chest problem and looked like an orphan, in grubby old trousers which had a hole in them. Horrified, Marlene could not bring herself to take him to her sister's flat; he needed medical care, clean clothes and a good bath, and there was only one person she could think of who could provide all three: her mother, who was living in the village of Croft, five miles from Warrington.

Florence Gibbons was equally distressed at Michael's condition. And although she had to work from 2 p.m. until 8 p.m., she agreed that the boy was in no state to go home to a mother who was working all day.

Florence quickly got organized: she put Michael straight to bed, then went to a chemist for medicine for his chest; she arranged for her youngest daughter, Elaine, to stay home from school to look after him in the afternoons; then she told Marlene to ask Reg for money to buy Michael new clothes.

Marlene reported back that Reg said he could not spare any money, so Florence went on a shopping spree in Marks & Spencers in Warrington with her own money. She bought Michael a whole set of new clothes – vests, pants, socks, shoes and a little blue waterproof winter suit, just like the one she had bought him as a baby. And she bought some Enid Blyton books which she would read to him. With no word from Maureen, and Reg not showing a great interest, Florence had no idea how long she would have the child. Certainly he would stay for Christmas. But what would happen afterwards?

Christmas arrived. Reg went to Barrow-in-Furness to spend the holiday with his relatives. Maureen went missing. Florence had a full house, and everyone made a fuss over Michael. If he noticed his parents were not around, he did not show it. He never mentioned them once.

Today, Florence recalls that Christmas fondly, if with a tinge of sadness. 'Michael was a fat, bonny little boy, with chubby arms and a mass of red curls, and was as happy as a little lamb. I'm sure he understood that his mummy and daddy were unhappy together – children do when they're intelligent, and Michael was a very intelligent boy. But we spoiled him rotten. We all felt sorry for him, particularly as he had been so unwell.

'He was such a gentle and beautiful child, you couldn't be cross with him. I remember putting a huge pile of hot mince pies on the kitchen table and Michael picking one up when he thought I wasn't looking. "Michael," I said, "that will burn you." But he just looked at me, with a cheeky grin, and shook his head, sternly. "Not hot, Grandma, not hot," he said, and proceeded to eat it. He was so cute and adorable.

'That Christmas, we all saw his musical talent. He had a little black and white banjo and would sing the song Maureen taught him – "Michael Row The Boat Ashore" – and "All Things Bright and Beautiful".

'I had no idea where Maureen was, but I knew that Marlene would have told her that Michael was in safe hands. Although she did not have the nerve to ring me because of the roasting I'd have given her, Maureen would have been happy for Michael to be with us, not with Reg. So I knew I was doing the right thing.'

Michael was contented at his grandmother's house, but it was not the right place for him in the long term, and Florence knew it. A week or so after Christmas, she decided it was best that he should be with one of his parents. There had still been no word from Maureen, and if Marlene knew where she was, she was not telling. So, the first Sunday in January 1963, Florence and her husband, Michael, put the little boy in their tiny Flying Standard car and drove to Denton to hand him back to Reg. First, though, they stopped at Maureen's rented room to pick up a canary they knew she had bought for Michael. The middle-aged couple who rented Maureen the room did not want Florence to take the bird, named Pepe, but she insisted because it meant so much to Michael.

Reg opened the door of 30 West Park Avenue, somewhat surprised to see his in-laws standing there with his son.

Walking in, Florence said, 'I'm bringing Michael back. He is staying here.'

According to Florence today, Reg replied, 'Why? He was all right with Maureen.'

'No, he wasn't,' Florence said. 'He's been ill. And I had to buy him a set of new clothes.'

'He had plenty of clothes.'

'Look here,' said Florence, 'that child didn't ask to be born. This is his home. Maureen helped you get this place. Michael isn't going back in digs. He's staying here.'

She looked at the child, sitting on the floor in the lounge, singing and playing happily and calling out to his daddy and she knew she was right. Evidently Reg thought so too, because shortly afterwards Florence and her husband drove home to Warrington, leaving Michael with him.

In the early 1960s, it was very rare for a man to be on his own with a child, and the responsibility worried Reg so much, he lost twenty-eight pounds in weight. But helped by Nellie and her family, he coped wonderfully. Unlike Maureen, he resisted the temptation to go out in the evenings, preferring to stay in and care for his child. Soon, they were safely settled in a happy routine, with Michael rarely mentioning his mother and Reg putting weight back on as his worries eased. It was the beginning of a father-and-son relationship that not only formed the basis of a happy childhood for Michael but gave him a sense of values that would determine the course his life would take.

It was also the start of his abbreviated name. Outside the house, he was still Michael; inside, to his dad, he was Mick.

For Florence, it was a relief that Michael was with his father. 'I was fairly easy in my mind,' she recalls. 'Reg knew deep down that it was right and proper for him to have the child. There was no way I was taking Michael back to Maureen, even if I had known where to find her. He had been in a terrible state and I knew he would get that way again. With Maureen working, he would be spending a lot of time with strangers and he would quickly have started fretting.'

That worrying, emotionally disturbing Christmas took its toll on Florence and she was ill herself for most of the next two weeks. She thought about her grandson constantly and, almost as soon as she had recovered, she told her husband: 'We must go over to Reg's to see Michael.'

On the third Saturday in January she bought some toys from Woolworth's in Warrington, and the next day set off in the ancient Austin for Denton. Her excitement at seeing Michael faded the moment she saw Reg's angry face.

'Michael's been in hospital, crying for you, and you never went,' he accused.

'What are you talking about?' Florence wanted to know.

'You *knew* he had to go into hospital,' Reg said.

'What do you mean, I *knew*? Who was to tell me? *You* didn't tell me, and I haven't spoken to Maureen since she left you.'

Michael had gone into hospital for an operation for a rupture in his groin, but to this day Florence insists she knew nothing about him having an operation. She was aware of the problem, but had no idea he had a hospital appointment. If she had known, she would have made sure she visited him, despite being unwell herself.

She says: 'Reg was in contact with Maureen and must have known for some time that Michael had to go into hospital early in January, but we never heard a word from him that Christmas – about Michael or anything. I'm sure Michael did cry for me in hospital, because we were very attached. But I'm equally sure Reg let him cry, so that he could come back and accuse me of ignoring him.'

The tense relationship between Reg and his mother-in-law now developed into something of a cold war, with both merely tolerating each other for the sake of the motherless child. Every Sunday for the next few weeks the old Standard would trundle up West Park Avenue and Florence and her husband would knock on the door, armed with little gifts for their grandson. Unwelcoming, Reg would greet them: 'You always seem to catch me in.'

★

And then, as spring began to brighten Denton's streets, the missing mother emerged from the mists and came into everyone's lives again.

She contacted Reg, saying she wanted to see Michael, and the following Sunday took the boy to her parents in Croft. During the months she had not heard from Maureen, Florence had been wound up, ready to give her daughter a roasting for her selfish, wayward behaviour. But when Maureen walked through the front door that Sunday afternoon, Florence greeted her warmly. She did not ask questions. And Maureen did not volunteer any information.

'I didn't judge, because I felt no one – not one person – was in a position to judge another,' Florence says today. 'If Maureen had wanted to tell me anything, she would have done. I didn't go on the attack. And she wasn't defensive. I just made her welcome and we both made a fuss of Michael.'

With relations with Maureen better, her parents did not feel the need to drive to West Park Avenue to see Michael; most Sundays, Maureen would pick him up and take him to them in Croft. Despite the emotional trauma of seeing his mother for relatively short periods before waving goodbye to her, Michael seemed happy and healthy enough. But, suddenly, he started getting chesty again; one Sunday, when Maureen stayed with her parents overnight, he coughed incessantly. Florence was worried. And when he had not improved the following weekend, she told her husband: 'This can't go on. We're going to have Michael here.' The next day she handed in her notice at the sweet shop so that she could devote all her time to caring for the child.

Evidently, Maureen was relieved. And when Florence and her husband arrived at West Park Avenue to tell Reg what was happening, he seemed to agree it was best if Michael lived with them. But something odd happened that Sunday afternoon which changed everything; it was a conversation Florence and her husband did not hear that drove the little boy they adored out of their lives for ever.

For Florence, the memory of that sad afternoon is as vivid today as it was then.

'We took Michael back to Denton to collect his clothes and toys,' she said. 'He was thrilled to be coming to live with us. Reg was quite pleased too, and started packing Michael's things. A few minutes later, when he'd got everything together and we were about to leave, Reg suddenly said, "Wait a minute. I'd better take him to Nellie's to say goodbye."

'He took Michael to Nell's home, leaving us in the house. We waited for what seemed ages and I began to sense something was wrong. After about half an hour we saw Reg coming up the road, carrying Michael. We went to the gate to meet them. Michael was crying, really breaking his heart. We all stood at the gate, Michael sobbing his heart out, saying, "Daddy, I can't leave you on your own . . . I can't leave you, Daddy."

'It was a dreadful scene, so upsetting for everyone. I just took hold of Michael's hand and said, "It's all right, Michael love, you stay with your daddy." Then I turned to my husband and said, "Come on, let's go. We can't take the child. We can't do it." I couldn't bear to see Michael pulled apart like that.

'We got in our car and, as we drove off, I said to my husband, "You know this will have to be a totally clean break." And I meant it.'

Two days later, says Florence, she received a letter from Nellie Spike telling her to leave Michael alone, because all she ever did was cause trouble and upset him. The letter, which also attacked her for being a bad mother, shook Florence.

'I was angry and upset,' she says. 'When I told Maureen, she blew her top.

'At the back of my mind, I think Reg and Maureen would have stayed together if Nell had not offered to look after Michael. It was Maureen's work that caused the problems, but she wouldn't have been able to work without Nell's help. And it was in her interest to help because she wanted Michael. I never did find out the truth behind that terrible letter, but I'm sure Reg gave her my address; I'd never met her and she had no idea where I lived. And all the time little Michael was breaking his heart at the front gate that dreadful Sunday afternoon, Reg was standing there, smirking, not saying a word. Something was said at Nell's, that's for certain.'

Having rejected Florence's offer to take Michael off his hands, Reg needed to get his life – and his son's – in order. Firstly, he asked Marlene to leave the house in West Park Avenue; he didn't fancy her in the least, but he did not want the neighbours thinking he had found a new bedmate now that his wife had gone. Secondly, he answered an ad in the local paper for a housekeeper.

And thirdly, he destroyed all photographs of himself with Maureen and flushed his wedding ring down the toilet.

He was bitter about the way things had turned out. But he was determined to make a fresh start and cope as well as he could with the responsibilities of bringing up a child on his own.

The housekeeper helped. She was an unmarried Cockney girl in her late teens named Beryl, who had a year-old baby. And she was gorgeous.

Reg smiles at the memory of her stunning, sexy figure. 'Word got back to Maureen's parents and they thought I was a right git,' he says. 'They thought I hadn't taken long to get myself fixed up. When I went out, all the neighbours would walk past with their noses in the air. They believed something was going on. But it wasn't.'

Beryl and her baby – whom Reg remembers as Marcus – brought pleasure into what had been an unhappy household filled with tension and bitterness. But, sadly, it lasted just three months: Beryl handed in her notice, saying she had to go back to London to be with her child's father. Reg was disappointed, not only for himself, but for Michael too. 'We were a nice, happy little family,' he says. 'Michael adored Beryl's baby and it was a great shame that it all came to a sudden stop.'

★

Having to spend nearly eleven hours away from home meant that Reg now needed someone else to take care of Michael while he was at work. To his relief, Nellie said she was happy to continue taking Michael to nursery school and would look after him until Reg got home in the evening.

For little Michael the arrangement was a happy one that would not only provide him with the feminine love and attention he lacked, but also shape his destiny.

For Florence Gibbons, however, the grandson she adored was, heart-breakingly, gone for ever. All she would have to remember his bonny nature by was a photograph of him that Christmas, which she hung on her living room wall – a picture that would gradually fade and remind her of all the missing years and what might have been.

2

The summer of 1963 was a musical milestone. The revolutionary Mersey Beat burst out of Liverpool, sweeping youngsters all over Britain along on a relentless wave of mass hysteria that spawned Beatlemania. The new sound shaped world music – and Michael's future. For at Nellie and Alf Spike's home in Manor Close, he was engulfed by four fun-loving, pop-crazy daughters, who exposed him every day to the energy, passion and joy that music can generate. In the week of Michael's third birthday on 8 June, there were four Northern bands high in the charts – The Beatles, Gerry And The Pacemakers, Billy J. Kramer And The Dakotas, and Freddie And The Dreamers. The Spike girls sang along to their and other hits, all the day and into the evenings, and took great delight in teaching Michael the lyrics. For such a young child, he was surprisingly bright in remembering all the words, but it was not just this that impressed the girls – it was Michael's voice. It was so sweet, so tuneful. The more the girls praised him and encouraged him to sing, the more Michael responded, showing no signs of shyness whatsoever. He had been taken from the quietness of his home in West Park Avenue into a house of non-stop sound and the good humour of a normal family, and he basked in the warmth of the attention lavished on him.

Nellie's sister, Margaret Kenyon, recalls: 'The girls looked on him as a little brother and they and their friends always made a fuss of him. He was very polite and well-mannered and forever on the go, tapping his feet to the music and humming. He was in his own little world.'

Next-door neighbour Jack Taylor remembers Michael well. 'Nellie loved him like he was her own child. She had always wanted a son, so she was delighted to look after Michael. Anyone who didn't know the background would have thought Michael *was* her little boy. She and two of her girls even had red hair, which made Michael look all the more like one of the family.'

If Nellie was busy, her eldest daughter would play mum to Michael, doting on him and taking him everywhere. When she got married and moved away, another daughter would step in and fuss over the child, so that he always had a caring mother figure.

Michael's third birthday that year fell on a Saturday. With Reg having his busiest day of the week at work, Nellie decided to throw a party for Michael. He received several presents, but the one he cherished most was a plastic guitar Nellie bought in Woolworth's. Like her four daughters, Michael adored The Beatles, and when he watched them on television singing their Number 1 hit, 'From Me To You', he strummed along and sang. He took that toy guitar everywhere – even to The Gardener's Arms, a pub on Stockport Road run by one of Nellie's friends, May Hammond. It was here that Michael gave his first public 'performance'.

May would sit him on the bar and he would entertain them and the regulars with songs Nellie's daughters had taught him. 'He sat there like a true professional, singing and strumming away,' says May's daughter, Freda. 'He knew all the words of all the current hits and wasn't in the least shy. Everyone thought he was amazing.'

★

In July Reg took Michael 100 miles further north to show him off for the first time to the Hucknall side of the family in Barrow-in-Furness, near the Lake District.

One of eleven children, Reg had been born on Friday 6 December 1935, at Reynolds Place on the Devonshire Road council estate, high above the town. He was one of twins, but, sadly, his brother Ronald died just four days after they were born.

The four years before the Second World War broke out were difficult for Reg's parents, but not nearly so tough as the twenty that followed the First World War. Six of Reg's brothers and sisters were brought up in a grim, poverty-stricken tenement block on Walney Island, where money was so tight that the eldest boy, Jack, had to put his pay packet on the table, unopened, until his twenty-sixth birthday. Today, aged eighty-three, he remembers standing in the cold, begging for food from workers streaming from the Vickers shipyard and across the bridge over the River Yarl.

Reg took Michael to see his brother George and his wife Barbara at their house in Salthouse Road, which they had bought the previous year. George and Barbara had eight children and, like the Spike girls, they made a fuss over Michael. Over the next sixteen years, the three-storey terraced house, a short walk from the docks, would be where Michael went for his summer holidays.

Michael's mother, Maureen, had been to the house too; Reg had taken her there shortly before they were married. Brenda, the eldest of

Michael's cousins, who was thirteen at the time, remembers her looking like an elegant model.

'She was very tall and slender and she had incredibly long nails,' Brenda recalls. 'She was very well dressed and looked as though she was well off. She gave the impression of a career woman who loved herself and wanted to go places. Although she did stick out a bit in the family, she didn't look down her nose. She seemed all right. I saw her only the once. After she and Reg were married, she never came here again.'

*

After leaving Reg, Maureen revelled in her freedom. During that summer of 1963 she started a new job and moved with Marlene to Whalley Range, a fashionable area of flats and bed-sits, popular with young people, nearer the city centre.

They rented the top flat in a three-storey house, and when a dashing Austrian engineer named Imre Kozarits came to the house, inquiring about the middle-floor flat, Maureen fell for him immediately. The landlord was not available, so Maureen showed Imre round. He was sixteen years older, but she fancied him on sight. And when he refused to rent the flat – because he was a night-worker and the people on the first floor were too noisy – Maureen said she would arrange for them to leave. She did, and Imre, a placid and easily persuaded man, moved in.

Imre got chatting to Maureen while decorating his flat and, after a few days, invited her out to dinner. A week later, she asked him to make up a foursome with her.

'She was pleasant company,' Imre recalls, 'but I was convinced she was going out with someone else and wasn't really interested in pursuing the relationship. Maureen said she was behind with the rent, so I paid it for two or three weeks. We went out a few more times, but then a friend of mine suggested emigrating to Canada with him and I decided to go.

'A day or two later, I came home to find Maureen crying. I comforted her, because I felt sorry for her. The next day, she told me she'd found another flat and asked me to move in with her. I was surprised because we'd been out only a few times and certainly weren't lovers. Anyway, I was going to Canada.

'For some reason I agreed to see the flat. Before I'd said yes or no, Maureen told me she had already informed the landlord of our current homes that we were moving out. Being a soft touch, I forgot about going to Canada and moved in with her. It was the worst decision of my life.'

*

16

For a night-worker, the flat Maureen chose in Keppel Road, Chorlton was hardly ideal; two doors down, three teenage brothers, named Gibb – later to become The Bee Gees – felt they had a future in the music industry and practised loudly day and night. If Imre felt peeved by that, it was nothing compared to how he felt four weeks after he and Maureen moved in.

One evening, she calmly announced that not only was she married, but she had a son too.

Imre was dumbfounded. And angry. He told her he would never have moved in with her if he had known, and he advised her to go home and try to make the marriage work, if only for the child's sake. But Maureen said she would never go back. The marriage was dead, she said. And she refused to discuss it.

'I didn't ask too many questions, or argue with her, because Maureen had a terrible temper and would go crazy over the least little thing,' Imre says today. 'I could never reason with her. But I was very, very unhappy, because I felt I might be breaking up her marriage.'

Imre dwelt on the problem for a couple of weeks, then decided he had to leave – for everyone's sake. When he broke the news to Maureen, she burst into tears and told him he couldn't go.

'Why can't I?' Imre asked.

'Because I'm pregnant,' Maureen said.

A caring, honourable man of principle, Imre decided immediately to stay with Maureen. Months later, he would discover that the supposed pregnancy was a callous lie, invented only to stop him leaving.

*

While his mother's topsy-turvy love life bounced along unpredictably, little Michael was in a settled routine that kept him, his father and the woman he now called Auntie Nellie very happy. Every morning at 8 a.m. Reg would wheel Michael in his pushchair along Moorfield Avenue, across Mill Lane and up Manor Close to Nellie's home, before catching a bus to Stockport. At 9 a.m. either Nellie or one of her daughters would take Michael by bus to the nursery, where he would stay until 3.30 p.m.

The adorable little boy with the chubby face and red curly hair, neatly cut by his father, quickly became a favourite at the nursery. He was always well dressed. He was polite. He was amusingly mischievous. And he was blessed with a precocious talent that quickly became a talking point among the nursery staff.

They discovered it when one of the trainee nurses made a little wooden guitar. There were dozens of other toys available, but Michael went straight for that eighteen-inch long green guitar in the music corner as soon as he arrived.

Irene Richards, former matron at the nursery, has never forgotten how Michael impressed her and her colleagues. 'I've seen hundreds of children over the years, but Michael has always stuck out because of the way he "played" that guitar,' she recalls. 'It didn't have a sound as such, but Michael made up for it as he went along. He'd go into what we called the Toddlers' Room and pretend to be a pop star, tapping his foot and rolling his eyes as he strummed the guitar and sang. It was obvious he'd seen a lot of pop shows on television and had been taught the words of songs. Other children would stare at him, transfixed, then try to imitate him. But no one could; Michael was unique.

'He would get quite carried away, in a world of his own, and the nurse in charge of the toddlers would have to insist he put the guitar down while she told a story, or got the children to do something else. Reluctantly, Michael would. But one got the impression he would be happy playing that guitar all day.

'He really was an adorable boy. He wasn't a crybaby, by any means, but if he did get into mischief and was told off, he would get terribly upset and cry buckets. His eyes would fill with huge tears which would run down his face. He would rub the tears with dirty hands, leaving his lovely little face all grubby.'

★

Maureen saw a long-term future with Imre and wanted him to meet her son. She was still talking to Reg, albeit briefly, when she took Michael to see her parents some weekends, and she asked him to let her have the child for a few hours on Saturdays. Reg met her in the centre of Manchester and handed Michael over, stressing that he must be returned to West Park Avenue at a reasonable time.

Maureen took Michael into the lounge of the flat in Keppel Road and introduced him to Imre, who quickly suggested that Michael called him Jim if he found Imre too difficult. A few hours later, Michael had him in fits of laughter, marvelling at his pop music knowledge.

Imre recalls: 'He took no notice of cartoons being shown on the television, but as soon as the pop programme *6.05 Special* came on, he sat on the floor in front of my chair, staring at the screen.

'I said, "Do you want to watch it?"

' "Yes," he replied. "I always watch it." And he did not budge until the programme had ended. He knew the names of every star, group and song on the show. When he heard a favourite singer or song, he looked up at me said, "I like that one," or "I like him." He sang along to the songs, rarely taking his eyes off the screen. He was like a little old man. At one point in the show, he looked up and said, "The Beatles are with it." I said, "Are they, Michael?"

'He said, "Yes. And Gerry And The Pacemakers are with it."

'I said, "Michael, I am with it." He looked at me closely, then shook his head. "No, you're not with it." I couldn't stop laughing.'

Imre liked Michael's confidence, self-assurance and openness, and looked forward to him coming to the flat. He would give the child a bath and chat to him about what he did at home, and was always amused to hear that Michael seemed to be interested in nothing but music.

'He was brainwashed,' says Imre. 'I told Maureen that someone must be teaching him those pop songs.'

If Maureen felt a sadness at all those months she had missed with Michael since teaching him 'Michael Row The Boat Ashore', she did not show it. As Imre admits, she was as 'hard as nails.'

He wasn't, though. And he felt so sorry for the boy having no mother, and a father who had to work, that he suggested Michael came to live with them.

'I believed that Maureen was pregnant and thought one more child wouldn't make much difference,' he says. 'But Maureen wouldn't hear of it. She said she was not very patient with children and Michael was better off with his daddy and his aunties.

'Michael had been to the flat about four times when Maureen had a row with Reg because he felt it was tearing Michael in two, going backwards and forwards between two homes. Finally, Maureen stopped seeing Michael altogether. When I asked her why she didn't even take him to her parents any more, she merely shrugged and said she felt it best to leave things as they were.

'I was surprised she wasn't bothered about Michael. I started to worry, thinking she might have the nerve to do the same thing with our child. I wanted to talk to her about it, to understand her reasoning. But I never asked personal questions because she'd always blow her top and tell me to mind my own business. If Maureen didn't want to talk about something, you wouldn't even be able to force it out of her with a pair of pliers.'

It was just over a year since Maureen had left Reg, and now, as Christmas approached, she decided she never wanted to see Michael again, either.

She walked out of her son's young life, in search of that greener grass, believing she was leaving him nothing. She was wrong. Maureen left Michael a huge slice of herself – the drive and determination to go after

19

what one wanted, and the ruthless singlemindedness to make sure one got it.

Ironically, as Reg Hucknall acknowledges, it would be these tough traits, not his own softer side, that would instil in Michael the strength and burning ambition to succeed in one of the world's most cut-throat industries.

But, in the faraway future, the emptiness Maureen had left would inspire Michael to write a haunting, melancholy song about his mother that would fulfil his dreams ... and draw her back into his life.

3

There were forty children at the Russell Scott Day Nursery's Christmas party. And when Michael was asked to sing for them, he could not wait. He strolled confidently across the polished wooden floor of the main hall, toy guitar in hand, and stood in front of them. Then he strummed and rolled his eyes and sang his heart out. He loved it. And the children and their parents loved him. They cheered and clapped and Michael looked out at them, beaming.

Irene Richards was watching the performance with Dr Alan Simpson. When the applause for Michael had died down, he turned to her. 'I reckon that boy's going to be a pop star when he grows up,' he said.

What Dr Simpson saw that afternoon was not just singing talent, but star quality: even at three, Michael could attract an audience's attention and maintain it. He had an exquisite soprano voice, but it was the manner in which he used it that made him exceptional. Being constantly taught, encouraged and flattered by Nellie's pop-mad daughters gave him an overwhelming confidence in his ability and appeal, making him immune to fear. This fearlessness, plus his skilful mimicry and childish cuteness, provided him with an enviable attribute that is the successful stage performer's stock in trade – charisma. Whether they were old, hard-drinking pub regulars, or toddlers at the nursery, Michael drew them like a magnet. They adored what he gave them. And he revelled in what he got back.

So it was really no surprise when, less than three years later, Michael got up on a stage for what could be loosely described as his first professional appearance. One of Nellie's daughters had got married, and family and friends were celebrating at a lively reception. A versatile young band thumped out a string of rock and pop hits, but there was only one entertainer the Spikes wanted to hear – Michael. And he did not need any encouragement.

To most adults, performing in front of so many people would have been daunting. But to Michael it was a joy. Asked if he wanted to sing, he nodded eagerly and almost ran on to the stage, clutching his treasured plastic Woolworth's guitar he had brought 'just in case'. Thanks to his four surrogate mothers, he was a walking jukebox of sixties' songs, and could have sung most of the current hits. But when the lead singer lowered the microphone and asked him what the band should play, Michael said, 'I Want To Hold Your Hand', one of his favourite numbers, which had been a hit for The Beatles at the end of 1963. He loved The Beatles: he had been taken to see *A Hard Day's Night* at the age of four and had learned to identify songs on the group's albums by the width of the grooves.

The reception went quiet. The band played the opening chords of The Beatles' classic. And Michael's golden voice filled the hall. To the Spike family, who had heard him so many times, it was enjoyable as usual, but only what they expected. To dozens of other guests, hearing Michael for the first time, it was a stunning and memorable experience and they all smiled and nodded knowingly to each other, acknowledging the child's talent. Michael finished to loud applause and a few cheers. He beamed at everyone, his face flushed with excitement. Then he took his bow, as Nellie's family smiled up at him proudly.

If Reg had been in the music business rather than hairdressing, it is possible that Michael's singing career would have taken off then. In the mid-sixties, young musicians in the north-west of England were dominating the pop charts. With the right push in the right direction, a charismatic six-year-old with a cheeky face, a good voice and endearing presence could have cashed in on the changing trends in the music business. As it was, Reg Hucknall gave his son's singing potential not a moment's thought. He was not aware of his son's musical talent and, even if he had been, he would not have pushed him to pursue a career in such a 'dicky' business as the record industry. Learning a trade and securing his future was far more important. For Michael, though, the thrill of earning long, loud applause for his singing would have fuelled his desire to perform.

He had already displayed a love for the limelight to teachers at St Lawrence's School, where he started in September 1964, three months after his fourth birthday. The school was 111 years old with grim facilities: the main assembly hall, which doubled as a dining room, had sliding screens which divided it into four classrooms, and the outside toilets – a forty-yard walk across the playground – were infested with cockroaches. The school may have been antiquated, but the staff were young and forward-thinking, and Michael found it easy to respond to his first teacher, Jean Breeze, who taught him to read. He showed no shyness, embarrassment or nerves when asked to read aloud to the class and within months was actually volunteering to do so, much to the delight of less-confident pupils, who hated the prospect.

Today, Jean remembers Michael as a lovely-looking, well-dressed, very appealing little boy, who was self-sufficient and not at all 'clingy' like some of the other children. He was mischievous but never naughty, and did not appear to be disturbed in any way by having just one parent.

'To me, he came over as a perfectly normal little boy, who coped very well with his situation,' Jean says. 'He was not a crybaby and, although I can't remember any bullying, Michael was confident in his own little body and would have been capable of protecting himself.'

Michael was cleverer than most of his class and quickly picked up writing too, although he did have a strange quirk that amused his second teacher, Marjorie Grantham. For some reason, he seemed to think that whenever he wrote down a letter that appeared in his name, he had to put it in capitals. And he would insist on doing so – even if the letters appeared in the middle of a word in the middle of a sentence. For instance, I wANt to bE A sINgEr. Marjorie never found out what prompted Michael to do that, but today his father jokes: 'Even as a kid, Michael obviously thought a lot of himself, and his name!'

*

A year later, with Michael settled in school, Reg decided he did not need Nellie Spike's child-minding services and instead trusted his son's after-school welfare to a warm and caring next-door neighbour, June Shaw, who had a son, Gary, eighteen months older than Michael, and a four-year-old daughter, Gaynor. It was an ideal set-up for all of them: the boys got on well and after school Gary would walk home with Michael; June welcomed the extra money Reg gave her for feeding and looking after Michael; and Reg, who would take his son to school in the morning, could rest easy, knowing Michael was in safe hands until he came home.

Michael loved going to the Shaws' house: June treated him like one of her own and Michael enjoyed feeling part of a family. He had been part of Nellie Spike's family too, of course, but all her daughters were so much older than him; now a playful and energetic schoolboy, he needed children of his own age around him. West Park Avenue provided that: most of the parents living there had young children at primary school, and Michael was never lost for friends – boys and girls. They all congregated at the top, where the road ends in a semi-circular cul-de-sac.

The children nicknamed that area 'The Circle'. And that's where Michael met and fell in love with his first sweetheart, Jane Spencer. She was a pretty girl the same age, who also went to St Lawrence's, and Michael was so smitten with her that he asked her to marry him. It is one of Jane's sweetest memories, for she said yes, and the two children went through a secret, make-believe marriage ceremony behind the rhubarb in a friend's back garden. The 'marriage' did not last, however. Soon Jane was joining in with other children, teasing Michael over his red hair, freckles and sticking-out ears. And Michael would hit back with any cruel jibe he could think of to hurt her. He succeeded – often. 'One particular insult I remember concerned some leather sandals,' Jane recalls. 'They had a buckle on the side and my mum made me wear them, even though I hated them. Knowing I didn't like them, Michael would make fun of me, calling the sandals "Jesus Creepers". I wasn't sure what he meant, but it didn't sound very nice and I refused to wear the sandals again. My mum went up the wall because I hadn't had them long. All in all, though, I liked Michael as a kid, even though he was quite a serious boy and a bit of a loner who didn't always play with the rest of us.'

The reason Michael did not join in may have been that he preferred singing to hide-and-seek, and that, in some of his pals, he had a willing and appreciative audience. One summer evening in 1966, for example, Bill Griffiths, the father of a friend, Johnny Griffiths, who lived opposite, looked out and saw six-year-old Michael standing on his garden wall, looking down at a handful of his friends sitting cross-legged on the pavement, gazing up at him.

Mr Griffiths remembers what happened next as if it were yesterday. 'Michael started to walk along my wall, singing a current pop song that was being played on the radio all day long. The kids were mesmerized. I was, too. When Michael finished, the kids all clapped and Michael gave a cute little bow. The confidence in someone so young was amazing.'

By the time Michael was seven, he was finding his feet at St Lawrence's. He was still one of the brightest and cleverest in his class, but was getting up to more and more mischief.

'He was a bit of a sod,' one of his classmates, Julie McCann, says candidly. 'He never did anything really bad, but always seemed to be in trouble. I honestly think he was doing it to get attention.'

The following year he was getting attention – but not of the right kind. The supreme confidence that had endeared him to adults had developed into a sort of cocky arrogance that certain boys did not like. Being clever and stealing the limelight in class was one thing, but being bombastic in the playground was another. One of those classmates, Frank Worthington, remembers Michael as an outgoing personality, who would never take no for an answer.

'He wasn't a bully, but he would put his point forward and always had to be right, ' Frank recalls. 'If you didn't agree with his point of view and tried to put your own forward, he would ignore you and change the subject, rather than admit he was wrong. A lot of kids didn't like him because he was loud and shouted a lot. He wasn't the type to be bullied, because he was fairly big for his age and would stick up for himself. So the kids who didn't like his attitude just ignored him.

'He was definitely one of the brightest in the class, though. He sat at the front and would nearly always have his hand up first with the right answer, while the rest of us were still thinking about it. And in playtime he would come out with long words the rest of us had never heard. We'd all look at each other, thinking: What the hell is he on about? If we asked, Michael always knew what those long words meant.'

Michael and Gary Shaw were like brothers. But, like brothers, their relationship was unpredictable. One day they would be close, sharing everything and going everywhere together, the next they would not be speaking. For Gary, a gentle, softly-spoken kid, it was a pleasing relationship, which he remembers affectionately. But it was also one that gave him a chance to experience, first-hand and at close quarters, the temperamental and cruel side of Michael's nature that would upset people in the future.

Gary says: 'When we fell out, it was usually over something trivial, but Mick would hold a grudge and give me the silent treatment for ages, sometimes weeks. He would make a point of playing with other boys, not me. He was trying to torture me.

'Once, when we were playing Monopoly, I went outside for something and looked through a window to find him slipping a couple of £500 notes under the board near him. When I went in, I told him what I'd seen and called him a cheat. But he denied it and got really angry. We had a row and I got the silent treatment. But then, just when I'd decided he was so upset he wasn't ever going to speak to me again, he would come up to me and everything would be fine – as though nothing had happened.'

After another row, over who was leader of the street gang, the two boys had a bare-knuckle fight in West Park Avenue, refereed by Johnny Griffiths, who was about two years older than Michael. The battle started seriously enough, with Michael and Gary slugging each other, cheered on by ten pals at 'ringside'. But just as things were warming up, a college student, who was staying with the Shaws for the summer holidays and looking after the children, rushed into the street. She called out: 'I'm cooking sausages and mash – how many sausages do you want?' Michael and Gary stopped fighting momentarily, and shouted out breathlessly: 'Two, please.' Then they carried on thumping each other. Being older, with a significant weight advantage, Gary got the better of Michael and Johnny Griffiths declared him the winner. The verdict did not go down well with Michael; he disappeared quickly into the Shaws' house and Gary found him on the floor, sulking and building up to some new mental torture.

Despite the unpredictability of their relationship, Gary speaks well of his childhood friend, although he does admit that he always felt, deep down, that Michael was trying to get one over on him and his sister, Gaynor.

'Although I was older, he could talk me into doing things I knew in my heart I didn't want to do,' says Gary. 'Even at eight, he was sort of streetwise, and knew what he was doing all the time. Gaynor and I were little kids, just going through life, but Michael always seemed to have an objective and knew precisely what he was doing, and why.

'I would be aware he was trying to fiddle me, but he would sweet-talk me and I wouldn't wise up until afterwards when it was too late. For example, we both had the fantastic Action Man toy and would swap clothes. One Christmas, I got the new skiing outfit, which had a smart red parka with fur round the hood, and a Union Jack on the front. Michael knew I'd had my eye on his Action Man's old frogman's suit and talked me into swapping. It wasn't until I looked at the suit properly that I realised I'd been done. The suit was missing so many things, it was unusable. I got a right roasting from my dad for letting Mick suck me in like that. But he was always so clever with words I never saw the con coming.

'He also talked me into selling him my bike – which was in better condition than his. We agreed a price and he promised to pay the balance within a week out of his pocket money. But he never did and, after several weeks of waiting patiently, I took the bike back. Michael gave me the silent treatment for weeks!'

For all his singleminded toughness, however, Michael could show a commendable sense of fair play – like the time he returned 50p to an old lady for not completing an odd job he and Gary had promised to do.

Gary says: 'We would go round the estate, offering to cut hedges and clean cars. One woman gave us 50p each to tidy up her garden, but Michael and I fell out shortly after starting the work, and we left the garden unfinished. I kept my 50p and didn't think any more about it, but it must have played on Michael's mind because he went back, explained what had happened and returned the 50p. He did have a nice side to him.'

It says a lot for Reg Hucknall that, despite the problems of bringing Michael up on his own, the boy never went short of the latest toys at

Christmas and birthdays. And the likeable, caring June Shaw made sure Michael didn't miss out on the attention most children get on their birthdays.

Sadly, June died in 1991, but Mrs Pat Clayton, who lived next door, remembers her organizing a party for Michael every 8 June. 'She always laid on a special day for Michael, with balloons and ice cream and games, and he looked forward to it all eagerly,' says Pat. 'He'd rush home from school, a big smile on his face, and play with his mates in the street, until it was time for them to go into June's garden for the party.

'Most of the other kids' mothers would make sure they bought him a present. We all felt he needed that little bit extra treatment and love because he didn't have a mother of his own. Michael was so appreciative. Once, I bought him a yellow helicopter model, powered by elastic. His eyes lit up excitedly and for the next few days he was flying it everywhere. I should have known better – it kept landing in everybody's garden!'

The concern of those neighbours would have done a lot to bring some normality to Michael's life, but it was impossible for him not to feel the odd one out at school at Christmas. Before the end-of-term party, for example, children went home at lunchtime to change into their 'best' party clothes and bring in their favourite toys. With no one at home, Michael would take his change of clothes in a plastic bag and stay with the teacher during the lunch break. Most of Michael's classmates were aware that he had no mother, but they said nothing. One, Wendy Maddocks says: 'All of us felt really sorry for him. But being the odd one out never seemed to bother Michael.'

This hard exterior, hiding what he must have been feeling deep down, applied to another emotional annual celebration – Mother's Day – when children would be asked to make a card for their mums. The teacher who had Michael in class that day would tell him, quietly and sensitively, to make a card for his father. Today, all those teachers remember him as a strong, independent child, who never showed any signs of being bothered or upset at having to do something different.

One would have forgiven Michael if any deep-seated resentment he may have been feeling had come out as rebellion or destructiveness. But throughout those early school years, Michael was, generally, a normal, popular kid, who worked and played hard and, until his last year, was well-behaved.

Out of school, though, he liked getting up to childish pranks, one of which was lying in the middle of West Park Avenue, waiting for a car to come. Pat Clayton admits he would frighten her.

'My kids would come running in, telling me that Michael was lying in the road again. I knew it was just a "dare" game, but I'd think: He's going to get killed, that lad.'

Pat thought her fears had come tragically true when Michael was run over – not when playing 'dare', but when simply dashing into the road without looking.

It happened one afternoon after school. Michael came out, saw Nellie, or one of her daughters, waiting for him on the other side of Stockport Road and ran across into the path of a car. He was taken to hospital and kept in overnight. Nothing was broken and he went home the next day.

'It was no wonder he was run over,' says Gary. 'He was one of those lads who was always in a rush and running everywhere.'

One of Michael's favourite targets for his practical jokes was Gary's younger sister, Gaynor. Once, at the age of eight, he and Gary stopped playing darts in the Hucknall kitchen to fill a cup with some water for Gaynor, while she was in the toilet. After Gaynor drank the water, she noticed there were some strange-looking bits floating at the bottom of the cup. Screwing her nose up, she asked what they were, and Michael could hardly contain himself as he told her it was Steradent. The cup was the one his father kept his false teeth in overnight!

Michael would also take delight in making Gaynor cry by climbing up a lamp-post and watching her being given a bath in the kitchen sink. Or he would infuriate her by wolfing down the early evening tea her mother had prepared for them, then rushing out and pinching her bike. 'I would get really annoyed,' Gaynor recalls. 'I'd go all round the estate, looking for him. He did that every night, but my mum never told him off. I think she made a lot of allowances for him.'

Gaynor's father, Bernard Shaw, also made allowances, although his patience was stretched one summer's day in 1968 when he took his own children and Michael on a coach outing to Chester Zoo with other parents and children from West Park Avenue. All was well on the way there: Michael sat at the front, his feet on a rail, singing. But once they were in the zoo, his excitement got the better of him: Gaynor and Gary were well-behaved and never left their father's side, but Michael was always jumping about and running off. Bernard's irritation with him grew and grew, and turned into embarrassment when he saw Michael pick up some stones and start throwing them at an orang-utan in an enclosure.

'Dad just stood there, not knowing what to do,' Gary recalls. 'In the end, he had to shout at Michael to stop. On the way home, Dad vowed he would never take him anywhere again.'

Johnny Griffiths' mother, Nessie, also has reason to remember Michael for his mischief. One summer afternoon, Michael hid in his front garden and picked off younger girls with his pea-shooter as they walked past. He caught Johnny Griffiths' sister, Mary, so badly on her legs that she ran screaming to her mother. An irate Nessie rushed out, looking for Michael, but he had disappeared, on the basis that unless he owned up Mary's mother would never know for sure who was responsible. Even if he had been spotted running off, Michael was the type of boy who would have played the innocent.

Pat Clayton says: 'Michael was cute and mischievous, but crafty, too. Most of the time we tended to let the kids get on with their games and sort out any trouble between themselves. But whenever one of us did get angry and take action, he would always stand back and let the younger ones take the flak. He'd watch, a cheeky grin on his face; then, once everything had got back to normal, he'd join in and start playing again. He was an impish little lad, but you couldn't help liking him.'

Being naughty was, of course, all part of being a normal little boy, but there was another reason why Michael got up to mischief: even at eight, he got bored quickly. John Burgess, another school pal, who lived nearby on Moorfield Avenue, says: 'We would call round to see each other and play with our Action Man models. But Michael always had a low boredom threshold. When that level was reached, his interest would suddenly drop. I'd be happy playing a bit longer, but Michael's thoughts would be on something else. As a kid, he was always a bit different. He was happy-go-lucky. Not a lot seemed to bother him. He let problems just bounce off. Looking back, it's as though he was a year or two older than the rest of us, in terms of what was going on in his head. I think he had a lot more in mind for himself, even as a little kid.'

John's mother would see both boys playing in a group in the street and sense that Michael was not 100 per cent involved. 'It's really difficult to explain,' she admits. 'He would be on the fringe, three quarters of him in the group, but the other quarter away somewhere, thinking of something else. I don't mean he was stand-offish – just not totally involved like the rest of them. I never regarded him as a mixer; more of an individual.'

It seems as if Michael was happy being in a crowd if he was the centre of attention; if he wasn't, his mind would wander.

Another Moorfield resident, Patricia Dewhurst, would often see him holding the attention of other lads in the street. 'I can picture him now, leg over his bike, with a group listening to him. He always stood out, not just because of his curly red hair, but because he was taller than the other boys and still wore short trousers. I remember thinking: What is it with this kid? – he's always got a crowd round him. He was a cocky little thing. Once, when he saw me walking past, he grinned and said,

"You all reet, missus?" I was surprised, and thought, cheeky little bugger. But there was nothing arrogant in him – he was just being cheekily friendly.'

By now, the little street entertainer's singing talent was well known in West Park Avenue: up to a dozen of his pals – girls as well as boys – would gather in front of someone's garden, playing hollow plastic tubes called kazoos, as Michael walked along the wall, singing. 'We were like his backing group,' Johnny Griffiths says. 'When he finished, we'd clap and he would bow, just as if he were acting a part.'

For all his confident, forceful personality and sometimes cruel streak, Michael did have a tender, more gentle side, although he let it show infrequently, and then only in defence of someone less fortunate or emotionally troubled.

Pat Clayton's son, Nigel, for example, was slightly backward and was teased mercilessly by kids in the street gang. They would not let him join in their games, and the few times they did include him, he would always be blamed if a game went wrong and they upset the neighbours. If a football went into a garden and the owner started shouting, the kids would immediately start chanting, 'Nigel did it . . . Nigel did it.'

Nigel, three years younger than Michael, seemed oblivious to the cruel jibes, but Michael wasn't. Something in him said, 'Hey, this is wrong, unjust,' and he would step in and stick up for him. And on the occasions when it did not suit his pals to let Nigel play football with them, Michael would put his arm round him and walk off, saying, 'Sod you lot – we're mates.' And he would sit on his doorstep reading books about trains to Nigel, or go into his house and play with him on his huge train layout. Sometimes he even took him to nearby stations to spot trains.

At school, Michael saved the blushes of a little boy named Johnny Gosling, who caught his private parts in his zip in the toilet. The pinch had drawn blood, but Johnny was too embarrassed to let anyone call a teacher. The painful problem was solved by an older boy who released the zip, while Michael guarded the door to stop curious pupils seeing what was going on.

One former pupil who remembers Michael's kindness is Iselle Gregg. Three days before Christmas 1970, her father died tragically, and pupils were told to be careful what they said to her when she returned to school in January. Most of the class either pretended nothing had happened or made a fuss over Iselle to make her feel better, but Michael showed her honesty and support.

Today, Iselle remembers: 'I was giving the milk or the chalk out with him, and, instead of saying nothing, he said, "I've only got my dad,

Iselle. But it's all right having one parent. It'll be okay, you know." It was a traumatic time for me and I was really low, and what Michael said was very comforting. He was the only one who could relate to what had happened to me. We shared something in common after that.'

If, at ten, Michael wondered where his mother was and what she was doing, he did not let on. His father never mentioned her name. And Michael never asked about her. The only relatives he had were the Hucknalls in Barrow, but when he went there for the annual two weeks' holiday in July, not one of the large family mentioned Maureen either.

It was as if she had never existed in their lives.

4

A lot had happened to Maureen in the eight years since she walked out of West Park Avenue in search of what she believed was a more satisfying life.

Having conned Imre Kozarits into thinking she was two months pregnant in November 1963, she went all out to have a baby and, the following August, gave birth to a boy. She and Imre named him Ricky.

Reg, who had no idea Maureen had another child, agreed to a divorce, and every couple of weeks she would phone him at the Stockport barber shop, asking when it was going to happen. Reg would say, 'I'm in no rush. I've no plans to get married.'

However, in 1967 Reg did agree to a divorce on the grounds of desertion and said he would split the legal costs 50/50.

Today, Reg recalls: 'An enquiry agent had to interview Maureen, so I rang to tell her he'd be round to her house between 10 a.m. and 1 p.m. the next day. To me, an enquiry agent meant somebody like Humphrey Bogart, but, bugger me, it was a woman who turned up on Maureen's doorstep. And Maureen opened the door, holding a baby.

'The enquiry agent asked, "Is that your baby?"

' "Oh, aye," Maureen said.

'With that, divorce on the grounds of desertion went out the window. Now I had no option but to do her for adultery, citing Imre Kozarits.

'Later, Maureen's mother wrote a snotty letter, accusing me of reneging on the deal to split the costs. But the truth is that it was a genuine misunderstanding. I'd told Maureen to expect an enquiry agent. I didn't think she'd be stupid enough to go to the door with a baby in her arms. She must have thought the woman wanted something else.'

Maureen married Imre in 1967 and, the same year, had another baby – a girl, whom they named Lyndsay. But when the baby was a year old, Maureen got the urge for freedom again and walked out of the family's new bungalow in Leigh, Cheshire, taking Lyndsay, but leaving Ricky.

Imre was pleased to get rid of Maureen. 'Marrying her was the greatest mistake of my life,' he says. 'I was never in love with her. I wish I'd never met her. When she told me she was leaving, I wasn't unhappy, but said,

"What about the children?" She said, "I'll take the girl – you keep the boy."

'I said, "You can't take one and leave the other – they're not animals. They have to grow up together, as brother and sister, not meet forty years later." I told her she should never have had children – she was messing up their lives.

'One Saturday morning I took Ricky to a park. When we came back, Maureen had left, with Lyndsay. I knew she was leaving me, but I never really believed she would take our daughter, and I was terribly upset.'

A few weeks later, Imre traced Maureen to a house in Bolton. She was living with another man. But then she disappeared again and Imre did not hear from her until she rang from Somerset, saying she was happy for him to have Lyndsay.

Imre recalls: 'She told me to meet her at a Birmingham police station and I went there with a friend. Maureen was driven there by another man. He waited in his car while Maureen walked in, pushing Lyndsay in a pram, and not looking the least upset or concerned. My friend said, "What kind of mother are you?" Maureen didn't bother to answer. She just turned and walked away.

'I was glad she was out of my life. I never felt comfortable with her. She was very materialistic and was always talking about money. Maureen was a hard, tough woman. I never saw her cry for anyone but herself – and then only out of anger. When I refused to argue with her, she would scream in temper. Once, she started banging her head against a door. I told her to use the wall, because it was harder. She took one of her stiletto shoes off and bashed me over the head with it. I was sitting in a chair at the time. Blood was running down my face.

'Maureen ruined my life, but at least she left me Ricky and Lyndsay. They're my consolation and I'm so very proud of them.'

As Maureen turned her back on her second family, still searching for that greener grass, Michael was out of her mind. Not once did she try to see him. Not once did she even send a birthday card.

Maureen's mother Florence says: 'She just vanished. She went off doing her own thing, as usual. She didn't want anything to do with Michael. And, much as my husband and I would have loved to have seen him grow up, we had no idea what he was doing or thinking.'

★

Michael was too young to take the Eleven-Plus exam in January 1970, so he was kept at St Lawrence's for an extra year. The positive side of this was that he was made a monitor, with responsibility for handing out milk, pencils, chalk and books. The negative side was that he had done the work the previous year and quickly became bored. He started to be cheeky, and distracted the class by chatting instead of working. Former pupils say it was a familiar sight to see him standing in the corner for being naughty, or being ordered to stay behind after school to see his teacher.

One time Michael was never in trouble was during music lessons. For most of the children, music with the prim Joyce Duxbury was a bore, because she made them sing dull, dreary hymns and very simple childish songs over and over again. But, no matter how repetitive the lessons were, Michael was always interested and keen to play a part: he would be one of five or six keen children at the front, near the piano, eager to clash the cymbals or strike the triangles; and he was the one Miss Duxbury picked to tap a stick for the class to stay in time when she was at the piano.

That autumn, Barbara Jones became deputy head and took over the music lessons; and she, more than anyone, must take credit for harnessing Michael's vocal talent. It did not take her long to see that he was a supremely confident boy, and an accomplished soprano, perfect for the school choir. And she made sure she flattered and encouraged him, as well as two or three other musically-gifted boys.

'I would organize two classes to sing along to the weekly BBC radio music lesson, and Michael was one of the more enthusiastic pupils,' Barbara remembers. 'Like other boys with good voices, he was a little cocky, but that never interfered with the lessons. He always took an active part in what I taught, and it was always a joy listening to him sing.'

When Mrs Jones called on Michael to stand next to her at the piano and sing solo to the class, he revelled in the limelight. Later, he was picked to sing hymn solos to the whole school at assembly, and revelled in that, too. For a kid who had performed publicly at six, nerves were not a problem. On the contrary, he always looked forward to being the centre of attention, doing what he knew he did well.

It was the same with reading from the Bible. Twice a week, a girl and boy were chosen to read a couple of verses at morning assembly, and Michael's confidence made him a prime candidate. Another able pupil, Diane Chapman, was always picked, too, and she remembers Michael well. 'We would be told to leave the classroom to learn what we would be reading at assembly the next day. We'd go in the cloakroom and read to each other for twenty minutes or so, then go back and read to the class. I was always frightened to death of reading to the whole school, but Michael never seemed to be nervous. I always made the odd mistake, but he would sail through it, word perfect.'

Coming up to eleven, Michael started taking an interest in girls and quickly discovered he had an advantage over the rest of the boys – his voice. The girls loved it, and would crowd round him in the main hall or playground, listening in raptures as he sang from his Beatles' repertoire, or whatever else was high in the charts. One of his favourites was 'Knock Three Times', by Dawn, which was Number 1 on Michael's birthday.

One of those who jostled among the throng to be Michael's girlfriend was Lynn Gooding. 'He was dead popular,' she recalls. 'He was *the* person to be with. All the girls wanted to go out with him because he could sing so well, and was such a bonny and bubbly person. He was always dressed smartly; sometimes he even wore a little green suit and a tie. And his hair was always neatly cut.

'He was always singing to himself, but whenever one of us asked him to sing something for us, he would do it. He'd stand there, singing an entire song, and by the time he'd finished, a crowd would have gathered round him. Everyone thought he was brilliant. He stood out from the rest of the lads and was quite full of himself. He would stand in the playground, girls all around him, looking at each of us in turn, saying, "You can be my number one girlfriend, you can be number two," and so on. At times, he had as many as five girlfriends!'

One of them was Wendy Maddocks; she loved his voice as much as she envied his plastic Woolworth's sandals. And one lunchtime, between the kitchen and the toilets, he gave her a long kiss, and later told her he loved her.

Today, Wendy says, 'I remember feeling lucky that it was my turn to be Michael's girlfriend. He must have planned that kiss, because he waited until we were alone, then planted his lips firmly on mine. It was a long kiss, and I was so surprised I could think of nothing to say afterwards.'

Michael certainly made an impression on Wendy's mother. Noticing his long fingers, she told her daughter, 'Long fingers usually mean talent. That boy is gifted.'

★

The talent with which Michael was endowed, however, would be submerged for the next five years as he battled to cope with the pressures of the most difficult period of his young life.

All but three boys from St Lawrence's failed their Eleven-Plus and went either to Egerton Park or Two Trees – secondary schools in Denton. Michael was one of the three boys who won a place at Audenshaw Grammar, a fifteen-minute bus ride from Denton. Although Reg Hucknall's own ambitions now were limited, he desperately wanted his son to have a good education, and he was prouder than he had ever been in his life when he heard that Michael's hard work had paid off.

Michael was pleased, too. But whatever pride he felt would be replaced by disenchantment, then resentment, which in turn would breed a rebellious streak, deep enough to alter the course of his life.

At St Lawrence's he had been an adorable, cheeky-faced favourite, fussed over by softly-spoken women, who loved his curly red hair and impish smile. At Audenshaw, he would be subject to a strict regime in which discipline was enforced by the cane, and the butt of the cruel jibes of bully boys, who laughed at his red hair and odd-shaped body.

The boy who had blossomed as a big fish in tranquil waters would be a tiddler, struggling for survival in a stormy sea.

5

His hair was a red rag to the bullies. It was thick and wavy and shaped like a triangle, so that it looked as if he was wearing a tall woollen hat. When the second- and third-year Audenshaw boys saw that flaming mass and the pale skin and freckles on that September morning in 1971, they could not believe their luck.

Bullying of first-year boys by those who had been victims themselves was a ritual that had been going on since the school was built in 1932; it was as traditional as the black gowns of the masters and the tough treatment they dished out. The older boys would call the nondescript eleven-year-olds cruel names like 'weeds', and throw their caps around, trying to make them cry. For most, the tormenting would end after the first term, but if a boy was singled out, it could go on longer, perhaps for the rest of the school year, and even into the next. The cruel teasing would progress to threats of violence and, for some hapless victims, the ordeal would turn into a terrifying nightmare, with them being dragged into the prefects' room by powerful sixth-formers and humiliated and beaten up.

Michael's red hair, making him stand out among the forlorn flock of little boys lost in the school playground that first morning of Audenshaw's autumn term, drew the bullies like a magnet. They did not know him, but they did not like the look of him. And they were going to make sure he got extra special treatment.

The first friends Michael made at Audenshaw, Gary Hulston and Frank Ollerenshaw, remember the prefects having a go at the younger kids, but giving Michael more stick than anyone else because he stood out. 'It was like *Tom Brown's Schooldays*,' Gary says. 'There was nothing you could do about it, though. You just had to put up with it, then try to bounce back.'

Gary and Frank immediately abbreviated Michael's name to Mick, as his dad had done – and it stuck. But the bullies constantly taunted him over his red hair, calling him 'Carrot-Top', 'Ginger-Nut' or just plain 'Ginger', after a character in the popular *Beezer* comic.

Mick began to dread going to school: the imposing building, tall and rambling in the six acres of playing fields, behind prison-like black iron railings, was an awesome sight for the boy. Barely eleven, he had come from a little school where, in his last year, he had been king pin in the top class: older than most of the other children, wiser in the ways of the school, and trusted in the enviable job of monitor. When he wasn't showing off and being naughty, he had been something of a teacher's pet because of his bonny look, happy-go-lucky personality and, of course, his golden voice.

At Audenshaw, everything changed from that daunting first day. The bullies were one problem, the teachers another: Mick was not terrified of them, but he did not like their no-nonsense, rule-by-the-cane approach, and the old-fashioned code they seemed to live by. They did not encourage individuality; they demanded respect and extremely hard work. What made that work even harder for Mick was that he was surrounded, and perhaps intimidated, by academically cleverer boys, destined for university and high-powered, high-salaried careers. He tried his best, but he was out of his depth and began to lose confidence. By the end of his second year, he was unrecognizable from the sprightly, run-everywhere kid, popular among adults and children alike. He had retreated into a shell, unhappy and withdrawn and, in an adolescent way, worried at where it was all leading.

At thirteen, his body began to change. And it made school life even more unpleasant. His arms and legs were growing quicker than the rest of him and he was developing a bit of a pot belly – a decidedly unsporty physique that amused bigger boys, known more for their brawn than their brains. One of them, Mark Fisher, would turn his exercise book over and sketch a lanky figure, with a pot belly and long arms dangling behind his back, like an orang-utan. Then he would draw a face with spots, a very small pug nose and tiny eyes, and finish it off with a ludicrous mass of hair, coloured red. Fisher would pass the book around to classmates, asking, 'Guess who?' If Mick was not aware of his work of art during class, Fisher would make sure he was afterwards. Calling Mick over, he would ask, 'What do you reckon? A good likeness or what?'

Today, Fisher, a scrap-metal worker, admits he and his burly rugby-playing mates saw the funny side of Mick's body. 'He really was an odd-looking character, particularly in sports gear. With long arms and legs and a short body, he looked a right sight in tight little shorts and a vest that never seemed to fit. But my drawings were like water off a duck's back to Mick. He thought they were funny and couldn't understand how or why I could be bothered to do them. He'd say, "You're mad." '

38

According to other classmates, however, Fisher has it wrong. Adrian Whittleworth, who was close to Mick in those first two years, says: 'He didn't like being teased. And he didn't like those cruel drawings. Fisher even got hold of one of Mick's own books, and drew those horrible sketches all over the front and inside. Once, I'm sure I saw Mick fighting back tears. It was not only Fisher who tormented him – it was the whole rugby crowd – Geoff Crossley, Jed West and Steve Halkyard. Mentally, they made Mick's life a misery.'

If it occurred to Mick to give Fisher a right-hander, he didn't go through with it. Fighting, it is clear, was not his style: he preferred to talk, not punch, his way out of trouble, and his fast tongue often got the better of classmates trying to put him down. Even at thirteen, Mick could be sharp and arrogant and capable of a quick, barbed retort, designed to hurt.

There was not a lot Mick could do, however, when a TV ad featuring a red-haired ventriloquist's dummy landed him with a hurtful, new nickname: 'Puppet Head'. The tag was picked up by one of his own form-mates, who thought the puppet looked like Mick. But the prefects took the taunt a stage further by making a similar dummy, with a red wig, and hanging a school tie round its neck like a noose. They called the dummy 'Hucknall' and hung it in a window above the door of their private room, so that it could be seen from the outside. Whenever they saw Mick, they would sneer, 'Hello, Puppet Head.'

★

Perhaps because he had been on the receiving end for so long, Mick indulged in a spot of uncharacteristic bullying himself one Saturday afternoon. He and a friend were wandering around the Clarendon Road area of Haughton Green when they spotted a group of boys, aged about ten, playing football in a field. Bored and looking for something to do, Mick asked if they could join in. The boy who owned the ball, Ken Laing, said, 'No, you're too big.' Mick took no notice: he took the ball off one of the other lads and started dribbling it and passing it to his pal. Angrily, Ken ran after Mick and rugby-tackled him to the ground. The ball ran free and one of the other younger boys picked it up. 'Right,' said Ken to a prostrate Mick, 'you're not playing now.' Immediately, Mick got up and smacked him in the face.

Ken recalls: 'I ran off crying to my mum. She came out and shouted to Mick, "Oi, you – bugger off." Mick and his mate legged it.'

★

Around this time, Mick met a boy who would become something of a soul mate over the next two years, and an important influence in the direction his life would take. The boy was Paul Sutcliffe, who went to Two Trees School with Mick's next-door neighbour and pal, Gary Shaw. To outsiders, Mick and Paul would seem to have had little in common: Paul, like Gary, was about eighteen months older, gregarious and worldly, with a love of life, while Mick was now shy, withdrawn and not that confident. But the two boys hit it off after meeting through Gary, and soon started seeing a lot of each other. In the evenings Mick would go round to Paul's home and listen to records – particularly The Rolling Stones – in Paul's bedroom. One album, *Sticky Fingers*, had a track called 'Sister Morphine' – and Mick loved it.

Paul recalls: 'We'd play the record again and again until we knew the lyrics, then we'd sit on the bed and sing the whole thing together. If one of us got it wrong, the other one would take the mickey and we'd start again. I'd start hitting some books with sticks, as if I was playing the drums. And we'd keep putting the needle back to the beginning, so that I could get the beat right. I was quite an extrovert and would get up and do my version of the Mick Jagger strut, dancing near the window and twirling the curtain around. But Mick was more restrained and stuck to singing. He had a good voice, but I wasn't listening to him – I was more concerned about how I sounded. We'd play records all the time up to 9 p.m.'

Mick was already doing a milk-round and now, at thirteen, he got a paper-round at a newsagent's in Moorfield Avenue, about a half-mile walk from his home. The owners, Derek and Audrey Jones, were so impressed with his intelligence and attitude that they quickly entrusted him with collecting money too. Every Friday evening, while on his round, he would have to collect outstanding paper bills from about sixty addresses and keep a log of the amount received. It was a privileged job for someone so young and Mick took it very seriously.

Mick loved his paper job – and not only because of the money he earned: there was a fourteen-year-old girl named Barbara Lees who worked part-time behind the counter, and Mick thought she was smashing. He was too shy to ask her out, though. Barbara knew Mick fancied her, because he blushed when he said hello, and went crimson whenever she said anything to him. Every Friday evening, he would come into the shop, call out, 'Hiya', then pick up the loose change for his collection float and rush out the door, too shy to say anything else.

The newsagent's was one of half a dozen shops in a small parade at the Two Trees Lane end of Moorfield Avenue. And since one of them sold fish and chips, it was not surprising that gangs of schoolchildren would congregate outside in the evenings. Mick attached himself to one of these groups, but he was not a whole-hearted gang member and, consequently, never fully accepted.

One of the girls in the gang, Bernadette Fleming, remembers him as a bit of a loner, who would mix in with them only if he had nothing else better to do.

She recalls: 'He'd be in the gang one night and not the next, whereas the rest of us would be around all the time. And when he was there, he would stay in the background, hardly saying anything. He was a bit of a misery, really. To be frank, I don't think he really liked our gang, because we were so rowdy. Once, upstairs in the bus after ice-skating in Altrincham, we all started smoking and singing a funny song, and Mick was so embarrassed he went and sat at the front with another boy, pretending he didn't know us. He wasn't one of the crowd. We just tolerated him.'

As at Audenshaw, Mick was viewed rather as a figure of fun, and the gang, particularly the girls, delighted in teasing him. A long tunnel in the woods at the back of the housing estate, for example, provided an ideal opportunity to have a laugh at Mick's expense. On winter evenings, the gang would venture into the woods and dare each other to run through the dark tunnel. They would dash off into the eerie blackness, with the very unathletic Mick trailing behind. Knowing he was terrified, the girls would emerge from the other end and start yelling and screaming, as if they had tumbled on some terrible sight. And they would collapse, laughing, as Mick staggered breathlessly out of the tunnel, looking horrified. 'He'd be effing and blinding,' Bernadette recalls. 'He was frightened out of his wits, but we all found it hilarious.'

When one of the gang's parents went out for the night, the word would go round that a house was empty and ready for a party. These impromptu occasions were called 'pile-ins' – and the cider Mick drank lifted some of his inhibitions and helped bring him out of the shadow of his shyness into the limelight as a pop star.

With the girls liking Motown stars, and the boys into heavy rock bands such as Hawkwind, Tangerine Dream and Black Sabbath, it was always a battle for control of the music. When the boys won they would turn the volume up, deafening the girls, then jump about, imitating their heavy-metal heroes, with any accessory at hand. 'I remember Mick grabbing an ashtray, and even a broom handle, and pretending it was a guitar,' says Bernadette. 'He'd shake his head as if he was the lead singer in a band. We all watched him and he loved the attention.'

To Bernadette and her pals, Mick was not an attractive thirteen-year-old. The bonny look he had had as a baby and primary school pupil had now vanished beneath the facial spots and incongruous body changes of puberty. He was not as ludicrous as Mark Fisher's bizarre sketches implied, but he did not have the looks that appealed to girls. He did not have the personality, either. If Mick had sung for Bernadette and her Motown-mad friends the way he had sung for the little girls at St Lawrence's, who knows what effect he would have had on them. But, with his voice breaking and his mind confused by the uncertainty of youth and academic pressures, his singing was silenced. As a result, he had nothing to offer but himself – a quiet, shy, oddball with bright red hair, a pale face and freckles. And it was not a combination to set young girls' hearts racing. As Bernadette says: 'Some lads would come into the group and we'd think: He's a bit of all right. But we never did with Mick. He didn't even get a rating.'

Sadly, Mick's social standing did not improve when he drifted out of that group and into another, somewhat more adventurous one that also gathered outside the Moorfield shops. The gang, which had a hard core of five – Elaine Adshead, Christine Watmough, Anne Bailey, Steve Ditchfield and Kevin Robertson – would buy a packet of ten No. 6 cigarettes and a bottle of cider and go to the St Lawrence's school building, which had closed and was being used by a judo club and a girls' brigade. To make the journey more interesting, the crowd would knock on people's doors and run off, in a game they called 'Knock-adoorrun'. And after they had had a drink and a drag in the darkened yard next to the old school, they would dare each other to put a hand through a window and turn off the lights, plunging the judo club or girls' brigade meeting into darkness.

Once, when some pensioners were having a party, Elaine started banging on the window and accidentally broke it. A handful of the more sprightly old folk came rushing out and Elaine, Mick and some other friends made a run for it. Unfortunately Mick was slow climbing over a fence and was quickly surrounded by irate elderly women waving walking sticks and shouting at him. He escaped unscathed, but with a stern verbal warning to behave himself in future.

For that sexually-curious gang of thirteen-year-olds, it was the game of Truth, Dare or Consequence that provided the most excitement. The game was all about sexual experimentation, and it quickly exposed and embarrassed Mick as the boy the girls least liked to kiss. Elaine was going steady with Kevin, so the other two girls, Anne and Christine, drew straws to see who would pair off with Steve and Mick to have a kiss and cuddle in the privacy of the school toilets. On this particular night, Christine drew Mick – which she most definitely considered the short straw!

Today, Christine admits: 'I didn't want to kiss Mick. He was the ugliest of our group, and not attractive in the least; we all thought him a bit naff. We must have been in the toilets for a good five minutes, but I don't remember having a good, long snog. I do recall Mick was very shy and kept his mouth shut tight all the time. But I was so young myself, I wasn't sure whether it was the right way or not. One thing I'll never forget about Mick was his generosity. If we didn't have the money for fags and he did, he would always chip in. He was very kind-hearted like that.'

★

Christine and Elaine liked Mick as a person, however, and they spent a lot of time together. He loved walking to the fields around Brinnington, near Stockport, with food for two horses they had 'adopted' as their own. The horses were on private land, but the field was out of sight of the owner's cottage and gave the children the chance for some illicit bare-back riding.

'We pretended they were ours, and convinced ourselves the horses were being neglected,' Christine says. 'Mick would take carrots for them, and, on the way there, we'd stop at a bakery to buy bread. We also took potato peelings in black buckets. We'd take it in turns to ride the horses and had a right laugh when someone fell off. The bigger horse was a bit wild and we got thrown off and kicked a couple of times.'

The woods off Mill Lane were a natural attraction for the kids in Haughton Green and Mick went there a lot with Paul Sutcliffe. Paul was not the type to sit indoors; he was the outgoing type who always liked to be doing things, and he widened Mick's horizons and made him less withdrawn. They would make camp fires, fix rope swings over the canal, or trespass on farm land – enjoying the exciting, if frightening, prospect of being chased off the land by an angry farmer wielding a shotgun filled with salt pellets.

When they weren't in the woods, Mick would spend time in Paul's back garden, fascinated at watching his mechanically-minded brother build or convert bikes from old frames and wheels abandoned around town.

'At that time, Mick was a shy, timid lad, who always appeared to have something on his mind,' Paul remembers. 'I like to think I helped to bring the best out of him. He was very good at impressions. He did Michael Crawford's "Frank Spencer", Harold Wilson, Eddie Waring, Brian Clough and Clive James, but only if I badgered him. He needed

43

encouraging, and certainly wouldn't do any in front of people he didn't know.

'I was crazy about football and we'd go up on Mill Lane and play fifteen-a-side. To be honest, Mick was the worst player on view. When we picked the teams, he was always the last one to be chosen. Nobody wanted him. Not that it seemed to bother him. He knew he was useless.'

The fact that Paul had failed his Eleven-Plus did not concern Mick. He looked up to him and could be easily influenced and persuaded to do things he probably did not want to do. Smoking, for example, did not interest Mick in the slightest. But Paul was curious, and one day, in the coalsheds behind an old people's home in Forest Road, he pulled out a Sovereign and lit it. After taking a drag, he handed it to Mick. 'Go on, try it,' he said.

Today, Paul smiles at the memory. 'Mick really didn't want to know about smoking at thirteen, but if I badgered him enough I could get him to do anything, and I kept on at him to give it a go. Finally, he gave in, but didn't inhale the smoke. "Go on, take some down," I said. And of course, he started coughing his heart up. I found it funny and when we were out with other friends, I'd ask him to do it again, and he would – for our entertainment.'

Another Two Trees boy who was to have a profound influence on Mick was Steve Howarth, who also hung around the Moorfield shops. Steve was fifteen, but for eight years had been called Lil, an abbreviation of 'Lilliputian', which his older brother, Derek, named him because he had been so tiny.

If Paul Sutcliffe was a soul mate who widened Mick's horizons, Lil was an aggressive doer who would show him what could be achieved with a little bit of self-confidence.

Lil started going out with Lynn Gooding, an intelligent, pretty girl, who had been one of three St Lawrence's girls in Mick's year to go to grammar school. She was popular with the boys, none more so than Mick; he had fancied her at ten, and he fancied her even more at thirteen. But he was too shy and timid to make a move and could only watch in adolescent envy as she started going steady with Lil. Lynn and a girl-friend, Venetia, were lucky enough to have horses, which they kept at a farm at the bottom of Town Lane, and the two boys would go down there to see the girls, and play on a rope swing across a nearby stream. Sometimes they would camp out in the woods at night in an old, weather-beaten tent, Mick and Venetia two shy children together in the shadow of a far more mature, more sexually advanced couple.

Today, Venetia admits: 'We were a pair of ugly gooseberries, who just tagged along because no one was interested in us. Lil and Lynn would be snogging away, while Mick and I just sat there, hardly saying a word. We were so shy that nothing ever happened. But I liked Mick. He was the only boy who didn't tease me for not having any boobs. I didn't wear a training bra, like all the other girls – just a vest – and I was so embarrassed I rarely took my coat off. But Mick accepted me for what I was, not for what was under my jumper, and I found that really nice. He was a lot quieter and more sensitive than the other boys, and didn't swear. He was more particular about himself, too.'

Over the next few months, the four of them, plus Paul Sutcliffe and a few others from the Moorfield estate, went around in a group, either eating chips with gravy, smoking and swearing in St Lawrence's church cemetery, a quarter of a mile from the old school, or dancing at the St John Fisher disco in Haughton Green. The disco was on Tuesday evenings, and before they went in they would buy the obligatory bottle of cider or cream sherry and pass it among themselves outside.

Again, the drink released Mick from his suffocating shyness. He was a Gary Glitter fan, and when the DJ put 'Leader Of The Pack' on the turntable, Mick was transformed. Suddenly he was that precocious six-year-old again, longing to perform, craving the attention. Throwing his arms in the air, he would do 'The Glitter Stomp' across the disco floor, to the delight of other dancers who would move back and encircle him, singing along with him and clapping in time to the music.

Mick revelled in the limelight, basking in the admiration of the watching youngsters, particularly the girls. But it was not only their applause that gave him a buzz on those Tuesday nights – it was the feeling of belonging. On that disco floor, doing what he knew he did well, Mick was no longer an unattractive misfit, part of the crowd but not quite accepted by it. He was out of the shadows and onto centre stage, and no one saw his spotty face, gangly body or red hair, only his talent for mimicry.

The thrill of it all boosted Mick's confidence, and he decided to ask Barbara Lees at the newsagent's to go to the disco with him. Over the next few weeks, his courage kept failing him, but one Friday, before starting his collection round, he hung around the shop until it was empty, then took the plunge. Barbara knew he had been building up to ask her out, but she turned him down flat. She liked him as a person but would never dream of going out with someone with red hair.

Today, she says: 'I didn't fancy Mick at all. He was so embarrassed when I said no, his face went beetroot and he quickly picked up his collecting book and money and left. I felt awful, because I was shy myself in those days, and made sure I was gone by the time he came back. I didn't want to go out with him mainly because of the red hair. But he also struck me as very strange. He dressed weirdly and was a bit of a loner.'

Mick knew his red hair was a turn-off; it was always at the back of his mind when he was trying to chat up a girl. But, in a perverse way, he was proud of it, because he felt it made him different, and in quiet moments he would say to Lil, 'One day I'm going to meet a bird who likes a guy with red hair.'

★

The girl he hankered after was Lynn Gooding, and when she and Lil split up, six months or so later, Mick thought he was in with a chance. 'Whenever we went out, he always wanted to know if she would be coming along, too,' Lil recalls. 'Lynn was going out with other boys at the time, but Mick would always be hanging around.

'One Saturday, we went shopping in Ashton and he bought her a Gary Glitter album. That evening a group of us, including Lynn, congregated in St Lawrence's cemetery, but Mick held on to the record for hours before he plucked up the courage to give it to her. She was pleased and, I think, agreed to see him a couple of times. But Mick read more into their meetings than was there.'

A few weeks later, just before Christmas 1973, Mick went to a party because he knew Lynn was going. And what happened there broke his heart.

Paul Sutcliffe remembers the night well. 'Lynn didn't want to know Mick that night. He kept sitting next to her, trying to talk with her, but she didn't respond. When he kept asking her if she would dance with him, she told her friends, "Keep him away from me."

'After a while, I noticed Mick was missing. He wasn't in the back room where the music was and he wasn't in the kitchen with the drinks. Finally, I found him in the front room. He was all on his own. And crying. Really sobbing. I knew why he was breaking his heart and I tried to pull him together. I put my arm round him and said, "Come on, never mind, there's more fish in the sea. Let's go and have a drink." The kitchen was packed, so we went in the back room, which was empty. I put on a Who record we liked and turned it up loud. As soon as he heard the music, Mick seemed to cheer up and we started dancing. We played it three or four times and Mick seemed to be okay.

'Some time later, though, he went missing again. Someone said he'd gone out the front door, so I went out, looking for him. I found him lying in the middle of the road. I asked him what on earth he thought he was doing and he said, "I want to die. I'm waiting for a bus to run me over."

'I just said, "Get up, you soft bleeder." Fortunately he did, and we went back inside. But that was the effect Lynn's rejection had on him. He was an extra-sensitive boy and he'd probably had enough of being turned down because of his looks.'

Today, Lynn cannot remember much about Mick's crush on her. She recalls him crying at the party but has no recollection of him asking her out. 'I felt sorry for Mick,' she says. 'He was really bonny when he was young, and he was such a nice person you couldn't dislike him. But he went off a bit as he grew up.'

★

It was the grammar school and all it stood for that had changed Mick. And as he began his fourth and crucial year that autumn, he was reeling from the final insult: he was relegated to the lowest group for O-level candidates.

It was D-stream. And, to everyone, D meant only one thing ... DUNCE.

Mick had tried his best for three years and it obviously was not good enough; the school, it was clear, had given up on him. His father was disappointed; he so much wanted his son to achieve academic success. But Mick was not bothered. That rebellious, couldn't-give-a-damn streak he had inherited from his mother came into play. If the school doesn't want to know about me, he decided, then I don't want to know about it.

6

That fourth school year was the turning point – the time Mick rebelled and opted out of all academic study. School, he had decided, was a waste of time, a necessary evil he had to put up with. If he was going to have to endure it for another two years, he would do so on his own terms. Work bored him, so he would not do it; he would mess around, be a clown, instead. The stiff and starchy school regime irritated him, so he would rebel against it. The masters' strict discipline angered him, so he would take the mickey out of them and all they stood for.

He quickly became a talking point in the staff room. Masters would talk about which pupils were pests and which were okay, and, according to geography teacher Ray Wood, Mick's name would always come up as a 'bloody nuisance'.

'At fourteen, he was incorrigible,' Mr Wood recalls. 'Being bored, he would become disruptive, pulling faces all the time and calling out. He wasn't stupid, though; he was an intelligent boy who simply found the grammar school not to his liking.

'The system was against his kind of personality. He hated the regimentation of "get up, sit down", when teachers came into the room. Lessons were conducted in an old-fashioned way, as they would be in a public school, with the teacher the big boss in front of the kids. And Mick couldn't stand it.

'What made it worse for him was that he was surrounded by so many bright boys – some who were destined for Oxford and Cambridge. Mick had more talent than many of the boys from working-class backgrounds, but he found himself out of his depth and eventually switched off. From his first year, he weighed up the situation, bit by bit, finally concluding: "This isn't for me. I don't like the system. I don't like many of the staff. I don't want to know."

'Having decided he didn't want to work, he had to think of something else he could do to pass the time. He could work a situation and play off personalities, and he'd find it amusing to manipulate a situation to his advantage, just for fun, to relieve his boredom.

'The school was a tough one. And some Friday nights, certain boys

48

would give a master a working-over for the aggro they'd gone through in the week. But that was never the case with Mick – he had no physical aggression and was never involved in the rough stuff.

'He was a cheeky sod, though. Most of the time, he'd have a grin on his face and when he talked to you, it would be tongue-in-cheek, so you never knew if he meant what he was saying. In these situations, he would be sharp and quick and you always felt he was getting the better of you.'

In Mr Wood, the fourteen-year-old rebel was lucky. The teacher had a keen sense of humour, and found the cheeky side of Mick merely high-spirited, a positive side of his personality. Other teachers, however, saw it as totally negative and thought Mick objectionable.

French teacher Harold Heywood, for example, found Mick casual and aloof, and did not like him at all.

'I felt I was bestowing a benefit on him by teaching him a second language to enrich his life, help him travel, get a job – but he wouldn't have anything of me,' says Mr Heywood. 'Some boys lapped French up and wanted to do really well. But Hucknall was at the other end of the spectrum. French was simply not on his agenda. He was treading water, thinking, "There's something beyond all this. I must get through this unnecessary process of being indoctrinated with French verbs and stupid childish stuff."

'I wanted his achievement in the language, but I didn't battle because I knew I would lose. I got that picture very quickly.'

Mr Heywood, who didn't 'battle', insists that Mick was not a smiler. But Ray Wood, who *did*, says his lasting impression of Mick is 'this carrot-top, smiling, laughing, full of beans'. Mr Wood, it is clear, saw a different side to Mick and, through his own effervescent personality, brought out the best in the boy.

'He was a jovial, happy sort of guy and I liked him,' says Mr Wood. 'I didn't think: You're a reject, pal, a waste of time – I don't want to know you. But teaching him geography was certainly a battle. I'd have to threaten him or play him along and encourage him to be actively responsive, rather than just a blasted pest.

'He sometimes liked geography, depending on what we were doing. I seem to remember him enjoying discussing the universe and the relationship of the planets. That summed him up. He would put effort into something only if it took his interest. Anything artistic, for example, would appeal to him. He had an artistic flair and would get a kick out of drawing a good map and being complimented on it.'

Art was the only subject to interest him. And even at that stage, the beginning of the build-up to O-level examinations, it seems clear that Mick had abandoned earlier thoughts of becoming an engineer and was planning to do just enough to get him into art college – and no more.

Walking along the corridor to the playground after a lesson, Ray Wood would try to encourage him: 'Come on, get your geography done. Get a few passes under your belt. You'll get a decent job afterwards.'

Mick would just laugh: 'I'm not interested in it,' he would say. 'I don't want to do it.'

And he meant it.

★

For a young rebel with no interest in school except the bell that signalled the end of the day's lessons, Audenshaw's army and RAF cadet forces could hardly have held a great attraction. But that winter of 1974, Mick, with Adrian Whittleworth, Frank Ollerenshaw and a couple of other pals, felt a strong desire to enlist. They chose the RAF section, run by a war hero named Geoffrey Eastwood, who had been awarded a Distinguished Flying Medal for his services as a wartime bomber pilot (and an OBE for Services to Training). He welcomed them into the force gladly.

Mick's decision to join Mr Eastwood's group of bright, highly-thought-of pupils surprised many, not least Harold Heywood.

'The RAF comprised the elite – chaps with personality, ambition and academic prowess – and Hucknall did not have these qualities,' he says. 'He was tolerably smart in his uniform, which helped him to qualify, I suppose. And he was individualistic. But cadet forces are about mucking in together on field days and camps – and Hucknall stood apart from other boys. He was a bit of a loner, if you like.

'At first, I thought he'd joined because he had vision and had some long-term project in mind. But then I thought it was probably associated with his rebelliousness against the academic discipline.'

The real reason was probably far simpler. The cadet force got together on Friday afternoons, meaning that members had to miss their last school lesson – in Mick's case, French. For a boy who did not have the language on his agenda, the RAF cadet force – despite the regimentation and discipline which Mick abhorred – presented a wonderful alternative.

Sadly, the love affair with Mr Eastwood's smart outfit was all too brief. Mick and his pals realized they had made a mistake after just three weeks, when the penny dropped that the cadets soldiered on after the rest of the school had gone home. En masse, they decided that the cadet force was an intrusion into their social life: Friday signalled the end of school and the start of the weekend and they wanted to prepare for that, not play at being airmen.

If Mick and his friends had thought it through, gone to Mr Eastwood and apologized for their mistake, things might have been different. As it was, the boys merely stopped turning up for the Friday meetings, then refused to return their uniforms. The school kept sending reminders, but the five 'deserters' ignored them. Finally, six months later, the Infamous Five were told they were being court-martialled and were to report to Geoff Eastwood.

They were ordered to stand to attention, but thought the whole affair funny and burst out laughing. After giving all five boys Dishonourable Discharges, Mr Eastwood tore into them: 'You idiots. You think it's funny – but it's not. This discharge is now on each of your military records – for life!'

The boys were given one last chance to return the uniforms – or pay a £300 bill. Each uniform found its way back to school. Fast.

*

For Mick and his close D-stream mates, lunchtimes could not come quickly enough: not only was it the half-way mark in the dreary daily slog, but it also meant time to eat, and Mick, Frank, Gary, Adrian and another friend were healthy, hungry lads. If it had been up to them, they would have headed the queue for lunch and been first up for second helpings, but the dining hall was controlled by a maths teacher named John Staff, who did not approve of them and restricted their culinary ambitions. The boys nicknamed him 'Greeny', because of his passion for green suits and shirts. He was a short Welshman, who controlled the dining hall with a keen eye and a rich, baritone voice. Sensing Mick and the group of D-streamers who came to the hall with him might be secret smokers, he would search them for cigarettes before letting them in. And he would take a delight in putting them at the back of the queue, so that most of the best food was gone by the time they sat down and there was no chance of going back for seconds.

Mick and his friends were no good at chess and were not interested in history, but they joined these societies when they learned it entitled them to an early dinner. Greeny was not impressed: he still put them at the back of the queue, still preventing them from getting seconds.

One lunchtime the boys decided something had to be done. They were all hungry, growing lads and fed up with what they felt was unfair treatment. They needed to make a protest. They needed someone to make their voices heard – someone with front, confident enough not to worry about being considered cheeky, and someone who could eat fast. There was only one candidate – Mick. He was brave about speaking up to teachers and was able to polish off a cottage pie, mashed potatoes and cabbage in just seventeen seconds.

Adrian Whittleworth recalls: 'We had races to see who could finish their dinner first and Mick nearly always won. He didn't eat – he just swallowed. And the whole table watched in amazement.

'Eating a plateful in seventeen seconds sounds impossible, but Mick definitely did it. He'd pick up the plate and shovel the food into his face and not stop until it was all gone. He just kept shovelling and swallowing, and his face would be red and his eyes bulging and filled with tears at the effort, but he never stopped until the plate was clean. It was a real competition to him. He never glanced at others he was racing – just kept going, like an Olympic contestant sprinting for the line.'

Frank Ollerenshaw says: 'We used to call him "Perpetual Motion", because he just kept going. He was undoubtedly the faster eater, but he nearly always won because the boy he was racing would make the mistake of looking at Mick's red face, tears in his eyes, and burst out laughing. St Trinian's had nothing on us. We had real fun at those dinner times – real crying laughter times.'

Chairman Mick's representations to John Staff for early 'seconds' call were nearly always met with a dismissive wave of the arm, but Mick's talent for impersonation did enable him to get some sort of revenge. He practised Staff's deep, rich voice until he had it off to a tee, then began echoing his lunchtime orders. When Staff spotted a boy stepping out of the queue for food and barked, 'Get back in line,' a similar-sounding command would come from the back where Mick was standing, po-faced, with his friends. As the early diners neared the end of their main course, Staff would boom, 'Any more roast potatoes?' And Mick would dutifully respond in a loud, Welsh accent, much to the amusement of his pals. Staff would look at the group and raise a knowing eyebrow, but never took it further.

With lunch over and time to kill before the first afternoon lesson, Mick and his pals would look for things to do. Extra study or revision was not something that sprang to mind; instead, they would congregate in the toilets – just across the yard from the dining hall – for a sly smoke, and any other idle, time-wasting pursuit that took their fancy.

A nearby newsagent made it easy for the rebellious fourteen-year-olds to buy cigarettes. The boys would pool their financial resources for a packet of twenty and a feeble-minded assistant would split them into fives and put them in toffee bags. Greeny was well aware of what was going on behind the closed lavatory doors, and he would burst in, unexpectedly, booming, 'Extinguish! Put that fire out!' Sometimes he would be carrying a bottle of water and when the guilty culprits opened the door, he would give them a soaking.

Greeny, it seems, was game for a laugh and in no way awesome, for one day Mick organized a spot of revenge that might, in other circumstances, have landed him in hot water. He talked other members of the unofficial Smokers' Union into filling a bucket with water and placing it over a partly-opened lavatory door, so that it tipped over onto whoever opened it. Then they, and a dozen or so other boys in on the prank, hung about outside the toilets, waiting for Greeny to arrive. He didn't let them down. He strode into the toilets – straight into the trap.

Frank Ollerenshaw will never forget the sight of Mr Staff soaked. 'He wasn't in a fit state to say extinguish anything, because he was extinguished himself,' says Frank. 'He had a bucket on his head and we were rolling about.'

It says much for the teacher that, although he knew who was responsible, he took no action.

When they weren't winding up John Staff, Mick and his friends would sneak into a gymnasium above the main hall and mess around with various apparatus, including weights. Even here, Mick took a delight in playing the clown to make him the centre of attention. Once he lifted a weight, marginally too heavy, and toppled backwards through a balcony rail. For a moment his pals thought he might be hurt, but Mick just sat there, the bar of the weight across his neck, and a stupid expression on his face.

Adrian Whittleworth, who was there, says: 'Mick turned everything he did into fun. He was always pulling funny faces. I'm sure he realized early on that he wasn't pretty, and decided to make use of his face in a funny way to make people laugh and like him for it.'

After school, Mick would travel home with Gary and Frank. Sometimes they would walk the two miles, saving the 2p bus fare, but most days they would get the bus and run the gauntlet of abuse from the unruly Egerton Park louts who got on a few stops later.

Mick would get off in Two Trees Lane and walk along Moorfield Avenue to the newsagent's, now taken over by a genial, fun-loving man, Keith Jaundrell, and his engaging wife, Sylvia. Keith was popular with other paper-boys because he liked a joke, but Mick did not want to be bothered by what he considered childish, time-wasting pranks. He rarely entered into the skylarking and spirit of fun Keith encouraged: he was there to deliver papers and be paid for it and that's all he was interested in.

Keith remembers: 'While we were waiting for the evening papers to arrive, I used to mess around with the lads. They thought they were the bee's knees at times and got a bit cheeky, so I'd pick them up, turn them upside down and spank their backsides; or else fight and roll around the shop floor with them. They all loved it. But Mick wasn't into that sort of thing. He would always be outside, waiting for the paper van to arrive. When it did, he'd come in for his batch and quickly disappear. He was there to do a job and wanted to get on with it.

'He was a serious boy, was Mick. Sometimes you would look at him and imagine him to be surly – especially if he had lost his patience with something. But I think it was just that he was a thinker. Certainly he was an intelligent lad, who I could rely on and trust 100 per cent. There were a few lads I wasn't keen on, but I liked Mick.'

Keith's wife, Sylvia, liked him too, although she found him a 'distant' boy who never talked much. 'He wasn't bad-mannered, but he was very within himself and hard to reach,' she says.

Not surprisingly for a young teenager who had lived without a mother for twelve years, Mick had learned to be self-sufficient. He would let himself into the empty house in West Park Avenue, change out of his blue school blazer, white shirt and red and white tie, and make himself something to eat to keep him going until his father came home around 6.30 p.m. Often, Reg would leave food prepared on the electric stove, which Mick would simply heat up; but if he had not, Mick would make himself something simple. Not that Mick was ever satisfied with traditional beans on toast: according to Lil, he would grate cheese into the beans, then, for some reason, add milk. Being on his own and an adventurous type, he began to experiment and discovered that curry powder could give the most mundane, unexciting dish a bit of a bite. This is how he developed an early liking of Indian food.

If coming home to an empty house and fending for himself bothered Mick, he never showed it. He had long since accepted being a one-parent child and never once referred to the woman who had brought him into the world. Once Lil's mother Jean brought up the subject and Mick reacted strongly.

She recalls: 'He didn't like talking about his mum, but one day I said that if she suddenly appeared on the scene and got in touch, he would welcome her with open arms. Mick shook his head. "No, I wouldn't," he said angrily. "There's no way I'd have anything to do with her after what she did." '

★

The under-age drinking law was no barrier to the rebellious Mick. He had flouted the law on smoking, and cocked a snook at the school's rigid

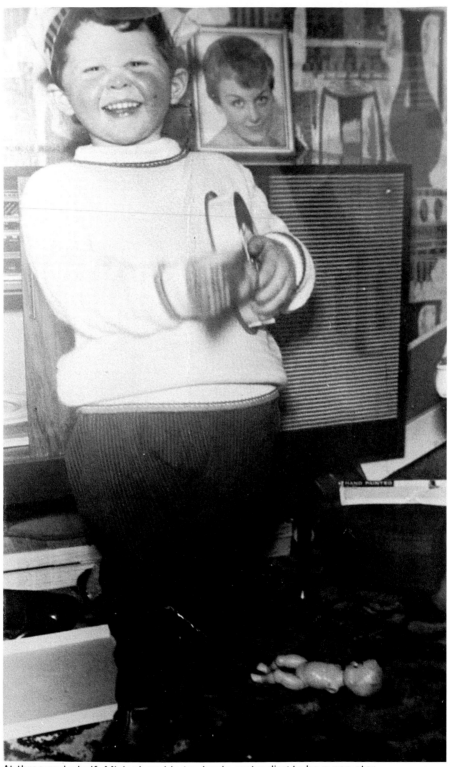

At three-and-a-half, Mick plays his toy banjo pretending to be a pop star.

Mick and Billy Grimshaw
at Santa's grotto in
Manchester in 1964.

Enjoying a summer's
day, aged four, with
childhood friend Billy
Grimshaw.

Mick, second from right, at a young
friend's birthday party.

Aged five in his first school
photograph at St Lawrence's
Primary School in Denton.

Above Reg and Mick, aged eight, gently holding the rabbit Reg bought him.

Right Mick's mother Maureen in 1967 posing for her local paper with her two children, newborn Lyndsay and Ricky, three. Mick was seven and growing up happily without her in Denton.

Leigh Reporter calling mothers and babies

BONNY BABIES and justly proud mums. Those are the ingredients of our successful mothers and babies feature.

If you live in the area which the **Reporter** covers—that is Leigh, Tyldesley, Atherton, Hindley Green, Boothstown, Mosley Common and Astley—you are eligible for inclusion. Provided you have a baby, that is!

Please write to the Pictures Editor, **Leigh Reporter**, Ducie Street, Leigh, or phone Leigh 71551 or 72723.

Mrs. Maureen Kozarits, 2, Arundle Drive, Leigh, with Ricky (aged three years) and nine-weeks-old Lyndsay. (W1590)

Above left Mick, second from left, aged six at St Lawrence's.

Left Aged seven at St Lawrence's.

The West Park Avenue gang on Mick's eleventh birthday.
Mick puts his arm around Nigel Clayton, the boy he
befriended. Far right is Mick's 'brother', Gary Shaw.

Playing while on holiday visiting relatives in Barrow-in-Furness.

Aged thirteen at Audenshaw Grammar
– bullies taunted him because of his 'woollen hat' hair.

Aged fifteen – now the rebel at Audenshaw.

Aged sixteen as a waiter at the Broomstair Working Men's Club.
People called him 'Mad Mick' because of his wild hair.

Maureen building a new life in the 1980s, her first son now forgotten.

regime in doing so. Now he was keen to see whether he could buck the legal system in a pub and get away with it.

Although he was tall for his fourteen years, he did not look eighteen, and almost certainly would not have been served had he walked into a pub on his own. But in Paul Sutcliffe and Steve Howarth, Mick had two pals who were well practised in the art of under-age drinking. Steve had been drinking since the age of eleven when he and his dad shared a pint after working together in the summer. And Paul had always looked older than his age; he even grew a moustache shortly after his fourteenth birthday.

The pub they chose for Mick's introduction to the public bar was in Denton. The pub was not an ideal choice because Steve's uncles were regulars, but the landlord was lenient and unlikely to turn them away. The three of them rolled up there one Saturday afternoon, just before Christmas.

Paul recalls: 'Lil and I were concerned that Mick would get us caught. And he was on edge because he was obviously the youngest. But we decided to front it out. We told Mick to follow us in and sneak around to a corner where he couldn't be easily spotted. Then Lil and I strolled up to the bar, bold as brass, and ordered three pints of bitter. No doubt the landlord had clocked Mick, but he was more concerned at taking the money and didn't say a word. We had two pints each that afternoon. Mick loved the experience. He was still a bit timid with us, but we brought him out of his shell.'

Certainly the drink did not do any harm to Mick's confidence. One Sunday night a few weeks later, he was knocking back the pints again, and was quickly in the mood for any bit of devilment his pals cared to suggest. For some reason, on the way home, Lil thought it a good idea to pop into St Lawrence's Church, which was holding Evensong. To Mick and Paul, it was a bizarre suggestion – certainly not one they would have dared make themselves. But, in their merry state, it sounded perfectly reasonable, so they walked in and stood at the back of the packed congregation. It was a solemn occasion, but the tippling trio saw a funny side and couldn't stop giggling.

'The vicar was talking in a peculiar sing-song voice and we were crying with laughter,' Paul remembers. 'People in front started coughing and looking round and, at the end of the service, an usher told us to leave and never to come back in that state again. But we were all young and uncaring and didn't give a damn.'

The three boys always went to Denton when they had money in their pockets. The pub was a fair trek, but it was the only pub where they were sure they would not be refused. They did not want to risk going into pubs in Haughton Green because publicans and regulars knew them and would probably have seen them earlier in the week in school uniform. After a few pints they would walk home, all sucking Polo mints so they would not arrive smelling of alcohol.

Having settled for a work-shy life of rebellion inside school, Mick took the soft option outside, too. With his confidence in himself growing, he began to smoke and drink more often. And when a friend of Lil's named Harry Bradbury said he had an easy way to make a lot of money, Mick could not wait to get started.

7

Harry's way to easy money was summed up in one word: theft.

He was an ex-grammar school boy with an agile brain, but he was also a lovable rogue, not fussed about how he made a few extra pounds. And he was something of an expert in the illegal art of stripping roofs of lead and selling it to a scrap merchant in the neighbouring town of Hyde.

Over a pint one Friday night in the spring of 1975, Harry told Mick, Paul and Lil that he had cast his expert eye over several old buildings in Denton and that they were ripe for stripping – particularly Mick's old school, St Lawrence's. If they could get a good wheelbarrow-load to the dealer on a Saturday they might get twenty quid for it. Mick's eyes lit up at the prospect of a fiver for hardly any work. So did Paul's and Lil's. The money was certainly one attraction, but the thrill of it all was another. The adventure appealed to the three of them, even if it was illegal, and they all agreed to meet Harry near the school the following Friday. The three older boys climbed on to the old school roof and started removing the 18 × 5 inch strips of lead fixed between the tiles. Then they rolled them and threw them down to Mick who waited below, ready to pile them into a wheelbarrow. When the barrow was full, the boys covered it with a piece of carpet, then pushed it into the old school's outside toilet where they left it overnight.

The following day they wheeled the barrow about two miles up Two Trees Lane, down the long and winding Mill Lane and into Hyde. The barrow was so heavy they could push it only twenty yards before having to stop for a rest. And by the time they reached the scrapyard over an hour later, their backs were aching.

'It was murder,' Paul remembers. 'And what made it worse was that all the time we were pushing, we kept thinking it may all be a waste of time. After all, we had no idea what the lead was worth. But then one of the staff weighed it and started counting out eighteen one-pound notes. I could have kissed him. We ran off on a high down to the canal to split the money up between us. We felt like kings.'

Having reaped such a reward for no more than a bit of labouring,

Mick could not wait for another Friday night job and was delighted when Harry announced the next target. That went off without a hitch and it was not long before Mick was looking forward to the Saturday morning trips as much as to his drinking. Sometimes they got as much as £40. To Mick, his share seemed like a fortune. With his paper and milk rounds, he was raking it in for a schoolboy not yet fifteen; often he made more in a week than his dad.

It seemed like easy money. But the lead adventures were not without their moments of danger and fear. Once, Mick, Paul and Lil went back to the old school building for some lead they had not had room for the first time. But they tried to do it without the expert guidance of Harry – and nearly paid for it. The three boys were all on the roof when they spotted an old lady watching them from a nearby house. They thought she was just nosey, and carried on with their early evening labour. But, several minutes later, a police car pulled into what had been the school yard. Paul and Lil got down from the roof on the other side, out of sight, and hid in the toilets. But Mick was not so quick; he was standing on the roof in full view as two policemen got out of the patrol car and looked up.

'What are you doing?' one asked.

While stripping the lead, Mick had spotted an old tennis ball in a gutter. Now, without saying a word, he went over to it and picked it up. 'I'm just getting my ball,' he said casually. The two policemen accepted his excuse and told him to come down. What they did not do was ask to have a closer look at the ball. If they had, they would have seen that it was threadbare and useless – certainly not worth climbing a roof for.

Paul and Lil, who were not discovered, found the incident funny. 'We called Mick a lucky bastard,' Paul says. 'But he was very quick-thinking, even at fourteen.'

The boys were breaking the law, of course, but they did not see it that way: to them, it was not so much stealing as scavenging.

Lil says: 'It was something a lot of other boys in the area seemed to be doing and we just jumped on the bandwagon. We never stripped new buildings – only ones that were about to be demolished. It was a serious attempt to make some money and we did well. When we got more confident, we would strip copper pipes and electrical wiring from behind walls in old houses. We got so good we could strip a house in an hour. If anyone asked us what we were up to, we'd tell them to bugger off; we didn't give a damn. We'd fill our wheelbarrow and push it to the woods and light a fire to burn off the rubber round the wiring. Then we'd go to the scrapyard for the weigh-up.'

Mick, it is clear, was no juvenile delinquent destined for a life of crime. With little to interest or encourage him at school, he was bored, perhaps a little lost, and eager for excitement as much as money. Certainly he went on those lead-stripping sprees with the adrenalin racing and not a little fear.

Harry Bradbury recalls: 'When I was around, Mick never got involved in the nitty-gritty of ripping lead off roofs – he wanted to be on the ground, so he could leg it first in the event of trouble. He was worried all the time about what his dad would say if he was caught. He was scared stiff of his dad.

'Me and the other two were happy to stay on a roof for an hour and a half or so to get as much as we could carry. But Mick was always on edge, anxious to get it over and done with. He only wanted a quick bob or two.'

★

Mick did have one brush with the law, however. When he wasn't increasing his alcohol capacity or relieving roofs of their lead, he would strip parts of abandoned bikes and rebuild them into his own designs, with cow-horn handlebars. Once, he was watching Paul and another pal, named Billy Inman, strip a bike he thought they had found dumped in a field. But the bike was stolen and the police caught them red-handed. Fortunately for Mick, his friends made it clear that he had nothing to do with the theft, and only Paul and Billy were charged. Later, they were bound over for a year at Ashton Magistrates' Court.

The bond between Paul and Mick was so strong that Paul, the stronger and more confident of the two, would go into battle for his mate. One day early that summer, his loyalty landed him in hospital with a broken finger.

It all began when he heard that Dave Sylvester, who also went to Two Trees, had stolen a bike Mick had spent weeks making.

Sylvester, so the grapevine gossip said, just walked into Mick's garden with a pal, Gary Doubleday, and helped himself. In the school corridor the next day, Paul confronted Sylvester and demanded he return the bike. Frightened, Sylvester sought the protection of his own strong-armed friend, Doubleday – a tough skinhead not known for his soft approach to life.

'He was like Sylvester's gangster and I was Hucknall's,' Paul remembers. 'We were having a go at each other in the school corridor and Lil, who had fought Doubleday, started arranging a fight. Other boys imagined I could fight because I could talk a bit and was very self-confident, but I wasn't the fighting type – I'd rather be playing football.

I couldn't back out, though, and agreed to meet at the Moorfield shops at 7.30 that night to sort it out. I was worried to death.

'When I told Mick, he didn't seem shocked or anything. He agreed to come with me, and that evening we went to the shops. When we turned and saw Doubleday, strutting around in his Doc Martens and jeans and black and white chequered driving gloves, surrounded by about twenty-five boys from school, I froze. I thought: Fucking hell, I'm going to get slaughtered. I didn't want to go any further, but I could hear them all whispering about what Doubleday was and was not going to do, and I couldn't back down. Mick was scared, too. Well, it's a daunting thing, walking up to twenty-five kids, most of whom are against you.

'Lil was making all the rules: shake hands before you start, no kicking when the other one's down, and all that. He was the Barry Hearn of the day. He wanted to see the fight. He had fought a draw with Doubbie and wanted to see how good I was. Mick stood there, just looking. He was probably embarrassed. He didn't ask me to get his bike back, didn't expect me to get in any bother over it. I'd got myself into it because I knew he couldn't stick up for himself against that lot.

'Anyway, we had this fight and I knocked the shit out of Doubbie. It didn't last long – ten minutes at the most – but there was a lot of blood and I broke a finger through hitting him so hard. I went to hospital and Mick told my mum and dad that I'd fallen off my bike.

'It wasn't in the rules of the fight that whoever won got the bike. But I knew where it was and, a few days later, Mick and I went there and got it. He was over the moon. I can't remember if he thanked me for battling for him, but I wasn't bothered – he had his bike back, and that's what mattered.'

*

For a while, early that summer, Billy Inman was on the scene, scrambling his moped in the woods. Which is why Mick came to get a punch on the chin – and a tattoo on his right arm.

Paul, who landed the punch, recalls: 'We had been watching Billy ride his motorbike in the woods when the chain came off. I was kneeling by the back wheel, trying to fix it, when Mick, without any warning, revved the engine. The back wheel span round, nearly taking my fingers off. I went spare. I got up, swearing blue murder, and gave him a right-hander on the chin. He went down and the bike fell on top, trapping him. Mick had done a bloody stupid thing. And he knew it.'

The tattoo, however, was a self-inflicted punishment, which Mick was persuaded to go through with after seeing a spectacular display of tattoos on one of Billy's pals, Michael Bradburn. One night, Bradburn met Mick and Paul at Billy's house, armed with some India ink, a needle, a lighter and a box of matches, and asked the younger boys what sort of tattoo they wanted. The three agreed on a simple crucifix-style cross on the forearm and Bradburn explained the procedure: they had to shave that part of their arm, and draw the cross with the charcoal from a burnt-out match. Then they would pierce the skin in the required shape, using a needle sterilized over a flame. They had to prick the arm until it bled, then add the ink.

Paul went first. He put his left arm on Billy's kitchen table and squealed as the hot needle punctured his skin. The others laughed, thinking Paul was not going to complete the job. But he did, albeit in some agony. Then it was Mick's turn.

'He was in agony, too,' Paul remembers. 'He had to do it on his right arm, because he's left-handed, and he had to keep stopping and wiping it because it hurt so much. He had to prick his skin hundreds of times to make the shape. But he did it, which surprised me at the time, because he was quite soft, really. Billy, though, bottled out.

'Mick and I were bloody sore afterwards. The area round the tattoo came up in a huge lump and we were convinced we had gangrene. It took a week to settle down, and then we had to resist picking the scabs because that would have made the ink come off. Mick was worried what his dad would say, so he covered his tattoo with a plaster.'

★

As his fourth school year ended, any worries Mick had that he had not worked hard enough for his O-level exams the following June did not show. It was as if he had already decided which subjects he was going to pass and which he was not. In the meantime, he was going to continue having a good time. He had got the taste for good Northern ale and could now hold his own with Paul, Lil and Harry, knocking back five pints on a Friday night without making a fool of himself.

Friday nights in the pub had become a ritual and Mick looked forward to them, particularly if the gang had done business with Freddie Pye and they had lots of drinking money in their pockets. But he was still a relatively quiet, shy boy, much in the shadow of his older, more gregarious mates; and this, plus the fear of getting home late and being locked out, seems to have prevented him from totally relaxing and enjoying himself – at least, until he had had a few drinks.

Harry recalls: 'Mick was terrified of his old fella. When we called at his house, for example, Mick would never invite us in. He would pull the front door behind him and whisper on the doorstep. If he wasn't ready, we'd have to hang about outside for him; we never went in. Then in the pub, he'd worry himself silly about being home before midnight because his dad would lock him out. But once he'd had a few pints, the quiet, shy bloke would vanish, and Mick would say, "Bollocks, I'm in the shit anyway, so I'm staying." Then he'd roll home about two or three, or even later.'

Mick's father laughs off the suggestion that Mick was scared of him, but admits he imposed a midnight curfew. 'You have to have rules, don't you? I had to be strict, keep a firm hand on him, or he would have been a tearaway. In some ways, I was old-fashioned. I never swore in front of Mick, but I would give him the odd right-hander if he stepped out of line. This wasn't often, because Mick was good lad, and a happy one. We were a good act.'

Harry is right, however, in thinking Mick's fear of his dad is the reason they were never invited into the house. Mick was aware his father disapproved of them.

As Reg says: 'Mick seemed to seek out older boys and I'd often say, "So and so is too old for you – why don't you knock around with boys of your own age?" '

Mick did not confide in his father about what he was doing or thinking outside school. And his father, it seems, did not ask. Which, in one respect, is a pity. Certainly Reg would not have approved of the drinking, let alone the stealing, but one aspect of Mick's adolescence was quietly concerning him: girls. Or, rather, the lack of them in his son's life.

Today, Reg freely admits: 'Having brought Mick up without any feminine influence, I was very worried he would turn out to be gay. I was very relieved, walking home with the weekend shopping one Friday night, when I saw him in a shop doorway with a girl. He called out, "All right, dad?" I looked over and thought, "Good luck to you, son – enjoy yourself." '

Having been enticed into smoking, drinking and stealing, Mick was all too eager to explore the virgin territory of that other so-called vice – sex. The problem was that he was not the type of boy who attracted girls easily. At just fifteen, he was still a spotty, gangly youth, with long arms, bright ginger hair and a red face, who blushed almost crimson, even at the thought of asking for a date.

He had fancied Barbara Lees the moment he saw her behind the newsagent's counter, but she had turned down his offer to go to the John Fisher disco because she did not like his red hair. With most of his pals boasting about the girls they had been intimate with, Mick was despondent about his failure to meet someone who found him attractive.

And then that August, he went to Butlin's holiday camp in Ayr, on the west coast of Scotland, with Lil and four other friends, and met a pretty, dark-haired Scottish lass.

She was twenty-one. And she didn't mind red hair one bit.

★

The trip was part holiday, part endurance test for a Duke of Edinburgh award. Lil had seen a leaflet about it at the Lancaster Road Youth Club a few months earlier and had talked Mick into going on it with him. The cost was £75, but it promised to be a good investment: part would be spent on a fifty-mile trek, sleeping rough; the rest of the week would be spent having fun at Butlin's.

The trip got off to a disastrous start. After travelling through the night on a coach, the group of adventurous teenagers arrived in Ayr to discover that their team leader had made a dreadful mistake: they were booked into another Butlin's camp nearly 300 miles away in Pwllheli in North Wales!

A Butlin's official was apologetic, but said there was nothing he could do: all the group's camping equipment was at Pwllheli and they would have to turn back and go there. The tired, hungry, disappointed teenagers were furious, none more so than Lil, who physically threatened the organizer, then threw his suitcase into the sea.

Finally, someone in the Butlin's hierarchy solved the problem by finding some spare chalets and allowing the group to stay at the camp.

'Our little lot were over the moon,' Lil recalls. 'We didn't give a damn about dedication and discipline and getting an award. We were there for a holiday. After a nightmare start, it couldn't have worked out better. Instead of having to walk bloody miles and sleep rough, we had chalets and the prospect of a lot of fun for a full week.'

For the first three days, Lil spent time at one of the two camp discos with a girl he had met on the coach. On the fourth night, he went looking for Mick and found him in the disco for over-eighteens, talking to two girls considerably older.

'I was amazed to see him so advanced in chatting them up, especially as he was on his own,' Lil recalls. 'I smiled at him and asked if he wanted a drink. He told me to get the girls one too, and came to the bar to tell me which girl he was trying to pull. When we sat down, I started talking to the girl Mick wasn't interested in and, before I knew it, Mick and the other girl were snogging. I was dead chuffed. It was all so new to him.

'He had a good old smooch with the girl on the dance floor, then said

63

he was taking her back to his chalet. He asked me to take the other girl to mine, but I'd been given a double chalet and the bloke I was sharing with wouldn't let my girl stay.

'We certainly interrupted something when we knocked on Mick's door and asked to be let in. He said, "What the fucking hell's wrong with your own room?" But he let us in and we stumbled through the darkness and clambered into a tiny single bed. Within seconds we heard a lot of grunting and groaning – and a lot of laughing – coming from Mick's bed. They were obviously enjoying themselves. I don't think the girl knew it was Mick's first time. I can't imagine he told her.'

In the morning, Mick confessed that he could have picked a better time for his first full sexual experience. But it did not bother him. Lil says: 'He was very happy – really pleased with himself. We were laughing and joking over breakfast. He had a huge smile on his face and it stayed all week.'

Overnight, Mick had become more confident, more self-assured, happier with himself and his appearance.

★

Back home in Denton, his new-found confidence paid off, and, much to Reg's delight, a petite, pretty girl with large breasts started knocking at 30 West Park Avenue. It was at a time when Mick had promised his father he'd given up smoking cigarettes.

'One day,' says Reg, 'I was coming home from work on the bus and saw Mick lying in a field next to this busty girl, with a cigarette in his hand. When he came home, I pulled him on it. "Copped you with a fag, with that girl," I said. Quick as a flash, he said, "I was just holding it for her." '

It wasn't true. Mick's adolescent flirtation with cigarettes would last another six months, before he discovered it could harm what he treasured most – his voice.

8

For four years, Mick's grammar school life had been a non-event – for him and his teachers. He hated everything about it and, nearly all the time, it showed in his casual manner and indolent look. But now, in his fifth – and O-level – year, Mick could see the light at the end of what had been a depressingly dark tunnel, and he perked up a little: it would all be over soon and he could concentrate on having a good time, without being told what to do. He did not know what he was going to do when he left, but he was certain he was leaving. Not once had he thought about staying on into the sixth form and taking A-levels, even if he had been clever enough. The last thing he wanted was the mundane routine of a nine-to-five office job. As soon as the summer term was over, he was going to leave – with as many O-levels as he could manage – and go to college for a two-year course: it would give him time to ponder his future.

With the end happily in sight, Mick began to enjoy art and economics, the two subjects he was reasonably confident of passing. And his interest was reflected in his attitude during lessons: both Ernest Walker and John Cumming remember him as a pleasant lad, who contributed to the class and caused no trouble at all.

'Some boys looked grim, but Mick was a positive sort of bloke and gave the impression he was pleased with what was going on,' Mr Walker recalls. 'He had a smile and I was always pleased to see him in a group because of it. Economics was the one lesson where boys *had* to join in; they couldn't just sit there, taking notes. Mick very much liked taking part in the political arguments. He loved putting his two penn'orth in.'

Probably more to the point, Mick liked Mr Walker and found it easy to relate to his style of teaching. Early on, the teacher shocked the group by telling them that Jimi Hendrix was his favourite guitarist. Then, when he was trying to bring complex economic theory down to basics, he would use footballers or pop singers as examples of why certain people earn a lot of money, so that the boys could understand more easily.

For Mick, it brought the subject to life, and the more he began to understand, the more he wanted to know, particularly when Mr Walker talked about the possibilities in life for people blessed with a unique talent, or who looked different in some distinctive way.

Mr Walker recalls: 'A mock exam question was: Why does a pop singer earn more than a coal miner? And I used to tell the boys that if they could do something that no one else could do, they could go a long way, whether it was playing football or a guitar, or singing. The boys liked this; it was something they understood.

'We talked about government and what a political party was and the general parliamentary set-up, and Mick was interested in that too. He and the other ten or so in the group liked the course because it dealt with things happening today, not yesterday.

'A lot of kids who have good memories feel safer doing something they can learn parrot-fashion and write down, but I'd rather have a boy who can argue a little bit. Mick was certainly one of those. He wasn't awkward to deal with and, as far as I was concerned, was not rebellious in the least. He was a damn good lad and I liked him.'

In that final year, Mick revelled in John Cumming's casual art class. Mr Cumming, a non-idealistic, bohemian type who admits he side-stepped the school system, ran the class like a little club, and Mick loved it. He and Frank Ollerenshaw and Gary Hulston would be encouraged to discuss the issues of the day as they worked; and the atmosphere was so relaxed that they often popped in there for a chat, even when art wasn't on the timetable.

Mr Cumming remembers Mick as a 'very mature, thinking' fifteen-year-old with an easy-going casualness, who was interested in debating important topics. 'He was a tidy boy, but he always seemed to be strangled by his clothes. He was neat, but he'd outgrown his blazer and it was always half-way up his arms. I regarded Mick and his pals as pleasant lads, who weren't going to get their art O-levels, so I decided I would make life pleasant for them and for myself. It was easy. They were absolutely no trouble. They weren't out to knock the system or upset me. They were all very dry-witted and treated me like one of the lads who could enjoy a joke. I did enjoy their jokes. And I hope they enjoyed mine.'

It seems clear they did. As Frank Ollerenshaw says: 'Mr Cumming was very forward-thinking and asked us to call him "Jim". We could go into his class and do virtually what we liked, as long as we produced something. Mick was very much into painting and was encouraged to paint what he liked. He loved it.'

Other teachers, however, were not so lenient. A chemistry teacher named Blundell, for example, warned one day he would 'slipper' any boy who did not do his homework. Mick did not do his, and the next day was called to the front of the class. He prepared himself for a gym shoe, but the teacher took off one of his own shoes – a Doc Marten.

Immediately, Mick backed away. 'I'm not having that,' he said.

'You are,' said Mr Blundell.

Mick turned towards the class theatrically, showing off. 'I'm not,' he said cheekily.

Other boys started laughing. So did Mick; he thought Blundell was joking. But he wasn't.

Pointing to a spot near his desk, he said, 'Bend over. I'm going to punish you.'

Mick shook his head. 'You're not going to whack me with that.'

It was a stand-off. Blundell could not administer his punishment unless Mick bent over, which he had no intention of doing. Meanwhile the class fell about.

Finally, Blundell ordered Mick to leave the room. Then he followed, leaving the class wondering who was going to win the battle of wills.

Today, Adrian Whittleworth says: 'Blundell could not be seen to lose his authority in front of the class. So whether he slippered Mick somewhere else or just told him to pretend he'd been punished, we don't know. Certainly Mick never said anything to me. I honestly think he enjoyed the attention, though.'

Audenshaw teachers, particularly the younger ones, were not averse to striking such deals with pupils, if circumstances called for it. Geography teacher Ray Wood, for instance, had to enter into a secret pact with Mick once – to save his own skin.

He recalls: 'Mick said something out of turn and gave me a supercilious look, which got me going. I went up to his desk and got hold of him. "Get down to the geology room," I snapped. "Now."

'Boiling mad, I marched after him. Don't ask me why, but there was a cricket bat in the geology room. I grabbed it. "Get over that desk," I thundered. "I'm going to give you some of this." He bent over and I whacked his backside.

'Mick, who was always fooling about, pretended I'd really hurt him and leaped forward in mock pain. He crashed into a six-foot high glass cabinet, sending fossils and bits of chalk and rock and splinters of glass all over the floor. I didn't know whether he had done it deliberately to spite me for cracking him one, or whether it was an accident. Either way I had a problem, because the cabinet and its contents belonged to the head of department.

'As we picked up all the bits and pieces, I said, "I'm not taking the rap for all this damage. Go downstairs and get an accident report form. Fill it in, saying you slipped on the wet floor." Mick filled in the form, then watched me sign it, laughing at the deal we'd struck to save ourselves. After that, we got on fine. Mick didn't bear grudges. He continued to be a joker and a damned nuisance in class, but I liked him.'

Mick's desire to impress the class with his clowning could have disastrous results, as one teacher can testify. He was a mature student being tested for a full-time job, a bizarre-looking character in his late forties, bald at the front, with long plumes of ginger hair coming out at the sides, and he had an odd accent. Seeing him as the perfect target, Mick made every lesson difficult by imitating his accent and making disruptive noises from the back. The teacher had little control, even when a school inspector sat in on one of the lessons: it was uproar from start to finish, with Mick showing off more than usual. Finally, the inspector left, relieved to escape the mayhem. As the door closed, the flustered student teacher, red-faced through embarrassment and fury, turned on Mick and snapped sarcastically, 'Thank you, Ugnall, you've just lost me my job.'

Mick just laughed.

*

What Mick would do for the rest of his life was something he would worry about tomorrow; today was for having fun, being answerable to no one, except his father. And in the autumn of 1975, with his O-levels only months away, Mick continued to put his leisure activity far ahead of school work. Despite that sexual success in Scotland, Mick's red hair and ponderous chat-up routine did not endear him to local girls and he was happier in male company, drinking with the Friday-night gang, or playing pool for money with Lil in pubs where the regulars were unaware of their potting skill.

'Mick and I were red hot at pool, and we'd be out most nights,' says Lil. 'We would go to The Highland Laddie and play guys in their twenties, even forties. We would let them win the first game and suggest playing for a pound or so. We would let them win again. After a few more games, we'd play for a fiver – but this time we'd make sure we won. Nobody could touch us. We'd be out most nights, and some weeks would pick up around £25 in winnings. I'd just started as an apprentice engineer, on about £16 a week and the extra bunce was good money. But to Mick it was a fortune.'

With money in his pocket, Mick was able to indulge himself on Friday nights, and his alcohol tolerance level had increased so much he was now able to knock back as many as twelve pints of ale. Mick took a certain pride in being a hardened drinker and part of an older crowd and had an ever-growing pot belly to prove it. He had little time for his Audenshaw school pals, particularly if they looked too young to pass

68

unnoticed in the public bar. And in Adrian Whittleworth's case, at least, he took a sadistic delight in belittling him over his failure to buy a pint.

'Mick was always teasing me,' Adrian recalls. 'It hurt me because, at fifteen, no one likes their maturity questioned – and anyway, I'd been getting served in lots of pubs when Mick wasn't around. One day, I met up with him and Lil and we popped into a pub where I'd had a drink only an hour before. This time, though, I was questioned about my age. I couldn't believe it. Of all the people to be there, it had to be Mick. And he loved it. When we got back to school the following week, he inflated the story out of all proportion to humiliate me. He could be hurtful to people he didn't much care for.'

The drink most certainly helped Mick's confidence: after five pints he would become the entertainer, making Paul, Lil and Harry roar with laughter at his latest impersonations, And when the group went to discos, Mick would even join in a bizarre game to see which of the four could get off with the most unattractive girl in the club.

The game was Harry's idea. He says: 'It was my idea and I called it "Trap a Pig Night". I would organize a bet on which of us could pull the ugliest bird. Mick didn't have the right patter for the sort of birds you got in the disco, but some nights he had a go and struck lucky.'

Striking lucky, it seems, was nipping outside and having sex in doorways down dark alleyways – quick, casual encounters with no long-term obligation on either side. At the end of the evening the girls would go one way, the boys the other.

'No matter what happened, our agreement was that we went home together,' says Lil. 'Sometimes we got the last bus, but if we missed it, we'd think nothing of walking the eight miles home – even if we had the money for a taxi. We were very close mates and it was more fun.'

It was at times like this, tanked up on ale and brimming with confidence, that Mick would come into his own as the talented impressionist, and turn the journey home into an event.

'He was hilarious after several pints,' says Harry. 'He would entertain us all the way home, not only with his impressions, but by singing, too. He had a brilliant voice, even then, and when we'd say, "Give us a song," he never let us down. He'd sing hit numbers of the day all the way through, really professionally.

'My claim to fame is that I used to sing with Mick all the time. One song we sang was the Marvin Gaye–Diana Ross number, "You Are Everything". I sang Diana's bit and Mick did Marvin Gaye. We sang at the tops of our voices in the street and, being full of beer, thought we sounded great.'

But it was the impersonations his pals loved; they never tired of them.

A favourite was one of Rolf Harris, which Mick did on the top deck of a bus, and Harry has never forgotten it. 'We were sitting at the back when Mick suddenly got up and started clambering over the seats. He pretended he was painting the ceiling, saying "and a little bit of red here, and a little bit of blue there" in an Australian accent. Upstairs on that last bus would be crammed with half-asleep drunks and they'd be swearing at him as he climbed among them. But Mick didn't give a monkey's. He always seemed to be full of beans at the end of the night, when he'd had a few.'

Mick's father had no idea about these Friday night excursions into Manchester's clubland; as far as he knew, Mick had been to the cinema or to a pub to play pool. Mick was worried about getting home after midnight, but Lil solved the problem by suggesting Mick slept on the settee at his house. It was ideal: Mick could roll in drunk at whatever hour he chose, and his dad was none the wiser.

'It became the regular thing,' Lil remembers. 'We were such close mates that Mick would even nick my bed. When we got home, he'd nip into the house ahead of me and run up the stairs and jump in. Even if I made it first, then had to get up to go to the loo, Mick would pinch it. I didn't bat an eyelid – just went downstairs and slept on the couch. We used to laugh about it and some nights when we were out, I'd say, "I bet you I'm in that bed before you tonight." My mum and dad loved Mick like a son. We always had a houseful anyway, and they liked him being around.'

One Saturday night, the boys didn't have to worry about who slept where – because they spent the night in separate police cells after a punch-up at the Elizabethan Hall nightclub in Belle Vue, a couple of miles outside Manchester.

Harry was at the bar, dancing around to a Bellamy Brothers song he liked, and eyeing up some girls, when a total stranger came up to him and, without asking questions, floored him with a right-hander. Some bouncers took Harry into an office, cleaned him up, and he returned to the noisy throng, none the worse for the punch and none the wiser as to who had thrown it. As everyone was leaving in the early hours, the same assailant punched another of Harry's friends and a mass fight broke out in the street. Within minutes, a police van arrived and Mick, Lil, Harry and another friend were bundled into it and taken to Whitworth Street police station.

Harry recalls: 'We were put into separate cells, then questioned, one by one, in the interview room. When one of us was in there, the others could hear screaming and shouts of "Get off me". It sounded as if the police were beating someone up, but we learned later that it was just a copper trying to intimidate the rest of us into admitting we had started the fight.

'We were kept in the cells until about 5 a.m. Then we were let out with a warning. Mick was the youngest, but all he was worried about was what his dad would say. Reg never got to hear about it, though, because Mick slept at Lil's as usual and never said a word about being arrested.'

Lil, a young fighter of some renown in Denton, was very protective towards Mick. Another night, at The Beer Keller in Manchester, he crashed a $1\frac{1}{2}$-pint beer mug on the head of a bouncer who had Mick pinned against a wall.

'He was about to punch him for some reason,' Lil says. 'When I whacked him, the mug didn't break, but it was enough to make him let go of him. Mick was my best mate and I always looked out for him. Some of the crowd who joined us for drinks thought Mick was a big-headed swine and didn't like him getting all the laughs with his impersonations and singing. They would start digging at him and Harry would wind Mick up to a point where he wanted to fight. But I'd step in and calm things down. They all knew that if they hurt him, they'd have to deal with me.'

★

Mick had never thought of waiting on tables to earn extra money, but when Lil's father, Arnold Howarth, told him what he could earn for a few hours' work, Mick was keen, particularly when he learned Lil would be doing it too.

Both boys were legally too young to work at Denton's Broomstair Working Men's Club, but Arnold said he could get round that: his brother-in-law, Alf, was a steward at the club and he would have a word with the secretary and fix for both boys to work Saturday and Sunday evenings. If the secretary knew Mick and Lil were under age, he did not show it, and they were told to report for duty the following Saturday.

Their hours were 8 p.m. until 11.30 p.m., and the wage £7. Tips, the boys were delighted to learn, could boost their take-home pay to £12, maybe more.

They were a good team: they split the bar's fifty tables between them, Mick working the right side, Lil the left, and pooled their tips. They quickly found a way of ensuring they were tipped for their services. It was crude but effective: they would serve the tables who tipped and ignore the ones who didn't.

Arnold Howarth says: 'If you didn't tip the first time you were served, you could shout all night, but the boys never came back. One couple who owned the chip shop on Moorfield Avenue were really tight and never gave anything. They would shout and wave their hands to get attention, but always ended up going to the bar themselves. I found it amusing.'

Lil says: 'Mick and I were a good double act. When the non-tippers moaned that we weren't serving them, we just shook our heads sadly and said we were rushed off our feet. Some customers insisted we had a drink instead of a tip, so we were able to indulge ourselves in a few pints while working, which gave us the best of both worlds. But, one day, some sourpuss complained that although we were old enough to serve booze, we were not old enough to drink it, so the boss knocked our drinking on the head.'

Despite the selective serving, both boys were well liked at the Broomstair. And they were so aware of their worth, they stuck out for an extra 50p bonus for working Christmas Eve. Ron Hill, then the club manager, is convinced Mick was behind the demand, although it was Lil who did the negotiating.

'Mick was the type to make the bullets, then get his pal to fire them,' says Ron. 'He'd say, "We could do with this or that," then push Lil to do it. The club offered them 50p each extra to work Christmas Eve, but they said they each wanted £1. The club secretary said he'd think about it but, by Christmas Eve, nothing had been decided, and the boys felt they were being cheated. They reported for work, but walked out after a few minutes, saying they would not be working unless they got what they wanted. Ten minutes later, the secretary went to a nearby pub, where both boys were having a pint, and agreed to pay the extra money.'

Today, Lil smiles at the memory of that minor financial tussle. 'We were at a bloody premium and we had them over a barrel,' he says.

Early in 1976, Lil noticed a change in Mick as they moved around the tables, collecting pots. Now, he was not so much interested in spotting a good tipper as watching the stage. The Broomstair, like most Northern working men's clubs, always had Saturday night entertainment, usually singers, and Mick was mesmerized by them.

'He would be working as usual, but his eyes would be on the singer virtually the whole time,' Lil recalls. 'I couldn't understand why he was so interested, because the singers were all over fifty and past it. When I asked him, Mick said he wanted to see how they did it. To me, it was just someone getting up and singing, but it was far more than that to him. He was interested in the detail of each performance, how they worked the audience and all that.

'Whenever we went for a drink to other working men's clubs, Mick's eyes would be glued to the stage and I would get hardly a word out of him all night. When he came to pubs with me to help sell raffle tickets for a children's charity, I'd be dashing around trying to persuade people to part with their money, and Mick would be sitting near the piano, listening intently to whoever was singing. He'd be totally engrossed, not at all interested in helping me sell raffle tickets.'

Music began to dominate Mick's thinking. He still went out with the Friday-night gang, but his heart was no longer in their riotous evenings; he would be subdued for long periods. Knowing his pals were not interested in music, he rarely mentioned the subject, but one night, during a serious conversation with Harry, he confided that he was in the middle of writing a song.

'I took the piss out of him for that,' Harry recalls. 'It wasn't the done thing to write songs. But Mick didn't care. He talked very seriously to me about the song. It was very important to him. We never asked to see what he'd written, though, and Mick never showed us anything.'

Winter turned into spring, bringing the June O-level exams nearer. For most Audenshaw boys, it was a time of near panic as they revised round the clock for the critical tests that would shape their futures. But, for Mick, the build-up was hardly a brain-taxing time that kept him awake at night. He wallowed in the casualness of the art room, revelled in the free speech of Ernie Walker's economics class, but did little else to change the general view that he would leave Audenshaw a relative failure. Mick did not give a damn. He was nearly through that long, dark tunnel; the light at the end was dazzling now, beckoning, inviting, and Mick basked in its welcoming warmth. Soon, he would be able to slam the door on his grammar school life, shutting out its painful memories forever. And it could not come soon enough.

After watching him drift aimlessly through another geography lesson, Ray Wood would taunt him: 'You bone-idle pig. You're going to fail everything here if you don't pull your finger out.'

But the well-meant cajoling cut no ice with Mick. Like French, the idea of achieving a long list of O-level passes was not on his agenda. He was reasonably confident of getting art and economics – and perhaps English – but he was not bothered about the rest. What good could they do him? It wasn't as if he had set his heart on a life in banking or insurance or some scientific post.

Far more interesting at that time was the latest classroom gossip: Frank, Gary and Adrian, it seemed, were thinking of starting a band.

The news was music to Mick's ears. Maybe he could get involved too. Maybe he could be their singer.

9

It was Adrian's idea. He was not musically gifted, but he wanted to be famous and not have to work any more, and thought forming a band the quickest way to do it. At first, it was just talk with Frank and Gary, and messing around in the dining hall on a snare drum borrowed from the music room. But then Adrian, whose mouth was bigger than his talent, spotted a synthesizer for sale for £200 in a local paper and saw it as the launch pad for his dreams of stardom. He paid the owner a £10 deposit, promising to pay the rest in similar instalments, and carried the synthesizer home. Excited, he took it to school and boasted to Frank and Gary: 'You guys are just playing at forming a band. I'm going to *do* it.'

Sadly, Adrian's big plans for himself crashed when he failed to pay the first two instalments on the synthesizer and his parents ordered him to return it. But his enthusiasm for starting a band rubbed off on Gary and Frank, and they decided to invest in a modest drum kit and guitar. They began practising and miming to records at Frank's house after school on Fridays. Frank was the drummer; he had been practising for years, although he had never been able to afford his own drums. Gary went on the guitar, despite being unable to play more than a few notes. And Adrian said he would stand up front as the singer.

Mick heard about the sessions a few weeks later and asked to go along. Gary and Frank did not object, but when Adrian saw him standing around listening to them, he was put out. He thought: This is *my* band – and it was *my* idea and I'm the front man. Who brought you in? He complained that Mick put him off, but Frank told him not to worry; Mick was only there to watch out of interest. Adrian was far from convinced; Mick obviously wanted to be involved. The warning bells sounded. A sixth sense told him he was on the way out and Mick was on the way in.

Today, Adrian is philosophical. 'It was never actually proved whether I had a voice or not, but Frank and Gary probably realized I couldn't deliver and felt I was a waste of time. They wanted someone else to sing. And Mick said he would do it. He was always going on about how he was cutting down on fags and taking honey and lemon to protect his voice. By then there was tension between us. We were rivals, not friends.'

It was this that probably prompted Adrian to put Mick down, saying his voice was 'dead strained'. Certainly Frank and Gary did not agree; they had heard Mick singing in class when the teachers were out of the room, and knew he was perfect for what they wanted. But it was not only his voice that encouraged them to welcome Mick into their group – it was his qualities of leadership.

'At first, the band was just something for us to do, but Mick made it serious,' says Frank. 'He sort of took over, organizing us and making sure we had a professional attitude and turned up on time for practice. He was dead keen, even then. We had spoken about the band at school and Mick probably knew that he'd be doing the singing if anyone would. Even if we didn't want him to, he was the sort of pushy type who would force himself in.'

So, while Mick took centre stage, Adrian faded into the shadows, nursing his hurt pride at being crowded out of what had been his creation. To make him feel worse, the band kept the strange name he had given it: Osiris. Adrian had stumbled across it during a visit to an Egyptian exhibition at Manchester University, and learned it meant not only 'God of Death', but also 'God of Rebirth'.

The irony would not be evident until more than a year later, when Osiris would die, giving birth to a passionate musical relationship.

★

A couple of weeks later, Glen Morby, a good guitarist and one of Frank's friends from primary school, heard about Osiris and asked to join. The jamming sessions became more regular, more serious; what had been merely an enthusiastic duo backing a singer now looked more like a band. Something was still missing, however – a bass guitarist. Glen said he knew just the lad – another Two Trees boy, who had also been in the same class as Frank at Manor Green Primary.

The boy, a quiet, shy type, had passed his Eleven-Plus for Audenshaw, but had shocked and disappointed his parents by insisting on going to Two Trees with his mates. At fourteen, he was playing chess with his father and beating him – even without using his queen! A patient, dedicated boy, he taught himself to play the guitar at eleven, by renewing a teaching manual from the library for six months until he had mastered it.

The shy boy was named Neil Moss, but everyone called him Moey. And when Mick met him in Frank's bedroom they clicked at once.

★

The O-levels came and went. Mick felt he had done enough to pass at least art and economics – enough to get into Tameside Technical College in September – but he was not bothered about the rest. What was far more important that long, hot summer of 1976 was a breathtakingly exciting and wild music craze gripping young rock fans on the underground circuit. It was called punk, and Mick first heard about it from Moey's brother, Ian, who had seen a London band called The Sex Pistols in Manchester in June. There had been just 200 youngsters in the Lesser Free Trade Hall that warm night, because The Pistols were barely known outside colleges and small London clubs. But they made a powerful impact and when the band appeared in Manchester again two months later, Mick and Moey made sure they were there.

They loved the new anarchic sound and style of the outrageous Pistols. But what impressed them more was the first support act – a new local punk band called The Buzzcocks. It was the first time either Mick or Moey had heard a sound like it; they were excited at the possibilities it presented for them. 'They were buzzing when they came home that night,' says Ian. 'Suddenly they realized you did not have to be in a band that copied The Rolling Stones. Punk was the most important music fad I turned them on to. If they hadn't gone to see the concert that night, they might have carried on playing "All Right Now"and "Satisfaction".'

That summer was the hottest of the century, and Mick spent many of the sun-soaked days cooling off at Denton's open-air pool with Gary Hulston and Bryan Dyson, another friend from Audenshaw.

Stripped to a swimming costume, Mick did not make heads turn: being a redhead, the sun burned him crimson, not brown; the long legs and arms, such objects of fun to Mark Fisher at school, were out of all proportion to his ribcage; and although only just sixteen, those Friday night pints had given him a pronounced beer gut. Mick was a strong swimmer, though, and took pleasure beating both boys and his next-door neighbour, Gary Shaw, when he joined them.

★

In September, with the heatwave continuing to break sunshine records, the sixteen-year-old Mick started at Tameside Technical College. He had passed only what he had expected – art, economics and English language – and planned to take a two-year advertising course. But, within weeks, he switched to art foundation, which meant re-taking geography O-level and studying for two A-levels.

Once more, he found himself out of his depth, surrounded by older, more academically-gifted students. But what he lacked in academic prowess he made up for in confidence, which, sadly, did not go down well with his colleagues. One of his lecturers, Michael Rooke, says: 'Shyness was not a feature of Mick's character. He was extrovert and articulate and liked showing off in group work. Some art students tend to be insular and inarticulate, and there might have been a tinge of resentment that Mick had a lot of self-confidence.

'But I warmed to him. At first he was immature and hyperactive, and survived on raw energy, as opposed to a straight, academic mind. But what he responded to was the sense that an event would take place.'

Mick had always enjoyed being different, not a follower of fashion, but the bohemian influence at college made him even more outrageous. His dress sense, always off the wall, became eccentric: he took a liking to red and white striped trousers, which he wore with sandals without socks, even when it was raining.

With his shoulder-length hair, he cut a Biblical figure and when he called at the home of Martin Kenyon – an old St Lawrence's school pal – in Doddington Walk one Sunday morning, Martin's mother exclaimed, 'Good God, Michael, you look like Jesus.'

'I've been to Oxfam for these,' Michael told her proudly.

'You look as though you have and all,' Mrs Kenyon laughed.

And Mick laughed, too.

He liked the novelty of such styles of dress, and adored the ankle-length grey trenchcoat he picked up at a flea market in Oldham. His weird wardrobe made him the talk of Denton and when he called on Gary Hulston, the boy's parents would laugh and call out, 'Mad Mick's here.' He would ride around town on his bike in his zany gear, oblivious to – or revelling in – the laughter he knew he generated, particularly when he started cycling to college wearing a World War II gas mask to protect his voice from car fumes.

Ken Laing, the little boy Mick had slapped in the football argument three years before, would see him walking in Denton in his trenchcoat, and think how weird he was. 'He always walked very precisely, very upright, and he would stare ahead, refusing to move his head. He was definitely wrapped up in his own world, singing in his head, maybe.'

At weekends Mick still worked at the Broomstair, but during the week and on Friday nights he was going to rock gigs in Manchester; and he now preferred the Whitegates pub in Hyde, where he and Bryan Dyson could go on stage and sing. That November, Harry Nilsson's 'Without You' had been re-issued, and Mick and Bryan would sing it full-blast, with Moey on piano.

With new friends in college and an absorbing musical interest out of it, Mick began to drift away from Harry and Lil and the Friday-night gang.

Lil would call round at West Park Avenue to take him out for a pint, but would find Mick engrossed in songwriting with Moey. 'Sometimes he would come out,' says Lil, 'but he began spending more and more time writing and developing the band. He was totally committed to it. One of the rare times I tempted him out, he ended up lying in the middle of Two Trees Lane, moaning, "I just want to be run over. I want to die."

'It was around midnight. We'd just come out of a pub and Mick was drunk. When I saw him lying in the road, I thought he was messing around. I said, "Come on, you silly bastard," but Mick started bawling his eyes out, and I realized he was in a state. I tried dragging him on to the pavement, but he was fighting and pulling back, so I sat down in the road with him and lit a cigarette. I asked what the matter was and he said he was upset because his girlfriend had left him. I didn't even know he had a girlfriend.

'I couldn't think of a way to get him out of the road, so I decided to be flippant. "When the car hits you, I'll call an ambulance right away, okay?" Then I looked down the road and saw a lorry turn into the lane. When I told Mick, he thought I was messing around. But then he heard it and got up pretty quickly and ran on to the pavement. I don't know about any girlfriend, but Mick was certainly depressed that night and wanted sympathy and, possibly, some attention.'

A clear sign that the friendship with Mick had run its course hit Lil – and Harry – one Monday night in November when they called at his house to borrow some money. Over the previous few months, money had changed hands in something of a ritual, with Mick lending each boy a pound on Monday nights and getting it back on Thursdays when Harry and Lil got their wages. But this Monday night, Mick refused to hand over anything. 'Sorry, lads,' he said, 'but I can't give you anything. I'm doing it for your own good. You're becoming dependent on me and you'll never get straight if I keep helping you.'

Harry and Lil were shocked; they were skint, and were relying on the money as usual. They tried to talk him round, but Mick's mind was made up.

Today, the memory amuses Harry. 'Lil and I would get paid on Thursday and blow it all by Saturday night, but Mick always had money at the start of the week. Lending us each a quid was fine for a while, but, eventually, he wised up that it was dead money. He would earn money on a Sunday, give us some on Monday, get it back on Thursday, then lend it to us again the following Monday. He said it was pointless for him. And he was right. Mind you, that didn't help us that Monday night. We were looking forward to having a few beers and were well pissed off when we realized we weren't going to be able to. What made it worse was that Mick was younger, and unlike us, didn't have a full-time job. We walked off with our tails between our legs and never asked him for a loan again.'

That was the beginning of the end of the relationship. Mick seemed to know where he was going and there was no room for anyone who didn't have something musical to offer.

Today, Lil says: 'The more Mick got into music, the more time he devoted to it and the less time he had for going out drinking. He would say he was going to be a singer and have a record out, but, to be honest, I wasn't interested and didn't think anything of it. I thought he might do reasonably well in a band, but that's as far as I thought. Quite frankly, I didn't like Mick's arty college crowd – they had different principles to me. So, after a while, Mick went his way and I went mine.'

★

Gary Hulston admits today that Osiris 'wasn't that serious as a band.' But to Mick it was. He seemed to appreciate, even at sixteen, that unless he took it seriously and gave it 100 per cent, he would not get anywhere. Which is why he traipsed all round Manchester for six hours with Bryan Dyson, looking for a particular microphone with a wire mesh mouthpiece. He would not give up until he found the right one.

Brian recalls: 'Mick had only about £30, but he was determined to find a shop with a particular make of mike – one of the best you could buy. We must have tried a dozen music shops between 10 a.m. and 4 p.m. When he bought what he was looking for, I said, "Aren't you going to swing it – you know, like Rod Stewart?" Mick said, "You *are* joking!" He did not see the funny side of that at all. Thirty quid was a lot of money and he didn't want to risk smashing the mike.'

The following Friday, Mick took the mike along triumphantly to Frank's house in Gibraltar Lane. 'He strutted into my bedroom in his camouflage army jacket, like, "Here I am – here's the singer",' Frank says. 'He had this mike. He was dead chuffed with it, but all we could plug it into was an amp/speaker, which the guitars were plugged into. So we had the guitars and vocal coming out of the same unit!

'Mick would stand on my bed, microphone in hand, and off we'd go with our version of "Jumping Jack Flash", or Free's "All Right Now", or a Status Quo number. Mick would jump around on the bed, loving it. He was deadly serious. If anyone fluffed, he'd say "Oh, fuck it," and be really annoyed. But if everything went well, he'd really get off on it.'

Despite the enthusiasm, Osiris was not much of a band. Gary, for example, was hopeless on guitar. Moey would painstakingly show him chords for certain songs, but Gary kept having to rest because his fingers ached so much. He desperately wanted to be good, though, and when Glen Morby was in full flow on lead guitar, Gary would lean out of the window and strum his guitar, so that girls listening below thought he was playing.

As historic summer heat gave way to early winter and welcome rain, the ambitious five trudged down Gibraltar Lane in the early evening, twice a week. They would go in the back door, where Frank's mother stood, making sure they took off their muddy shoes and left them outside. They would go upstairs to Frank's bedroom, and practise non-stop until the noise got too much for Frank's parents.

Frank's father, also called Frank, says: 'We'd put up with the racket for about an hour, then I'd go and bang on the door to tell them to pack it in. The noise used to travel through the valley at the back, as well as to houses next door, and I was worried about the neighbours. To me, it was just a din. I didn't think any of the boys had any talent.'

But the boys were not put off by the less than enthusiastic review; they even wrote their own song. Mick had the idea, while rehearsing one night in Frank's bedroom. Gary Hulston was strumming on guitar, with Mick singing, making up the words as he went along. The band got as far as they could that night, and by the next rehearsal Mick had written four verses. After three rehearsals, it was finished – a love song, which they called 'Time Over Matter'.

Frank says: 'It was actually quite impressive. It was Mick's title and words, but we all chipped in a bit. We all agreed that if any of us got famous, we would all get together and record it. It hasn't happened yet.'

One night that November, Gary arrived at the house, bubbling. His swimming club, Onward Dolphins, was arranging a disco for younger members on Saturday 4 December and the secretary had agreed for Osiris to perform there.

The Methodist church hall in Hyde Road, was not the most glamorous of venues – and they weren't being paid for it. But it didn't matter. What was important was that the band would be playing live. In front of people. Their first gig.

For all five boys, it was an exciting prospect. For Mick, it was thrilling. And for the next few weeks he talked of little else.

*

They got a shock when they arrived at the church hall late in the afternoon that Saturday. They assumed they would have the stage to themselves, but the disc jockey, who would be playing records for the kids, had a large, professional-looking mobile unit with multi-coloured flashing lights, and it took up most of the raised platform that served as the stage.

There was an argument: Mick and his pals pointed out there were five in the band and they needed room for their instruments. The DJ hit back, saying he would be working for several hours while the band would appear only briefly, while he had a break. He needed the whole stage for his equipment.

The five boys had no option but to use some plywood boxes to build a makeshift stage at the other end of the hall. It was not ideal, and certainly not what they would have chosen for their live musical debut. But they had no choice. And anyway, they convinced themselves, the audience would be as young as nine, and unlikely to be critical.

After making their preparations, the band went home, returning to the church around 8 p.m. to find the hall filled with around fifty pop-crazy children, dancing to all the current hits. Nervously, all five boys sat around, waiting for the DJ to signal he was ready for a break. He did, just before 9 p.m. Eagerly the boys picked up their instruments and went to their makeshift stage to assemble their two amplifiers and Mick's microphone, adrenalin pumping through them.

The children of Onward Dolphins who were there that chilly December evening are hardly likely to remember the brief but noisy debut of that band bearing the strange name Osiris. The first number was 'Silver Machine', a deafening song made famous by the heavy-metal band, Hawkwind. And the kids could not believe it: they gathered round the 'stage', staring up at the red-haired boy leaping about with the microphone and his four friends pounding out the heavy beat.

The end of the number brought just a few polite claps. But Osiris had got the taste of live performance and went swiftly into David Bowie's 'Rebel, Rebel', followed by Led Zeppelin's 'Whole Lotta Love', then another Hawkwind belter, 'Seven by Seven', followed by The Stones' 'Jumping Jack Flash'.

The kids were beginning to love the music: it was loud, but it was exciting. But parents who had turned up to watch over the younger children hated it. So did Penny Harrison, the swimming instructor who had organized the disco. And after five deafening numbers, she told the band, 'That's enough. Stop that horrible row.' When they took no notice and carried on playing, she strode across the hall and pulled out the equipment's electrical plug.

Mick and the rest were upset; they thought they were going to do at least forty-five minutes and they had been cut short after little more than twenty minutes.

Today Gary's mother, Jenny Hulston, recalls: 'Penny Harrison was a great person, but the music the boys were playing wasn't her thing. She couldn't take it, and wanted to get the disco back to what it was, so that the kids could dance. My husband and I were annoyed at the time, because it was the boys' first live show and, after all, they hadn't asked for payment. We wouldn't have asked them to stop because the kids were loving it, and the noise didn't really matter.'

Despite the disappointment, the band were thrilled by the experience. The audience had not been as wildly appreciative as they might have wished, but then Osiris was probably the first band they had seen play live; perhaps they were in a state of shock.

'I can't remember any reaction at all,' Gary recalls. 'It was probably deadly silence, or maybe a few polite claps. But we weren't bothered in the least. We took no notice of what anyone thought – we were just dead chuffed that we were on a stage.'

Referring to that short-lived debut in a tiny church hall as a 'gig' makes Gary and Frank smile now. But it was no laughing matter in 1976. They were ambitious, if inexperienced, sixteen-year-olds and they saw it as just the start of their musical career. None was more convinced of that than Mick.

'He was always more serious than us about the band,' says Frank. 'If anyone ever fluffed anything, the rest of us would let it go by. But Mick used to go mad. If there was any bossing about, he was the one who did it. He was definitely behind everything. He wanted it right.'

While the rest of the band enjoyed that memorable Saturday night, Mick was a little subdued. The band had made an impact, as he knew it would. But there had been many mistakes. He knew they could do better. And next time they would.

10

They did not have long to wait. Mick asked the Broomstair if the band could play a gig at the club in February and, although George Welsby admitted he had not heard the expression 'gig', he persuaded the committee to give Mick and his pals two half-hour spots during a mid-week disco.

Knowing their audience would be older and more critical this time, the band stepped up rehearsals. They abandoned Frank's bedroom because of the noise, and met instead at Gary's house as often as they could. By February they had practised all the numbers they had done – or had planned to do – at the Methodist church, plus their own composition, 'Time Over Matter'. They had tried to write others, but never finished them because they felt the songs were nothing compared with that first effort.

If the swimming club disco had been exciting, the Broomstair appearance was positively thrilling: not only did the band have a proper stage, with 150 expectant teenagers waiting to cheer them on to it, they had their own dressing room too! To Mick, particularly, the whole affair was deadly serious; he even had an argument with one of Frank's college friends, who was hanging around the dressing room. Mick felt the band should have some privacy while preparing to go on stage, and said so. Frank's friend objected but even at sixteen Mick had a way of making his point. After a few heated words, he got his way.

The band's first half-hour went without a hitch. They left the stage to cheers from their friends and headed for the bar to celebrate. This was understandable, in view of their age and lack of experience, but it illustrated that not all the band had the same professional approach as Mick. Gary did not know when to stop drinking and had difficulty playing when he went on the stage again. But the second set went as well as the first, and they sang 'Time Over Matter', for the first time in public. They went down so well they were cheered back for an encore.

Afterwards, the band was enthusiastic. All in all, the gig had gone well, and they looked forward to the next one. As Frank says: 'Considering that some of us couldn't play a note a few months before, we'd done bloody well to learn so many songs. We were raring to go.'

They began looking around for premises where they could practise; if they were going places, they needed more than a cramped bedroom to flex their musical muscles. Within two weeks, they found what they were looking for, at the Pitt and Nelson pub in Ashton, a fifteen-minute drive from Denton. Excitedly, they threw themselves into yet more practice, polishing up the numbers they knew, learning ones they didn't. For Osiris, they all thought, it would be a new beginning.

It was the beginning of the end.

★

Another teenage band – named Purple Haze after a Jimi Hendrix hit – was also using the Nelson for practice and, after a week or so, they started jamming together. Musically, Purple Haze were more gifted, with newer, more expensive instruments, and they delighted in showing off how much better musicians they were. The competitive element began to niggle Mick and Co., and they would leave the pub depressed at having their limitations exposed.

Mick, more than anyone, saw the writing on the wall. Punk was gathering pace in the wake of the outrageous Sex Pistols, and two new singers named Elvis Costello and Ian Dury had captured Mick's imagination. His fascination with the musical changes strengthened his friendship with Mark Reeder, a college friend, who had been one of the earliest supporters of Osiris. Mark, who worked in Manchester's new Virgin record store, had his finger on the pulse of the punk scene, and fuelled Mick's growing enthusiasm. Mick desperately wanted to be part of the latest musical revolution, but knew it would not happen with Osiris. He lost interest in the band, and without his motivation it disintegrated. Moey went off and teamed up with other musicians; Mick started going to more and more gigs, looking for opportunities for himself.

Towards the end of April he found one, thanks to Mark Reeder. Mark introduced Mick to Barry Stopford, another Audenshaw old boy studying at Tameside. The boys did not know each other well, but now a solid friendship developed, based on their shared musical interest. During that May, they decided to form a band – Barry on lead guitar, Mark on bass guitar, Frank Ollerenshaw on drums and a lad named Loz Green on keyboard. Mark, who had a fascination with Eastern European culture, came up with the innovative if bizarre name: Joe Stalin's Red Star Radio Band.

The band promised a break into something new, but Mick q̶
became disillusioned. Barry had great musical ability and they spe̶
hours in his bedroom trying to write songs, but Barry hated all-out
punk, and, in the end, they settled for playing their own versions of
standard rock hits. Joe Stalin's covers were better than anything Osiris
had produced, but that was poor consolation to Mick. He wanted to
express himself differently. He wanted to be original.

His dissatisfaction with rock came out in a mickey-take impersonation
of Robert Plant, lead singer of the heavy-rock band Led Zeppelin,
singing 'Dazed and Confused'. The takeoff was brilliant and Mick would
do it during Sunday afternoon rehearsals at Ashton's Guide Bridge
Theatre and at Joe Stalin's gigs. But those close to him knew that the
impersonation was a protest at having to perform the same boring rock
numbers.

All that mattered to Barry was playing correctly, the way other classic
guitarists had made their names, and he would lose himself in long solos.
But Mick felt the energy and spontaneity was lost playing like that, and
he began floating between other local bands to satisfy his hunger for
something newer and more challenging.

Mark Reeder, who today runs his own record label – Masterminded
For Success – in Berlin, remembers a row over The Sex Pistols. 'Barry
said they were crap, they couldn't play. Mick kept telling him that it
wasn't the playing that mattered – it was the energy and power behind
it and the statement the band was making. Barry was proficient, but
there are only so many solos one can put up with. The jamming sessions
at his house always ended up with him showing off.

'Mick saw the future in punk. Rock didn't mean sod all. And during
rehearsals he would say, sarcastically, "Shall we play some
Hhhhrrrock!" – rolling his r's ridiculously, taking the piss out of the
word as much as the music.'

★

On Saturdays, Purple Haze performed between professional acts at the
Broomstair, and they got chatting to Mick while he was serving drinks
and asked him to join them. The band were also doing cover versions of
heavy rock numbers and – worse – cabaret sets of current chart hits. But
Mick agreed to rehearse with them in St Anne's Primary School,
opposite the Broomstair, the following Saturday afternoon and to
perform in the club in the evening.

He quickly made an impression. Paul Moody, the band's leader, who
played keyboard, says: 'My cousin Phil had been doing the vocals, but

it was a case of "Shut up, Phil." Mick was always
was a mistake, it was rarely down to him. He could
ings did go wrong – like, "Let me know when it's
he would shake some menthol snuff on to the back
snort it to clear his nose and throat. It struck us as a bit
Mick was not your normal kid. I don't know where he got
but he seemed to think it helped keep his voice in good singing

Mick's appearance at the Broomstair the next Saturday amused the
regulars: as he took off his white waiter's jacket and walked on stage for
the first half-hour spot, they taunted him with shouts of 'Get off and get
me a drink,' and 'Hey, pot collector, give up that nonsense.' But they
kept quiet when he sang and, judging by the applause after each number,
enjoyed his performance. The second set was well received too, although
some of the older, more sedate members were shocked by the noise.
The closing number was Deep Purple's 'Sweet Child In Time', a loud
song they had deliberately kept until the end. In a slow prelude to the
deafening climax, the lyrics say 'You'd better close your eyes', but Mick
sang 'Close your *ears*', before belting out the rest of the song.

It is unlikely the Broomstair faithful gave that performance another
thought but, to Mick, the evening was a knockout: he had been paid for
the chore of waiting on tables *and* for doing what he enjoyed most.

It was a short-lived alliance with Purple Haze, as they all knew it
would be. Mick made no secret of the fact that he hated their repertoire
of commercial hit-parade songs, and was always talking about writing
his own material. He wanted to progress. The band knew they didn't fit
into his plans. 'It was obvious Mick was going places,' Paul Moody says.
'He looked different to the rest of us and was into different music. Even
at seventeen, he was a classic front performer. He would get hold of the
audience and his voice had an incredible range.'

Mick was still in Joe Stalin's and continued trying to write with Barry
Stopford. But the gap between their tastes was widening still further.

★

In Manchester that 1977 summer, there was a club called Waves, which
was notorious for all forms of drugs. Mick liked only the occasional puff
of cannabis, but one night he found himself in the club talking to Moey,
who introduced him to two of his closest friends from Two Trees School,
Craig Paolo and Neil Smith. The three of them had joined up with two
other lads, Phil Bentley and Martin Kenyon, and formed a band named
after a Humble Pie song, 'Four Day Creep'. Mick was interested that

Mick in his British Rail uniform at the Palm Grove Club in Bradford in 1978.

The Elevators at the Palm Grove in Bradford in 1978.

The Frantic Elevators. From left to right: Moey, Mick, Brian Turner and Kevin Williams. Kneeling is photographer Richard Watt – the fifth Elevator.

Mick, third from right, looking smooth in his studio at the Polytechnic's art centre.

Mick, third from left, in the Poly art class of 1981.

Knocking back the Guinness with Brian Turner in Clynes Wine Bar.

Mick and Kevin at Adams Club.

The Frantic Elevators at Adams Club in Liverpool.

Mick and Moey at the
UMIST gig. They were still
making music but had
started to drift apart.

Performing with The
Frantic Elevators at the
Band on the Wall.

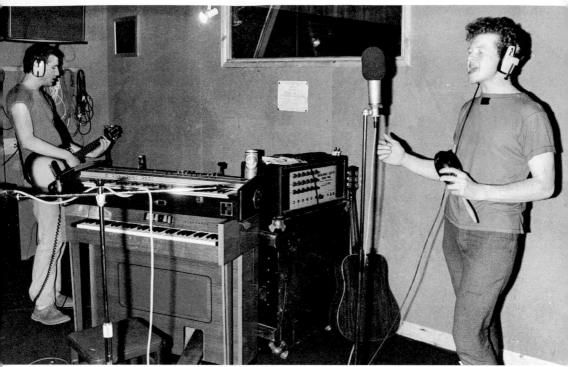

The studio where Mick recorded 'Holding Back The Years' for the first time in 1982.

Rehearsing in Brian Turner's flat
– the room where Mick finally left the band.

Below Mick and Mog at Simply Red's first gig at the Poly in 1984, when they appeared as World Service. Mog was later told to remove the CND sticker to protect the band's image.

Above Mick with Brian Turner, left, and sharing a cigarette with another friend.

An early Simply Red gig.

Moey had written dozens of songs with Craig, and when he was asked to jam with the band at Neil Smith's Ashton home, and in a spare upstairs room in the nearby Halfway House pub, Mick accepted at once.

It was yet another band banging out covers of Rolling Stones, David Bowie and Free hits, but Mick threw himself into practices enthusiastically. Although he was a newcomer, he was not afraid to speak his mind, even take control if he thought things were not going the way he wanted. And he was never reluctant to pick up a member of the band for making a mistake. Not being a great diplomat, he often ruffled a few feathers.

Once, rehearsing in the pub, Martin Kenyon messed up the rhythm on the drums, and Mick reacted rudely.

Martin has never forgotten the experience. 'He stopped everything, jumped behind the drums and literally nudged me off my seat,' he recalls. 'He nicked my sticks, then did the business on the drums, saying, "You do it like this – not the way you've been doing it." I was a bit pissed off and felt a prat, obviously, because I'd never had any drumming experience and he was a lot better than me.

'He wasn't nice about it at all. There were no apologies. He just gave me the sticks back and said, "Right, get on with it" – that sort of thing. I felt I wanted to thump him. In the later stages of his relationship with the band, he was like that to me quite regularly, and was always bawling and shouting at the band if we weren't performing the way he thought we should.'

Neil Smith agrees: 'He had a musical head on him and his amazing voice stuck out even then. But he did like to orchestrate things and would not be slow to tell us if he thought we could play a certain thing better. He knew Moey and I were dropping acid a lot of the time, but he never preached to us about not taking it. He just wasn't interested himself. To him, music was everything – not drugs.'

In 1977, £30 was a small fortune to Mick. But when Neil said that was what he wanted for two public-address speaker columns, Mick didn't hesitate; his commitment to music was so great he had to have those speakers – even if it meant scraping the money together. In the end, that's precisely what he had to do.

'I agreed to let him pay in instalments,' says Neil. 'He would turn up at rehearsal every week and give me five quid, or whatever he could afford. Sometimes it would be a load of change. But he paid the whole lot over five or six weeks.'

Sometime in July, Frank Ollerenshaw became fed up with the sameness of Joe Stalin's and joined another band. Mick quickly replaced him with Steve Tansley, another Denton boy, who had played with Purple

87

Haze, but in his heart Mick knew that he himself would not be in Joe Stalin's much longer. He and Barry were beginning to argue.

Mark Reeder says: 'The differences between them grew too great, Barry couldn't accept that something new was happening within the music industry, while Mick had become more and more radical. It was only a matter of time before they split.'

Early that August, Mick was depressed – unsettled and confused about his future. He was due to start his second year at college the following month, but was no nearer to deciding what he was going to do when he left. All that interested him was music. All he really wanted was to do something new, be different. When he looked around, he saw the impact punk was having. And the more he looked, the more he liked it. What was depressing him was that, no matter how many gigs he went to, no matter how many new bands he saw, he could find no one with the spark to light the flame of his ambition. No one he felt he could work with and create that something 'new'.

And then, one Saturday night, when Four Day Creep were appearing at a Broomstair Talent Night, Mick got chatting to Moey over a pint. What they discovered about each other would change their lives.

Both boys found they had a lot in common. Both were fed up with not getting anywhere with what they were doing, musically. Both wanted to do something new and exciting. And both saw the potential in punk.

They talked and talked. And then they walked home together, still discussing their dreams, their hopes for the future.

By the time they got to Haughton Green, they had decided to form their own punk band, singing only songs they had written themselves. It was, they both agreed, the only way to get anywhere.

*

Any lingering doubts Mick had that he and Barry should go their separate ways were removed a few days later. Mick was at Mark Reeder's house with Frank when the phone rang. It was Barry. Mark turned the ear-piece round so that Mick and Frank could hear.

Frank remembers the conversation well. 'Barry told Mark he was sick of Mick and the punk thing and wanted him out of Joe Stalin's. And he wanted me back in, to replace Steve Tansley on drums. Mick was shocked at what he was hearing, but he had the attitude: "If that's what he wants, that's it." '

The showdown came the following Sunday morning after practice at the Guide Bridge Theatre. Three representatives from a record company were there to listen to the band and were impressed. But Mick and Barry started a blazing row in the coffee bar afterwards and it ended with Mick shouting, 'I'm leaving.' A minute later, Mark Reeder said he was quitting too.

For Steve Tansley, it was an unsettling experience. He had been with Joe Stalin's just three weeks. And the band was breaking up in front of him.

He recalls: 'I went from one guy to the other, trying to sort things out, but Mick and Mark were adamant they were going. The record people stepped in and said it wasn't a problem – all they needed was another singer. I was in a quandary. Barry wanted me to stay, but I hardly knew him. The only one I knew was Mick, and he made up my mind for me. He said he was going to form a new band and I could be the drummer if I wanted. It was odd, being asked to join a new band just weeks after starting in a different one, but I felt I had to latch on to Mick, so I told Barry I was leaving too.'

★

For someone seemingly so desperate for a songwriting partnership, Moey was remarkably casual. High on anticipation and eager to start, Mick expected to see him a few days after that Saturday night talk, but Moey did not turn up for two weeks. When he finally did arrive at West Park Avenue, however, Mick's disappointment turned to delight, for Moey produced the outline for a song he had written. The two boys disappeared upstairs to Mick's bedroom to start working on the lyrics and opening chords. The song was called 'Marion'. It would be the first product of the Hucknall/Moss partnership.

The band Mick and Moey were going to form needed a name and an image. But, first, it needed musicians. Mark Reeder warned that he was planning to begin a new life in Europe, but agreed to play temporarily, and the three boys began practising in Mick's bedroom – Moey on electric guitar and Mark playing bass on a converted guitar, with the first and second strings missing.

Mark recalls: 'I played through a bass amplifier with all the treble off. It didn't sound brilliant, but it was good enough for those early sessions. Mick would have the outline of a song and we'd work through it as a threesome. He and Moey wrote very basic bass lines and it was up to me to provide some flair. When Moey and I left the house, Mick would work on the song and finish it by the next rehearsal. We'd practise it one more time and it would be done. After that, it was simply a question of what the drummer should play, and where there should be a break. We would have a completed song after just three rehearsals, at the most.

'Mick's life revolved around what we were doing; he was set on making a political statement and leaving his mark on the world. Moey felt the same, if to a lesser extent. Personally, I wasn't bothered, but I went along with them because they were talented and I liked them. Certainly I didn't want to see them die out simply because they couldn't find a bass player.'

Mick kept his word to Steve Tansley and asked him to be the band's drummer. Steve had not given punk much thought, but he agreed immediately, and a week later joined the other three in Mick's bedroom, tapping out the beat to the new songs with his hands. If Steve felt uneasy about some of the compositions, he kept his mouth shut. What was happening in that tiny room was far better than any of the punk happening outside, he felt. And he threw himself into it wholeheartedly.

Steve recalls: 'Mick didn't want the shouting type of punk band; everyone was doing that. He was an intelligent guy and he wanted his words to be heard. He was also clever in playing punk with real musicians, which no one was doing. All four of us were into making the band work. The music was a switch in style from Joe Stalin's, and no one mentioned that band again.'

★

When it came to a name for the band, Mick and Moey were sold on 'Elevation', a track on an album by the band Television. But Moey's brother Ian convinced them it could be bad for business, because it sounded like a hippy band left over from the sixties.

Ian suggested they settled for The Elevators. Mick and Moey amended it to The Rancid Elevators, but they dropped that too when Mick saw an advertisement in the *New Musical Express*, asking, 'Have You Gone Frantic Yet?' Both he and Moey thought 'Frantic' went perfectly with 'Elevators', but Mark Reeder said it was 'crap, pathetic crap'. He did not argue, though, because he was still planning the move to Europe and did not think he would be in the band long enough to worry about its name.

Something else Mark swallowed was the decision to credit every composition under H/M, for Hucknall and Moss, even if he or Steve came up with the idea. Deciding on their songwriting credit illustrates how forward-thinking Mick and Moey were for seventeen-year-olds without even a demo tape to their name.

But it did not surprise Ian Moss in the slightest, however: 'They both saw themselves as the new Lennon and McCartney or Jagger and Richards. They felt they were part of that tradition, and wanted to be treated with the same respect. I didn't take the mickey. They were deadly serious.'

Late that August, Mick's transformation from disenchanted, bored 'Hhhhrrrock' singer to passionate punk performer was almost complete. The only aspect of the change that bothered him was his appearance. He was excited about the new ideas The Frantic Elevators were developing and he wanted to look as fresh as he felt. But with flared jeans, an old Yes T-shirt, scruffy training shoes and shoulder-length hair, he looked every inch the person he didn't want to be: a rock singer. New clothes meant money and, that summer, he did not have much; they would have to wait. But the hair was something else. He had no excuse there.

Shortly before he was due back at Tameside Tech for his second year, Mick spent a week with his cousins in Barrow. One day, he went to the beach on Walney Island with a pair of scissors, and, in a symbolic gesture, started chopping at his hair. More and more of his curls fell on to the soft sand and, by the time he had finished, the thick red mass that had been his trademark was reduced to a ragged crop. It was a drastic new look, but a necessary one for an ambitious teenager desperate to cut all ties with the mundane music he had come to loathe.

11

The students gathered outside Tameside College got a shock that September morning. A few had seen Mick during the summer break, but not one of them knew anything about his startling new look. Waiting around in the sunshine while lecturers processed their names, Mick stood out from the crowd as much as he had on that awesome first day at Audenshaw Grammar School six years ago.

The flares and trainers had gone; now, he wore shiny cherry-red Doc Marten boots, with the laces visible below tight drainpipe jeans. Gone, too, were the naff jackets he had worn over the Yes T-shirt. Instead, he wore a white nylon wind-cheater. And the crude crop he had chopped himself had been fashioned by his barber dad into a smart crew-cut, as favoured by US Marines.

No one needed to ask Mick what had brought about the change; the tidal wave of anarchic musical rebellion had engulfed not only London, but Manchester, and it was plain to see that Mick was caught up in it, too.

That did nothing to lessen the shock of the change. Mick's college pal, Alan Fell, was amazed by it. 'It was really quite incredible. Led Zeppelin and Yes had gone right out the window. To me, Mick did not want to go unnoticed. The change of appearance was saying, "Hey, look at me – I'm here! I've arrived." But, in fact, it was rather unnecessary at college. People were drawn to him anyway, mainly because of his unusual personality. The way he conducted himself, you knew he wasn't going to end up in a nine-to-five job. You knew he was going to be something. It wasn't his artistic competence – it was his confidence. He was a one-off.'

That confidence had been boosted by Mick's first year in college and what he had learned about life outside it. He had made astonishing progress after starting the fine art course late, far behind other students, and could more than hold his own in heavy art discussions. He would love having passionate debates in college and, whenever he went swimming with friends at Ashton Baths, he would talk non-stop about impressionism while breast-stroking the lengths. Alan Fell sums him up:

'He had read a great deal and was very knowledgeable. But he never shut up.'

This knowledge, and the confidence that came with it, made Mick appear cocky and arrogant and he was always ready to speak his mind, often with an abrasive honesty which did not always endear him to fellow students.

Every week, students on the course had to produce a painting or drawing, which would come in for mutual criticism on Friday mornings. Most students would sit on chairs, offering quiet, diplomatic comment designed to encourage, not hurt. But Mick would sit higher up, on a table, and verbally slaughter every piece of work presented, with little regard for feelings or embarrassment. He did not seem to care what he said or who he upset.

Alan Fell recalls: 'Mick didn't give a toss about swearing – even if the tutor was there. It was nothing for him to look at someone's work and say, "That's a heap of shit" – or worse. Quieter ones on the course would not get a chance to say much, but that's why Mick was so vocal. He realized people were more subdued than him and thought: Why not control things? It was easy for him – his personality was so strong, he even dominated some of the tutors! Looking back, I think all that bluntness was bravado, and not to be taken seriously. I don't think he intended to do real harm.'

Mick got his fair share of stick, but it did not upset him. Girls apart, he had never seemed to care what people thought of him; adverse criticism was like the proverbial water off a duck's back. In the work studio, for example, he would love singing loudly, and was not bothered in the slightest when other students yelled at him to shut up. And, on the bus to college with Alan Fell, he would act stupidly, unconcerned by the irritated looks of other passengers.

Alan explains: 'If the bus was nearly full and there wasn't room next to me, Mick would sit, say, six places away and still carry on a full conversation. He would chat away to me at the top of his voice, about all kinds of things, while looking out the window. People would give him all sorts of weird looks, wondering who on earth he was talking to. They must have thought him mad, but Mick didn't give a damn. He thought it funny. I did, too, although it was stupid, and a bit embarrassing.

'But that was Mick. He was an interesting person, without any malice, but, to be perfectly frank, most people found him a pain in the arse at times.'

To people on the music scene, however, Mick's eccentric image cut no ice. They thought he was plain daft and scoffed at the energy he was pouring into punk.

Neil Smith summed up the feeling of many when he accused Mick of selling out. He says: 'Like a lot of musicians, I felt a bit snobbish about the whole punk thing. Most of what was being produced was a load of dross and everyone who'd heard Mick sing thought he was wasting his talent. He and I had a heated debate about it one night in Waves and Mick put up this deep argument about why he and Moey were so into punk. He went on and on for ages, determined to get his point over to me.'

For every Neil Smith, there were dozens more who disliked Mick and mistook his non-stop enthusiasm and dedication for cockiness. Mark Reeder spent a lot of time defending him against those who didn't understand his motives or his dedication. 'They'd come up to me and say, "How can you bear to be with Hucknall? He's such a wanker." They didn't like him because of the way he looked. They thought he was a complete loony and mistook his enthusiasm and aggressive energy for arrogance. Although he shocked people by his appearance, Mick was, underneath it all, dead sensitive and had a softer side. He was, in London terms, a diamond bloke, capable of really touching little gestures. And his enthusiasm was quite unbelievable.'

If it had not been for this enthusiasm, energy and belief, it is almost certain The Frantic Elevators would not have got off the ground floor. Mark was adamant he would not be around long. Steve Tansley was keen, but hardly an inspiring leader. And Moey, the talent Mick needed to ignite his own musical spark, was unreliable, still unsure how serious the band was supposed to be.

All the running was made by Mick. And it was not easy.

Says Mark Reeder: 'Moey would simply not turn up for rehearsals, and we'd all be waiting around, not knowing what to do. Sometimes I'd be delayed at work and would arrive an hour late, which would really piss Mick off. He'd scream and shout at me for wasting valuable time and accuse me of not taking the band seriously enough, which I wasn't. But he ranted more out of frustration and disappointment than anger. The whole thing was so terribly important to him, he wanted to get on with it, to practise and be good enough to be booked for gigs. I wasn't surprised. With Mick, it was always 100 per cent – never 90.'

Moey's unreliability centred around a different group of friends, with lower, less demanding, goals than Mick's; teenagers who believed that taking drugs, and breaking the law generally, was an acceptable way to spend a day. Moey got caught up in their wayward lifestyle and, just before Christmas, it backfired on him, putting the immediate future of The Elevators in jeopardy.

He and a pal were stopped by police while driving a car. Moey was only a passenger, but the car had been stolen, and Moey was arrested. He was bailed to appear in court in January, on a charge that could result in being locked up at a time when Mick and the band needed him most.

★

That Christmas Eve, Mick pushed Moey's problems out of his mind and went on a local pub crawl with a group of his old friends, including Lil and Gary Shaw. Over a pint at The Jolly Hatters on Stockport Road, Gary responded to an invitation from the compère to go on stage and sing. He staggered forward drunkenly, preparing to sing Rod Stewart's 'Maggie May', but the others pulled him back to stop him making a fool of himself. Instead, Mick took the microphone and said he would sing himself. He chose a Frank Sinatra classic and had the packed pub cheering with his brilliant, finger-snapping impersonation of the great man's stage act.

That song was 'My Way' – a fitting choice for a seventeen-year-old determined to do what he believed in, despite the opposition of all those who thought him weird or mad, or both.

★

The New Year got off to a violent start. Mick was punched by another young musician, jealous of his growing relationship with Moey; then Mick and Moey were attacked and beaten up by a group of anti-punk thugs after watching a band perform in Manchester. Both incidents happened on the top decks of buses. The first was a personal matter: Craig Paolo had spent years writing songs with Moey and was upset that he was now working so closely with Mick. While the three of them were drinking with some other pals in The Phoenix, Craig started picking a fight, and on the bus home it boiled over.

Craig says: 'Mick said, "Punk is the energy – it's here to stay, man, it will be here for ever." That made me see red and I snapped. I smacked him in the mouth, pretty hard, and he fell off the seat. I started kicking him and he was crawling around like a baby, too frightened to hit back. I was jealous that Moey had left me to work with Mick. I couldn't believe that they'd formed The Frantic Elevators. I was upset that all the songs I'd written with Moey were wasted and I was blaming Mick. Finally, Moey pulled me away, saying, "Leave him alone – you're killing him." I stopped and we all sat in our seats, not saying anything.'

The second punch-up came the day before Moey's court appearance. He and Mick were travelling home after a mid-week punk night at a Manchester club, called Rafters, when six louts from a notoriously tough estate gave them a working over for being punks. The next day, Moey appeared in court with a black eye and was sent to a remand centre for three weeks. Mick was not in court, but he showed his allegiance by turning up at college, sporting black eyes of his own and a badge he had made, urging 'FREE NEIL'.

Far from being ashamed or humiliated by his wounds, he took a certain pride in them. According to lecturer Mike Rooke, he turned them into a status symbol.

'It was very much part of the New Wave and punk psychology to be seen as the victim – not strong and macho, but quite weak,' says Mr Rooke. 'Mick shifted away from any pity he got into the "I've been beaten up on a bus" attitude – which is quite an achievement for a seventeen-year-old. He turned the beating round to his advantage and talked about it to the class.'

Several days later, however, Mick was not so cocky when he went back to Rafters with Moey's brother, Ian – and saw the thugs who had beaten him up. He kept quiet for a few minutes, then told Ian he was leaving. When he explained why, Ian said he would deal with it.

Today, Ian recalls: 'I told Mick that nobody was going to intimidate us. I went over to their crowd and asked who had had a go at Mick and my brother. I was passed from one to the other until I got to the leader – the biggest one. He said he didn't want any trouble. I asked for his glass of beer, then poured it over his head. He just stood there, in shock. No one said a word and I walked back to Mick. Obviously, the gang didn't fancy any trouble that night.'

★

By the time Moey was released the next month, The Frantic Elevators had eight songs virtually complete, but they needed somewhere more spacious than Mick's bedroom to give the numbers the full treatment and bring them to life. Mick and Pete Dervin – one of Moey's school friends who had become a Frantic Elevators fan – trekked round count-less pubs in Denton, looking for a large room to rent, but landlords took one look at their weird appearance and shook their heads. 'We got all sorts of excuses, but basically it was our rough-and-ready look that put people off,' Pete admits.

Mick had an idea: the Broomstair's committee had been good to him in the past; maybe they would allow the band to practise there after the club closed on Sunday afternoons. Thinking about it, he could see many objections, particularly about the noise disturbing the neighbours, but he had nothing to lose by asking.

Secretary George Welsby was concerned about security, and told Mick he stood a better chance if he asked the committee personally. The following week, Mick sat before them, not fazed in the least by the stuffy, formal surroundings. Some of the older, more old-fashioned members objected to his request, but Mick talked them round with a polite, well-considered argument, plus a promise to keep the noise to a minimum. He walked out of that committee room pleased with himself: the band had an ideal place to rehearse from 3.30 p.m. until 7.30 p.m. If he could motivate the others to turn up on time and dedicate themselves to making the most of those four hours, The Elevators might begin to sound like a professional outfit.

In a little over three months, Mick would be eighteen. Many of the boys who had joined Audenshaw with him in 1971 were now immersed in A-levels or apprenticeships, their heads filled with dreams of traditional success and secure futures. For Mick, the future was less exciting than the present. He had just two loves in his life: art, which fascinated him, and his band, which obsessed him.

And, that spring of 1978, he threw himself into both with a single-minded strength that would shock, often upset, people inside college and out of it.

★

At college the hyperactive, immature first-year student, barely tolerated by his more educated contemporaries, had become a considerable force in the classroom, capable of off-the-wall, zany behaviour. Once, for example, Mick was part of a pottery class asked to create Noah's Ark. He produced a speedboat with a giraffe at the wheel.

Another day, Mike Rooke asked his twenty-five students to present an original event, containing elements of surprise. They had to act out something – either in pairs or on their own – which would capture other students' imagination and make them react. Most of the students opted for predictable scenarios, but Mick had worked out something out-rageous. When it came to his turn, he walked over to a window and opened it. With the students expecting him to act out a sketch featuring the window, he climbed out on to a ledge, about three inches wide, and thirty feet above the ground.

While Rooke and the class looked at him, horrified, Mick put his palms against the glass and started inching along the ledge to another window ten feet away.

Today, Rooke admits: 'I was standing there, shaking. I've seen students do some strange things, but that was beyond belief. Everybody was stunned. I thought he was going to sing something, or perhaps shout obscenities out the window. When he climbed out, I had visions of him falling, or someone below seeing him and calling the police. It was such a relief for all of us when he made it to the next window and climbed in.

'We discussed why, perhaps, Mick had gone beyond the parameters of the task. But performance art is, in a sense, to do things which break the rules. And Mick had achieved precisely that. The reaction of the other students was mixed. Some thought he was a fool. There were difficult dynamics between him and the rest of the group. It wasn't a lovey-dovey atmosphere, because he was so different. He had an energy about him and the others saw him as a bit of a show-off, an idiot. He found himself set apart quite often.'

Another task students were set was to teach the others a dance. Mick borrowed a book on traditional ballroom dancing from the college library and got all the class involved. 'It was memorable, like a real event, and everybody joined in for the sake of having a good laugh,' says Rooke. 'Those sessions allowed Mick to demonstrate his creativity. Many young-sters don't find themselves until they are seventeen, so he was just beginning to have that confidence to branch out. He was assertive and took an idea by the scruff of its neck, which is perhaps why people were jealous of him to a certain extent. He didn't suffer fools gladly and could be brutal and a tinge insensitive at times. Some of the class, who were older and more intellectual, thought he was a bit of an upstart, a bit of a squirt really. I found him arrogant and self-centred, but I warmed to him because he was off the wall and a keen, committed student who was eager to learn and do well.

'He had a singlemindedness and seemed to be sure he could deliver. And he was very aware of his bodily presence, too. As a teacher, you expect to take the space and control and communicate, but when Mick walked into a room he would take the space and you'd find yourself stepping aside, thinking: Over to you – you do it!'

Mick impressed Rooke with his voice, too. The class were given two weeks to make a pop record and, although he had help from other students, it was Mick who produced a catchy song with keyboard and drums backing. He sang the song on tape and Rooke can remember listening to it, thinking: This boy can really sing.

Today, he says: 'The tune was not very sophisticated, but it was a commercial sound and it was evident that Mick had the talent to make it in the pop music field. He was going to be a rock star, and art was a sort of day job.'

★

Throughout that spring and early summer, The Frantic Elevators sweated hard – at the Broomstair on Sunday afternoons, and at Mick's house on Tuesday nights – polishing their eight original numbers and working on others. Five of those numbers were 'Marion' – the song Moey had brought to Mick's house that first evening – 'Production Prevention', 'Voice In The Dark', 'Passion' and an outrageous offering that included the lyrics: 'If you want to turn me on, turn the fucking telly on, don't switch the radio on, 'cos Tony Blackburn is a cunt...'

Mick and Moey were inseparable, getting together every night either to write or to go for a drink and talk about music. They would shut themselves away in Mick's bedroom, and swap ideas: not all their songs were hard punk with crude words, however. One of Mick's earliest efforts was a slow, haunting number, for which he drew on the most significant and emotional experience in his life for inspiration – being abandoned by his mother as a child.

Mick never spoke in depth to his friends about Maureen, and his father says they never mentioned her in the house. But a clear sign that Mick did, indeed, think about the woman he never knew shone through in a precocious display of his songwriting talent in that back bedroom. He had written only a couple of brief verses of the song, but Moey liked them and they started putting a tune together. Whether the lyrics were too personal and Mick, at seventeen, was not confident enough to sing them publicly, only he knows. But that song, which he called 'Holding Back The Years', would stay locked away behind his bedroom door while The Frantic Elevators poured their energies into punk's more basic sounds.

They were excited at securing their first gig – supporting Sham '69 and Bethnal at Rafters – but worried about two problems threatening their performance. One was Mark Reeder, who was under increasing pressure at work, and who was still determined to move abroad. He kept telling Mick and Moey they had to find a replacement but they never took him completely seriously, particularly when he gave in to their pleas and bought his own bass guitar. Nevertheless, it was a nagging worry that would not go away. Fortunately, one of Mick's Tameside pals was showing interest in the band. He was a good bloke and very enthusiastic. His name was Brian Turner.

Another problem was a public address system. The band had been making do with amps, begged and borrowed from a variety of people, but with June and their first gig not far off, they needed a proper system, something that would show off the sound they had been working so hard to produce.

Steve Tansley solved the problem. He worked in the case-making department at the Magnet Southern wood factory, and found time to make some plywood cabinets to hold twelve-inch speakers. Getting them to the Broomstair for practice the following Sunday posed a further problem until Martin Kenyon offered to pick up the cabinets in an ice cream van he had bought for a new business he had started.

The PA worked perfectly at the Broomstair and the band were excited at the thought of impressing the Rafters regulars with their unique sound. But when they went there, two hours before the club opened, they got a shock. Sham '69, who were top of the bill and on last, had set up their own PA, and were not prepared to take it down. The stage was too small to hold the two PA systems, so The Elevators had no choice but to ask Sham '69 to let them share their system. For some reason, it was Mark, not Mick, who sorted it out.

Mark recalls: 'I talked to some roadie, who was very reluctant to help. He finally said he could do it – for £10. We were only getting thirty quid for the gig, but we had no choice. Even then he was difficult. He wouldn't let us touch the mixing desk and gave us just a brief sound check to make sure our instruments were working. We were still sorting out the set-up when people started coming into the club.'

Despite the setback, The Elevators went down well. They played their repertoire of eight numbers, all of which were punctuated with outbreaks of shouting from the audience – a sign of approval in the anarchic world of punk in 1978. Mick threw himself into the role of Mr Angry, returning every scream of abuse with a tirade of his own.

Steve Tansley says that, even at eighteen, Mick was a brilliant front man, with a knack of quickly getting an audience on his side. 'They hurled abuse at him and loved it when he hurled it straight back. He had a rapport with the crowd, even if they were being nasty. No matter how frightened he might have been, it never affected his performance. He related to the audience as if he wasn't on stage, and joked them round. He worked hard and really sweated and, by the end, he was buzzing.'

For Mark Reeder, the abuse of the punk audience was amusing – all part of the entertainment and a recognition that a band existed. 'In those days, you spat at your idol,' he says. 'It was great fun and I laughed myself silly.'

But Mick did not approve of the joviality. Scowls, not smiles, were more in keeping with a new musical fashion that had spawned Sid Vicious and Johnny Rotten, and when Mick saw Mark looking as if he was enjoying himself, he told him to cut it out.

To Mick, punk was no laughing matter; it was their future. If The Elevators were to make a name for themselves, everyone had to take it deadly seriously.

12

At punk gigs, fighting was expected: it was an accepted part of the night's entertainment. The more the band was abused – either verbally or with spitting – the better they liked it. Not only was it reasonable behaviour, it was a compliment; a tribute that the band was so nasty, it was good.

But at The Elevators' second gig, at Pips, Mick was shaken by the violence – because it started before the band had played a note! He was chased around the club by a huge punk with a Mohican haircut, braces and Doc Martens, seemingly intent on doing him physical damage.

Steve Tansley recalls: 'He looked as if he wanted to kill someone. Mick ran on to the stage and hid behind my drum kit, sending everything crashing. The Mohican ran up after him and Mick dashed off to the side. But the bloke went after him. I don't know what happened because I was setting things up again. Mick turned up twenty minutes later when we were due to start the gig. We were worried for him.'

The mad Mohican had set the mood for the evening. Midway through The Elevators' set, a fight broke out and fans of a rival out-of-town band advanced on the stage, wielding sharpened car aerials and throwing beer glasses. Mick and Moey were the targets and they did not need much persuading to leave the stage while the fighting went on. The top-of-the-bill singer, John the Postman, rushed out, smashed a guitar, then threw it into the grappling mob. A few minutes later, the fighting ended and the punks who had started it ran out of the club. Mick and his pals piled into a transit van with another Manchester band and drove around the city for half an hour looking for them, unsuccessfully.

'It really went off that night,' says Pete Dervin. 'The car aerials were lethal – they could easily take someone's eye out – but Mick and the others couldn't see them because of the lights on to the stage. When I told him, he said, "Fucking hell, that's dangerous!" '

A few weeks later, it was the band themselves who had to make a run for it when Mark Reeder started another bit of club bother by calling the manager of another band a moron. The Elevators and their followers escaped in their van.

Around this time, The Elevators became one of thirty bands in the Manchester Musicians' Collective, formed to provide gigs for new groups at the Band On The Wall and an equal share of the takings. They appeared on a rota basis and, one night, Neil Smith went to check them out. He had heard good reports, but when he saw the band for himself, he wasn't impressed. 'They were crap, and I told Mick so,' he says. 'The lyrics were merely controversial and Mick wasn't making the best use of his voice. What I said didn't cut any ice. Mick was totally absorbed in the punk thing.'

That summer, Bryan Dyson, an Audenshaw pal he had gone swimming with the previous summer, appeared back on the scene. Mick had got him a job, waiting on tables at the Broomstair at weekends – although, typically shrewd, Mick secured all the tables with good tippers for himself, leaving Dyson the tight-fisted members. During the week, Bryan took a keen interest in The Elevators and, mainly because his parents had a phone, became a manager of sorts, ringing northern clubs, often as far away as Derby and even Newcastle, to try to organize gigs. They did not always insist on a fee for appearing: gaining experience was far more important. Bryan would happily agree deals that gave the band free beer in return for performing. Getting to venues was never easy. They were forever cadging lifts from friends who had cars or vans and often, when they were unsuccessful, they had to travel by bus.

Martin Kenyon's ice cream van would have been perfect, but he could never guarantee finishing work at a regular time. It was a fun vehicle to go out in, though, and when Martin was free and they were not performing, he would pick up Mick, Moey and Pete Dervin and drive them to various pubs in Denton and Hyde.

The band supported Sham '69 again in front of more than 7,000 people in Bury, and took part in a massive Rock Against Racism march through Manchester, as well as performing at various smaller venues. But of all the gigs they played that summer, it was one at Oldham's Tower Club that remains the most memorable. Not for its success, but for its sheer awfulness.

Mick was bellowing out one of the band's own compositions when a group of louts at the bar decided to liven up the proceedings by singing The Beatles' 'Yellow Submarine'. It was picked up by more and more people until 200 or so were singing at the tops of their voices, drowning Mick's voice and the backing.

Steve Tansley recalls: 'We were all pissed off. Mick put his mouth right over the mike and screamed, "Shut up, you fucking bastards." He was so mad, his face was bright red. A big black guy came up to the stage, wagging a finger at Mick, and threatened to thump him for being lippy. They stared at each other, then the guy walked off. Mick immediately turned to us and said, "Right. That's it. We're packing up." And we did.

'Mick disappeared and we didn't see him until the end of the night when we went to our van. He was slumped nearby, half a bottle of Scotch in his hand. He was so depressed by what had happened, he had drowned his sorrows.'

Mick began spending a lot of time with Moey's brother Ian. They would go to gigs at The Electric Circus, The Ranch and other Manchester clubs, then back to Ian's house and stay up until the early hours, drinking, playing records and chatting about music.

'Talking through the night about music was Mick's great passion,' says Ian. 'Once we both started, we went on and on, and before we knew it, it would be getting light. I never found Mick a great wit or the life and soul of the party, and he had an abrasive manner at times. But he was easy to get along with and you could always have a good chat with him.'

Evidently, they could have a good laugh together too, and one night they got drunk in The Spreadeagle in Ashton. The pub was notorious for burly bikers, and Mick and Ian were out of place. The atmosphere was icy, with the bikers staring, trying to intimidate them. Mick and Ian were too drunk to notice, and when the jukebox played a song they both liked, they staggered to their feet and started strutting around, oblivious to their grim-faced audience. 'We must have looked like a couple of drag queens,' Ian says. 'But we were in a world of our own and didn't care. We enjoyed geeing them up, and it was all the more fun because there was the risk that someone would take offence.'

The friendship led to Ian forming his own band. He was at the Broomstair one evening, watching The Elevators preparing to perform, when his brother and Mick invited him on stage to sing. Delighted, Ian sang a few numbers, one of which was a mickey-take of an Elevators song, 'You'. It consisted of shouting that one word from beginning to end, and Mick and Moey loved Ian's version. Later, they pressed him to start his own band and a few months later, he did. For some reason, he called it The Hamsters.

Being a couple of years older, Ian was often asked for advice, and around that August he was called to arbitrate in a dispute over what sort of music The Elevators should be playing.

Mick and Moey were keen to experiment, but Mark felt the band should continue belting out noisy punk sounds. Ian sided with Mark, but Mick and Moey decided to go their own way. This was the beginning of the end for Mark. It was time, he decided, to do something about his dreams. It was time to go abroad and do something on his own. He told Mick and Moey that they should contact Brian Turner to ask him if he would join the band as his replacement.

Mick knew Brian wanted to be in the band. They had met through Adrian Whittleworth and chatted a few times at The Concorde, a teenage disco in Droylsden. Brian was at Tameside Tech, too, and was aware of the band's problems over Mark's desire to move abroad.

When it seemed inevitable that Mark was going to leave, Mick agreed to give Brian an audition. Brian was delighted, but he had a problem: he could barely play a guitar, much less afford to buy one. But, three days before the audition, he scraped together £20 and bought the cheapest bass guitar he could find. Then, somewhat desperately, he set about trying to learn something that would impress Mick and Moey at the audition in Mick's bedroom the following Friday night.

It did not matter. The audition sounded professionally daunting, but it was nothing more than a casual jam session; Mick and Moey had, more or less, made up their minds about him. What mattered more than Brian's bass-playing was that he was a good bloke. He liked getting drunk and stoned. He made them laugh with clever one-liners. And he was keen to play in the band. That was good enough.

When Brian went to rehearsals, he found it hard mastering even the easiest bass lines of The Elevators' songs, and Mark began to worry that he would be no use to the band. But Mick and Moey did not seem concerned, so he stopped worrying and finalized his plans to move abroad. Even when it was clear that Mark was going, Mick and Moey would not accept it was for good; they thought he wanted a long holiday because he was fed up with the pressures of running the Virgin store. The fact that Brian was a poor replacement did not bother them.

It seems that Mick's priorities had not matured: he was not yet aware that, to be successful, you had to get rid of the second-rate. Brian was a good bloke, who fitted in and did what he was told. That, for Mick at eighteen, was good enough.

It bothered Steve Tansley, though. He liked Brian as a person, but not as a musician. A drummer and a bassist needed to be in sync, to have an affinity, but Brian was a raw beginner and did not have a clue. It gave Steve the hump.

To make matters worse, the Broomstair had given in to local residents' complaints about the band's noisy Sunday afternoon rehearsals and told Mick he had to find another location. For a few weeks the band used the youth club in Lancaster Road, Haughton Green, but it was not right; they needed somewhere bigger that they could use more often. The only person likely to find suitable premises was Mick; he was the driving force, the one who always made things happen. But, that autumn of 1978, he was more concerned with starting a two-year course at Manchester Polytechnic, studying for a fine art degree. Moey, as usual, could not be relied on to do much apart from write songs and turn up for gigs. He quit a job – putting up neon signs – after being sacked from Oldham Batteries following the stolen car incident, and now seemed happy on the dole. Brian was still struggling to find his feet in the band, while Steve was getting more depressed than ever.

It had been a miserable, unproductive couple of months, and Mick decided that if The Elevators were to take off, they needed (a) a proper manager, and (b) a slice of luck.

The first was easy: their friend, Pete Dervin, had been following the band almost from its inception and was ideal; he was on the phone, and equally important, was 100 per cent trustworthy.

One day in October, shortly after starting at the Poly, Mick stopped at Pete's house in Osborne Road, Denton, with 200 business cards the band had paid to have printed. In the middle, they read FRANTIC ELEV-ATORS MANAGEMENT. And, much to Pete's amazement, his name and telephone number were at the bottom.

Today, Pete says: 'I wasn't particularly keen to do the job, but was flattered to be asked. I was on the same wavelength as Mick, and he knew I wouldn't rip the band off. In practice, the job wasn't so hard as it might sound. Mick knew so many people, he'd just pass their names to me and I'd give them a call. Other than that, I just handed out the business cards to whoever I thought might be interested in booking the band. I also had to arrange the van hire to get us to and from gigs.'

The slice of luck Mick felt the band needed came when he spotted an advertisement for a rehearsal room in Little Peter Street, in the Knott Hill industrial area in the city centre. The room was in a three-storey disused cotton mill warehouse, converted into practice space for up-and-coming punk bands by Tony Davidson, who owned a small independent record label called TJM.

The only one of the twenty-two rooms still vacant was in the basement. It had no windows. It was damp. And, at £18 a week, it was not cheap. Surveying the room with Moey, Mick said they had no choice: they would have to make themselves afford it. And to get the best value for money, they would make sure they used the room as often as possible. Before they started there, however, the band suffered a setback: Steve Tansley said he could stand it no longer, and was leaving.

Today, he admits: 'We had been doing so well and I was all fired up, wanting and expecting to go up a cog and do more and more gigs. But all we'd done since Mark left was rehearse at weekends. I felt I was back where I was before I joined the band. Brian's lack of ability had got to me more and more; he simply couldn't play bass guitar to the standard we needed. When I complained to Mick, he told me not to worry – we could break Brian in and the band would recover and get better. But I wasn't convinced. One day, I couldn't take it any more and put my hands up and said, "I can't see this going anywhere, Mick – I'm leaving." '

The band needed another slice of luck. And they got it when Tony Davidson came up to them after a rehearsal and said, 'I think I have a replacement drummer for you.'

His name was Kevin Williams, a motorbike-mad Oldham lad with long, blonde hair. He worked in a printing shop next to the rehearsal rooms. Kevin had started playing the drums at the age of eight and had been practising on his own ever since. It had always been his dream to play in a band, and he now, at work, would listen to the noise next door, wishing he could be part of one.

When Tony Davidson told him that Steve Tansley was leaving The Elevators, Kevin asked Tony to tell the band he was interested in joining.

Mick was delighted. He popped into Kevin's printing shop and said, 'Right, I'll see you in the cafe after work for an interview.'

Mick could not keep the appointment; he was involved in work at the Poly, and arranged for Moey and Pete to interview Kevin instead.

As with Brian Turner, the cafe meeting was not so much an interview as a quick chat. Moey, particularly, had no idea what to ask Kevin. According to Pete, he just said, 'All we want is someone who can keep a beat,' then went off to get a cup of tea.

Pete says: 'While he was gone, Kevin asked me what The Elevators were like. I wound him up, saying they were complete crap – but he didn't seem to mind. He said he *could* keep a beat and we agreed, there and then, to take him on. Despite what I'd said, he was delighted. He wanted to be in a band so much.'

Kevin got a severe shock, however, when he started. He had his own drum kit and could play well, but he knew nothing about timing, and Mick had to put him through a relentless schedule to break him in for a gig already booked at the Band On The Wall. Rehearsals went on for five hours a night for ten consecutive nights and by the date of the gig, Kevin's fingers were covered in blisters and cuts. He said nothing to Mick or the others and went on stage, prepared to suffer in silence. Although his hands were sore, he got through the first two numbers, but in the middle of the third, those fifty hours of non-stop drumming – coupled with first-gig nerves – took their toll: cramp began to tighten in his hands and arms and it got so bad Kevin had to put his drum sticks down and stop playing.

Mick glared at him. 'What the fuck's the matter?'

Kevin shrugged and shook his head. 'I can't do it,' he said, helplessly.

Mick went over to the drums and started hitting a beat with one hand, while holding the microphone with the other. 'Just sort yourself out,' he hissed, icily.

Happily, Kevin managed to massage the cramp out of his hands, which in turn loosened the muscles in his arms, and he was able to play the fourth number and complete the performance, albeit through gritted teeth. But it was hardly the debut he had dreamed of all the years he had longed to be in a band.

★

For the next few weeks, Mick and Moey took the 210 bus to that drab warehouse in Little Peter Street virtually every night to organize more practice. Tony Davidson was impressed with their dedication but not with their music: he found it dire and drab, and not worth putting out on his Indie label. But he liked Mick's voice, his strong, passionate views on music, and his sincerity about what he wanted to achieve in the business.

Undeterred, the band pressed on, and their dedication was rewarded shortly before Christmas when they were offered an attractive gig, supporting a promising band called The Undertones at The Factory in Hulme. It was a boost that gave The Elevators hope for the approaching New Year, and it was made sweeter with an offer from a pal, Steve Mardy, to drive them to the gig in his Escort van.

Sadly, what happened after the band's 45-minute performance that freezing December night soured what should have been an enjoyable and exciting experience.

First, The Undertones were held up by the weather and failed to make the gig. Then Alan Wise, who ran the club, told them he could not pay the £25 they had expected.

Mick was furious and shouted and screamed at Wise, demanding the money. When he realized he wasn't getting anywhere, he turned to Moey's brother, Ian, for help. Ian talked Wise into promising to book the band for the next support gig, but could not budge him on the money.

'It was scandalous,' Steve Mardy recalls. 'But that was the scene then, and it happened time and time again. Bands got stamped on and they had to learn to fight for their money at the end of the night. Mick didn't give up easily that night. He told Alan Wise he wanted a fiver for my petrol and said he wasn't leaving until he got it. Wise didn't want to pay up, but finally handed over the money. Then he said, "Right, Hucknall, I've only lent you that fiver. Next time you play here I want it back." When I heard that, I was so disgusted I turned and walked out of the room. I imagine Mick screamed at Wise because he wouldn't take that kind of shit quietly.'

★

If the band was to stand any chance of interesting record companies, they had to have something they could hear. But there was a problem in producing a demo tape: money. They had checked the Yellow Pages for all the studios in the area and found the cheapest quote was £150 – a small fortune to four young people, one of them living off a £1,300-a-year student grant and another on the dole. But Mick insisted that the money *had* to be found, and suggested they thought of things to sell. He set an example by building a bike, then selling it to someone at the Poly. Moey had nothing to sell, but he agreed to put away some of his dole money every week. Two months later, the band had the necessary £150 and organized a van to take them and their equipment to Great Western Studios, in the city centre, one Saturday morning. All were excited, particularly Mick. He felt they had four good songs, and he was determined not to leave the studios until they had perfected at least a couple that would do the band justice.

The studio, on the second floor of another converted mill, was very basic: for soundproofing it had old, threadbare mattresses and bits of carpet nailed to the walls; in the so-called mixing room next door, the controls were primitive and out of date, and were worked by an ageing, long-haired relic from the hippie era.

Pete Dervin remembers: 'We had no idea what to do. The hippie told us to do the numbers and leave the rest to him – he would lay down the basic track of each one, then take certain bits out and leave others in. Mick and the band had made weird musical accessories, such as a Squeezy bottle with dried peas in it, and I was given something to rattle. The band did the first number two or three times until the vocals were right. Mick was always very precise about that part because he and the rest agreed that, unlike with a lot of bands, the words should be heard, not just screamed out. Mick and Moey spent a lot of time in the mixing booth. It was another part of the business they wanted to learn and understand, and they took a keen interest in what the hippie was doing with each of the songs.'

Nearly nine hours later they left the studio, Mick clutching a precious demo tape containing the four songs. All five lads were exhausted, but optimistic. The helpful hippie had said the songs were good. And so were their chances of getting a record deal.

★

The hippie was wrong.

One of Mick's friends at the Poly made five cassettes from the master tape, which were then sent to record companies – picked because they sounded friendly or had an attractive logo – and two weeks later, the band found themselves with a small but nevertheless depressing pile of rejection letters. The responses varied from the reasonably polite: 'We are not interested in signing any New Wave or Punk bands at this time,' and 'We have bands like yours on our books already,' to the blunt: 'Thank you, but we're not interested.'

It got to a point when the band had so many negative replies, they saw the funny side and started taking the mickey out of themselves. One night, after drinking cider and messing about with Tarot cards all day, they decided to write a humorous letter to Virgin.

Despite falling into bed semi-conscious, Pete remembers the night well. 'We'd had that many rejections, we were killing ourselves laughing about what to do next with our tapes. A Tarot card that kept coming up for all of us translated as "Softly, softly, catchee monkey", and for some reason it tickled us. We all started chipping in silly things about monkeys to put in the letter. The more we drank, the sillier we got. Mick was trying to write the letter and I can remember slurring, "Put something serious down, because you've got to treat these people seriously." Mick was so drunk he actually started writing "I am putting something serious down because you have got to treat these people seriously."

'That letter was so much of a piss-take, I couldn't believe Mick sent it. But he did. And we got a reply. It was most encouraging: "Although we are not interested in you at this time, we do think you have a better chance than most of rising above your local scene." '

One response they did not appreciate, however, was from the BBC's dour Liverpudlian disc jockey, John Peel. Pete recalls it saying something like: 'Thanks for the cassette, boys – I'm sure you're going down well in your local scout hut.' To rub salt in the wounds of their pride, Peel enclosed a photograph of Tony Blackburn.

That sarcastic note apart, the rejections were not so much a surprise as a disappointment; the band all believed in themselves so much.

13

They became known as The Dying Band. They wrote a morbid song, with Mick singing plaintively to a monotonous drum beat, and they performed it so often it became a running joke among bands rehearsing above them at Little Peter Street. The song was only ninety seconds long and the lyrics were so limited that the title – 'Every Day I Die' – was repeated eight times after two brief verses. But The Frantic Elevators found it hard to get it right and Mick was obsessed with perfection so much he insisted on singing it again and again, sometimes all day, much to the amusement of the other rehearsing bands and Tony Davidson himself.

'The sound was something out of a house of horror movie and, at first, it drove everyone mad hearing it on and off all day,' Tony remembers. 'But in the end we all ended up laughing. One day someone said, "Oh, no, not again – The Dying Band are back from the dead." And the name stuck. The basement was very gloomy and damp, but they seemed to like it. Once, they asked to be moved, but when I said I could arrange it, they said they would stay where they were. The dismal surroundings seemed to suit their music – and Mick's mood. He was very frustrated and depressed at that time. They rehearsed every night, and all day Saturday and Sunday, and I remember thinking that they should have many more songs in their repertoire. But they were restricted within their musical limitations.'

Ironically, it was the record everyone had laughed at that helped clinch a record deal with – Tony. He had not been impressed with their first demo, but when Mick and Moey persuaded him to watch them perform that January, the potential in Mick's voice persuaded him to change his mind and he agreed to sign them as his fifth band. He was not prepared to draw up a legal contract, however, much less pay an advance on royalties; instead, he agreed to wipe off the band's £80 rent arrears, and include them in the TJM tour of the north of England in the forthcoming spring. It was hardly a spectacular entry into the recording industry, but for four broke musicians it was something to celebrate: they were going to cut a record and tour with four other bands.

That disc – an EP – was recorded the following month at Smile Studios, a former RAF hut in Chorlton-cum-Hardy, which Tony hired for £600. There was one song on the A side – 'Voice In The Dark' – and two on the flipside – 'Every Day I Die', and another Elevators composition, 'Passion'. It took the band one day to record the three songs to everyone's satisfaction and another half day for the studio producer, Steve Fowley, to complete the mixing.

Today, Tony Davidson admits: 'Smile wasn't the best studio but it was adequate, and Steve was a lovely bloke, who produced a good sound. Mick and the band were nervous on the day, but he was, without doubt, the leader and got them organized. It was all very light-hearted. Nobody was under any illusion that we were cutting a hit that would make us rich. It was obvious the musicianship wasn't brilliant, but Mick's voice shone through. So, when we mixed the record, we faded the music into the background and pushed Mick up.'

Advertisements were published in the local press, announcing that The Frantic Elevators' record – the *Life And Death* EP, featuring 'Voice In The Dark', 'Passion' and 'Every Day I Die' – would be released on 7 February. But it was not: the 2,000 copies pressed did not leave the production factory. When Mick demanded to know why, Davidson made one excuse after another, and disappeared for long periods. The band coped with their frustration and irritation by throwing themselves into yet more practice in the dank basement that had become their second home. Often, they would spend the night down there. They would rehearse all evening, have a few relaxing drinks in the pub, then go back and try to sleep on the rotting carpet that was so damp it had grown a furry fungus and turned green. They would wake up in the morning and start playing again.

★

One bright prospect on the horizon was TJM's forthcoming Identity Tour of the North in February, in which Davidson had promised to include The Elevators with his other bands, V2, Slaughter And The Dogs, and Skrewdriver. After the disappointment of their record delay, The Elevators were sceptical that Davidson would keep his promise to take them on tour, but he did, and they appeared at The Rock Garden in Middlesbrough, in front of nearly 800 people, for the first performance of an expected twelve-date tour. As it turned out, only five venues were played. But that first one was a success, if only because of the way Mick coped with a hostile audience.

Tony Davidson remembers: 'He handled a tough situation very well.

He told them, "Stop fucking spitting and listen to the music." And they did. You could see Mick had bottle, and was very professional, even then. He was using that tour as an educational experience, learning to control an audience and developing his personality.'

The tour was not a success; some of the gigs were so badly attended that the bands did not get paid. At one gig, in Derby, a Pakistani club-owner could afford only half the agreed fee because of the poor turn-out, but offered to make it up to them by laying on a banquet of Indian food in his restaurant next to the club. It was hardly a big reward, but was gratefully accepted, particularly by Mick who was developing a passion for Indian cuisine. They did not get such a tasty result at a club in Sheffield. The promoter ran off with the night's takings – and none of the bands received a penny. During the tour, The Elevators also performed for the first time in Liverpool – a city that would become significant in their careers.

Mick and the band were pleased with themselves. But, back in Manchester after the tour, they had to face a harsh fact: they were popular, and young people in the city took them seriously, but compared with established bands, such as The Buzzcocks, Joy Division and Slaughter And The Dogs, they were decidedly second division.

One of the reasons for that, of course, was the lack of musical talent. Most people who saw them came away, thinking: Mick's got a great voice, but what else has the band to offer? Another reason was they did not look the part.

Ian Moss, who was at the Middlesbrough gig, says: 'At that time, there was a certain look bands were expected to conform to, and The Elevators did not, by any means. Their music was as aggressive as other punk bands, but their appearance was more middle of the road. Their hair was a bit too long and their checked shirts and jeans that were not quite tight enough were just a touch out of date. They were neither one thing nor the other, and didn't quite fit in.

'They created mayhem in Middlesbrough and were pestered for auto-graphs after the show. And some of the first division bands said some flattering things about them. But Mick and Moey knew that all of it counted for little unless the press were writing about them and they had a record out to cash in on the publicity.'

*

Shortly after the tour, The Elevators got a major break – a prestige gig at the famous Liverpool club, Eric's, which they had heard so much about after their gig in the city with TJM.

Conditions could not have been worse on the night they were due to play: thick snow created havoc on the roads and none of their friends had a van available. To make matters worse, Mick was in London on a Poly trip, and the chances of him making it back north in time for the gig were slim.

Brian, Moey and Kevin met at Little Peter Street and persuaded a cab driver having a snack in the cafe to take them to Liverpool and bring them back after the gig for £30. They did not have that money, but promised to pay it out of their performance fee.

The traffic was nose-to-tail most of the way to Liverpool and the three of them felt they would be lucky to get there at all, let alone that night. Staring out at the snowbound road, they thought of Mick: if they were struggling in Manchester, how on earth would he get to Liverpool from London? A band without a singer was pointless. Even if they got to Eric's, would it all be in vain?

In the end, they made it. Optimistically, they started setting up their gear. As the time they were due on stage drew nearer, there was still no sign of Mick, and their spirits sank. Just when they were thinking it had all been a wasted and costly exercise, Mick walked in. He was snow-swept and shivering slightly. But he was bubbling with enthusiasm and raring to go. Moey, Brian and Kevin gave a cheer and round of applause and they all got ready to go on stage.

The club's owner, Roger Eagle, was deeply impressed with the attitude of the band. He loved an enthusiasm for music and, on that freezing night, a warm bond was formed between him and The Elevators that would last several years and have a crucial effect on Mick.

Much to their surprise, that July, Tony Davidson *did* release 'Voice In The Dark' and the two other tracks on the EP the band had recorded four months before. The delay had taken the edge off the band's excitement, but they were delighted when they saw the finished product: on the front cover of the sleeve was the title, 'Voice In The Dark', on a black background; on the back was a photograph of each member of the band, their faces blacked out like silhouettes and hardly recognizable. To most, the cover looked cheap, but to Mick and his fellow Elevators, it was perfect: they wanted to create an air of mystery. On the record, Mark Reeder and Steve Tansley were credited because, even though they had left the band, they had contributed more to the songs than Brian Turner or Kevin Williams.

Moey, however, did not have his name anywhere on the record. Even though he would make no money from it, he feared the Department of Health and Social Security might see it and start asking questions about his unemployment benefit, so he 'appeared' under the name Neil Smith – borrowing the surname of his close pal from Two Trees.

Two thousand copies of the record were pressed and it went to Number 8 in the Alternative Charts on 21 July, although how it got there is a mystery: the record did not achieve the sales to warrant climbing any chart. Only two magazines bothered to review it: *Sounds* was mixed and non-committal; the *New Musical Express* merely said it was 'a bit different' and 'off the wall'.

Soon it was evident that the air of mystery that Mick and Moey were so keen on was working well: the record was so deep in mystery that few people had heard of it, let alone listened to it!

Tony Davidson recalls: 'I rang my distributors, Red Rhino, and told them I had a single by The Frantic Elevators, and they said, "The Frantic What?" When I explained, they said the punk craze was dying down, but I persuaded them to take five copies.

'It was left to me and one of my employees to go to every record shop we could find and force the disc on them. The final total sales were about 450, but about half that was the result of a blag I pulled off with a distributor in London. He wanted only two copies, but I told someone in his office that there had been a mistake and that, in fact, the order was for 200. Amazingly, I got away with it – and came away with the money for 200.

'Mick and the band kept asking me how the record was selling and I had to be brutally honest. They were realistic and accepted that they were up against a lot of decent bands.'

It was not all gloom and doom, however. Moey received a letter from a stranger in London, saying he thought 'Voice In The Dark' was brilliant and this encouraged them. 'Wow,' one of them said, 'somebody likes us in London.'

Mick and the others in the band took several copies of the record, but none of them would hear of giving any away; even Moey's parents had to buy one. Mick, particularly, was less than generous, even to a friend at Poly who had a New Wave single out himself.

Nick Manning got chatting to Mick as they walked to All Saints Park after a mass media studies lesson.

'When I heard about his record, I told him about mine and suggested we did a swap,' Nick remembers. 'Mick said, "No. If you want it, you'll have to go out and buy a copy." So I did. I really liked it and told Mick so. He said, "Good. Make sure you buy the next one, because we're going to be big one day." He said it very calmly, with absolute conviction, and I believed him. I didn't go away thinking he was a bighead. I thought: Yeah, I bet he bloody well will be. He had a certain presence that left you in no doubt that he was dedicated to being good at music.

'He would turn up for our lesson on Fridays looking knackered from his gigs. His face would be red and his eyes puffy from fatigue and it struck me he was putting more effort into his music than college work. He was completely different to everyone else. He had very short red hair and a rugged ruddy face like a fisherman's. And he used to ride home on an old-fashioned bike, wearing a long, charcoal-grey trenchcoat, looking like someone out of the 1930s Depression. He wasn't one of the lads, by any means, but he was a nice guy – not really loud or full of himself – who stood out as a character.'

★

Mick felt the best way to overcome the failure of 'Voice In The Dark' was to get back in the studio and record other material he felt was better. He pestered Davidson to invest in the band again but, typically, Davidson kept making excuses and putting them off.

Frustrated once more, Mick talked the band into putting their own money into another demo tape to try to persuade Davidson to change his mind. And on 15 August they all piled into Steve Mardy's Escort van for the trip to Cargo Studios in Rochdale. The studios – used by The Fall and other prominent new bands – would cost £10 an hour, but Mick was sure it would be worth it.

Steve, who had started his own heavier punk band called The Hoax, remembers: 'Mick and Moey knew what they wanted, and from the moment they started at 10 a.m., they were in control, making every minute count. While Brian and Kevin stood around looking nervous, they sat in the control room, telling the engineer, Colin Richardson, what sound levels they wanted.'

One of the songs The Elevators laid down that day included a reference to an Irishman named Michael who was in charge of security at Little Peter Street. He was forever whingeing, and when asked to do even the smallest task, he would always whine: 'I don't know . . .' Mick and Moey called their song 'Never'. And it began: 'Uh, I don't know . . .'

★

The demo did the trick. Davidson liked it and agreed to record another Elevators record. But this time, he said, he wanted more than a hand-shake and a verbal agreement. Delighted, Mick and Moey signed a contract on 31 August. A few days later, the band went back into the studio to record the new material: 'Hunchback Of Notre Dame', 'I See

115

Nothing And Everything' and 'Don't Judge Me'. Mick was optimistic: at last, he thought, they were getting somewhere.

Sadly, it was a short-lived optimism. Again, Davidson delayed pressing the record. And, again, fobbed them off when they started asking why. One of the reasons was that Davidson had been hit by a big rates demand and had no money to invest in the band. But that cut no ice with Mick. Davidson had signed a contract to bring out a record – and Mick felt he should honour it.

Today, Davidson explains: 'The punk boom had passed. You couldn't just put out anything and hope it sold. You needed something different, and The Elevators didn't have anything. They were practising virtually five days a week and should have had a flow of songs. But they didn't. I couldn't possibly take a chance on them again. Even if I had had the money.'

The Elevators felt trapped: they wanted to leave Davidson and try their luck elsewhere, but they had signed a contract tying them to TJM. Relations between Davidson and the band deteriorated and then, one wintry night, Mick, Moey and Pete Dervin met two record producers who said they wanted to record The Elevators on an exciting new Indie label. Breaking the contract with TJM, they said, was easy.

Unfortunately, it was not. Davidson made it clear that if the band wanted to leave, it would cost them.

'They were being a bit childish,' Tony says today. 'I'd invested money in them and lost it. If they were going to leave, it was only fair they should give me my money back. I wasn't a Big Brother-type record company, but I had taken a chance on them when no other label would.'

The band were in an impossible situation: they had little enough money for life's essentials, let alone cash to buy themselves out of a record contract. And anyway, it struck them as absurd that they should have to pay anything when they had not earned a penny from the deal.

Over a pint, they hit on a solution: if Davidson would not give them the contract, they would have to take it.

'We felt we had no option,' Pete Dervin says. 'We decided to break into Tony's office, steal the contract and rip it up. His room was on the ground floor, but it wasn't easy getting in, because he was always buzzing in and out, or hanging around. Finally, one of us got in, but couldn't find the contract. I remember Mick being extremely pissed off, because he knew TJM would stop the band doing anything else with another company.'

The band had no choice but to stay put. Angry and dejected, they went back for yet more practice in the dismal basement room where the water, like tears of frustration, streamed down the walls.

And then, just before Christmas, Mick could stand it no longer. He confronted Davidson and demanded to know why he still refused to release them when he was doing nothing for them. This time Davidson agreed to let them go. He appreciated that Mick had a brilliant voice, but he could not see the band improving. And in any case, cash problems were forcing him to rethink the future of TJM.

The New Year was just around the corner. And for Mick and his band of hopefuls it would herald a new beginning.

14

That new beginning came in the tall, imposing form of Roger Eagle. He was – and still is – a cult figure on the Northern music scene, known for his knack of spotting talent early. In the sixties he was the disc jockey at Manchester's Twisted Wheel Club, which featured Rod Stewart (or Stuart, as his name was spelt then) and The Yardbirds. Roger put on various young hopefuls, including David Bowie and Led Zeppelin, at The Stadium in Liverpool, and in 1977 opened a club in the city that would become nationally renowned for encouraging young performers and putting musicians and their managers in touch with each other. The Sex Pistols played there. So did The Stranglers, Elvis Costello and Orchestral Manoeuvres In The Dark.

Roger and his partner, Peter Fulwell, called the club Eric's. And for Mick and The Frantic Elevators it would become a base where they were always warmly welcomed – and a launch pad for a new and exhilarating life that would make them more popular and successful in Liverpool than in their home city.

Roger had liked Mick the moment he saw him, shivering with cold but burning with enthusiasm, that snowy March night the previous year. He loved musical passion and he loved talent. And Mick was bursting with both. Showing that enviable knack that made him a legend in the industry, Roger took Mick under his influential wing, and began feeding the youngster's insatiable appetite for music from his vast record collection, said to be the largest outside the BBC. He took delight in playing blues singers Mick had never heard of. And when he saw the reaction, he started lending him his treasured, very rare imports of the legendary soul singer, James Brown.

Many of the soul and blues sounds Mick was being introduced to were on a huge Wurlitzer jukebox in the corner of the club, and he would drag other members of the band over to the jukebox and try to convert them, too.

Roger's liking for the band's attitude generally, and his admiration for Mick particularly, prompted him to make The Elevators his 'first reserve' at Eric's – a band he could rely on to appear at short notice if he was let down. Being accepted by such a prestigious club proved invaluable, and the band were quickly offered other gigs in Liverpool. Early that year, they began to see their future there.

Travelling to the famous Merseyside city became something of an outing. Normally, the band would arrive late in the afternoon, take the ferry over to Birkenhead and have a few pints in the Duke of Norfolk, a pub made famous by The Beatles, before going back to the city for their evening gig. Not surprisingly, the talk often revolved around John, Paul, George and Ringo, and Mick would draw comparisons, saying that, like them, The Elevators were having to spend years on the small club circuit, learning their craft. Coincidentally, on stage, Mick started to sound like John Lennon and he would wear a Lennon badge on his trenchcoat. When Pete Dervin mentioned the similarity with the Beatle, however, Mick was annoyed. He did not mind the comparison – and accepted certain similarities in their upbringing – but hated the idea that he was blatantly imitating Lennon.

Personal criticism was something Mick did not like. After one gig at Eric's, for example, a music journalist called him a wimp – and Mick went spare. It was not so much the word he objected to – although at the time he didn't understand what it meant – but the context in which it was used. Another of the minor acts appearing that night had looked like damaging The Elevators' instruments, and Mick complained. Unfortunately, his whingeing was overheard by the music journalist, who found the row story more interesting than the concert review he had been sent to do. Under the headline 'CAN WE HAVE OUR INSTRUMENTS BACK?' he wrote a critical piece about The Elevators, stating that they were 'fronted by the wimpiest singer to come out of Manchester...' When Mick discovered what the writer meant by 'wimpiest' he was offended, and angry, too, because he felt the band's performance had been good.

★

When Martin Kenyon – or Gary Livesey, one of Kevin's friends from Oldham – was not around to drive them to gigs, another friend Mick had met at the Poly, Gwynn Jones, would help out, usually hiring a blue Sherpa van for £9.50 a night. The back of the van was totally sealed off, with no windows or access to the driver and passenger, and when the equipment was loaded on, the band joked that it was like driving 'with a coffin in the back'. For Mick, however, it was no laughing matter being cooped up in the rear, engulfed by nauseating smoke from cigarettes and cannabis. He now enjoyed smoking and getting stoned, but he was concerned about the effect of the smoke on his throat, and always made sure he sat in the front.

This did not always go down well with his pals, particularly Pete. 'We were always rowing about who was going in front with the driver,' he remembers. 'I hated it in the back because all the others smoked, and after a few hours in there, I'd feel as though I was dying. Mick would really wind me up. The moment the van was loaded, he would get in the passenger seat and refuse to move. I'd be desperate to sit in the front, but he wouldn't budge, no matter how much I argued. He became a real prima donna, saying things like "I've got a night's work to do." '

Even at nineteen, it seems, Mick was fully aware that his voice would be his fortune; he was genuinely keen to protect it. He still drank lots of hot lemon and honey. And now, supping five or six pints before a gig, he would mix blackcurrant with his Guinness, because he had been told it would soothe his vocal cords.

'He was one of those people who was always looking after himself,' says Pete. 'He was always getting notions in his head about what he should drink for his voice, and what he should eat. Once, he told his dad to put him on a strict vegetable diet, which he felt would keep up his strength for performing.'

Personal hygiene, too, was high on Mick's agenda. 'When I called for him, he always seemed to be cleaning his feet,' says Pete. 'He wouldn't wash them quickly, like most people – he'd take great care, cleaning each toe immaculately.'

★

The Elevators were now being booked for a gig virtually every week, and certainly never less than every other week, often supporting prominent bands. Their hard work was paying off: the band was more confident, more professional and even more dedicated, and Mick and Moey were convinced they were getting somewhere. Not that anyone would have guessed it, had they seen the two boys in that hired van after some of the gigs. They both took themselves very seriously and would be extremely angry and depressed if they felt a performance had not gone well. 'Moey would sit in the back, his head on his folded arms, really upset, and Mick would be in the front, looking the same,' says Pete Dervin. 'To me, they never seemed to enjoy all the experiences to the full, because they took themselves so seriously.'

Although still in his teens, Mick knew that getting to where he wanted to go was a serious business, and that nothing should get in the way – even girls. There were never such things as groupies with The Elevators, and when chances did present themselves Mick did not want to know. Pete says: 'One night, in Liverpool, two girls asked for a lift back to Manchester and it seemed obvious there would be some fun on the way. But when I mentioned it to Mick, he wouldn't have it. "What do you want them along for?" he said. So they didn't come.

'Mick's devotion to the band and anything connected with it was so strong it often shocked me, particularly where girls were concerned. I just couldn't understand why he couldn't have a girlfriend as well. Once I asked him about it and he looked at me as though I was mad. He was learning the guitar, helped by Moey, and he said, "I don't want a girlfriend. I haven't the time – I'm too busy with the band and learning the guitar." I was amazed. I thought: How would a bloody girlfriend stop you learning the guitar? But Mick didn't see it that way. He was the type who would really focus on what he wanted to do. Having made up his mind to learn the guitar, he didn't want any distractions.'

★

That March, Eric's club was closed after being raided by police invest-igating claims of £20,000 debts to breweries and unpaid VAT bills. A mass march, backed by appeals in local newspapers, was organized to try to save the club, but it never reopened.

If it was a blow to The Elevators, it was disastrous for Roger Eagle, who retreated to a caravan in the Welsh countryside, well away from angry creditors. The depth of friendship between Roger and Mick was such that the beleaguered club owner invited him to spend a long weekend with him and, over the occasional joint, they discussed music – and The Elevators' future.

Despite his financial problems, Roger held on to Eric's Records, a company he ran with his partner from 4 Rutland Avenue in Liverpool. To Mick's delight, Roger said he would demonstrate his belief in the band by producing a single.

For a group who, just a few months before, had been trapped in a worthless contract with Tony Davidson and hoodwinked by empty promises of other would-be entrepreneurs, it was an exciting time. After all, the Indie market was foundering in the wake of the demise of the punk movement, and many better, more experienced, bands than The Elevators were struggling to get deals of any sort.

Excitedly, on Thursday 22 June the band piled into Gary Livesey's car for the thirty-mile trip to Cargo Studios in Rochdale, to record their second single, 'You Know What You Told Me', and one of their earliest songs, 'Production Prevention', throughout the night. Gary, then working as a part-time cabbie to supplement his small wage as an apprentice engineer, agreed to drive them to the studios for free, then pick them up in the morning.

When Mick got out at West Park Avenue the next morning, he said, 'Thanks a lot, Gary. When I'm rich and famous, I promise I'll pay you for the fare.'

'Right, that's a deal,' Gary replied, adding jokingly, 'And if you don't, I'm going to come looking for you.'

They were both laughing as Gary drove off and Mick went into his house to go to bed.

Today, Gary is not upset at all that he never got paid for that 120-mile journey. 'I didn't mind driving them for nothing, because being part of the band was fun; I liked helping them. It wasn't as if they were making anything out of that trip themselves. When I arrived to pick them up, they took me into the studio and played me the tracks they had laid down. All the boys were shattered, having had no sleep, but they were delighted with what they had done, and seemed very optimistic for the future. Mick, particularly, always believed they were going to make it and that everything they went through would be worthwhile in the end. I must say, though, that I always found him a bit reserved and difficult to get to know. Somehow, he didn't seem to fit into the direction the band was taking.'

What hopes the band had for that second single were dashed when Roger Eagle's own optimism about his financial future proved unfounded. Reluctantly, he admitted he could not release the record until his cash flow improved. In the meantime, he said, he would do his best to book The Elevators at as many venues as possible.

Eagle was true to his word: the next five months were busy and, for the first time in their brief history, the band saw some worthwhile return for all their travelling discomforts and hard work on stage.

What clearly distinguished The Elevators from other hopeful bands was the prolific writing of Mick and Moey. They were getting on well, and it showed in their musical output. They lived for music, each drawing confidence and enthusiasm from the other.

Ian Moss, Moey's brother, who was still heading his own band, The Hamsters, says: 'They were a good team, constantly reassuring each other. They were both very intense, very passionate about their music and shared a common goal. Mick had tremendous self-belief and he drove Neil on to achieve things. Mick was emotionally and mentally tough, and very organized, whereas Neil was moody and erratic. But they became so close they were like brothers. Certainly Neil was closer to Mick than he ever was to me.

'My own band would gladly postpone rehearsals to go off for a few days' drinking, but Mick and Moey would never have tolerated that. They were constantly displaying their belief and there was never any pretence that The Elevators were a democratic band. Mick and Neil were the leaders. And the others often had to bear the cross of their passion – like rehearsing on Christmas Day, for example.'

By mid 1980, the songwriting duo, who saw themselves as another Lennon and McCartney, had written fifty-four songs. And at a gig at The Mayflower, a converted cinema in Belle Vue, they decided to play the lot when less than thirty people turned up. Most bands would have honoured their commitment and got off stage quickly, but Mick saw the positive side of what looked like a negative situation.

Ian Moss, whose Hamsters came off after their obligatory thirty-minute spot, recalls: 'Mick's attitude was: "Right, we'll get something out of this". And they played for over two hours. It was like having a human jukebox on stage. In those days, it was unthinkable for even a major band to have so many songs in its repertoire and play for so long. But Mick and Moey seized the opportunity to make the point that they were different – and worth taking seriously. They were terrific that night. Everyone enjoyed them.'

Mick and Moey were always supportive to Ian and The Hamsters and enjoyed it when both bands managed to get bookings at the same gig. But that summer the agreeable double act came to a sour end after an ugly incident in which a Hamster threatened Brian Turner with a knife. It happened after a gig in the village of Nelson, near Burnley, when one of the audience invited the bands and their friends to a party. For some reason, he decided to pin Brian against a wall and hold a knife against his throat. Ian and the other Hamsters, used to his wild and unpredictable temper, thought little of it, but Brian was terrified and Mick and Moey were furious. Although the episode passed without injury to Brian, it severed the connection. Nothing was said at the time, but when Ian invited The Elevators to join The Hamsters on a gig in Coventry a few weeks later, Mick and Moey refused point blank. They said they would never play anywhere with them again.

For more than a year, Pete Dervin had arguably been the band's most loyal friend. But the band had now performed at close on 100 gigs, and the drudgery of travelling up and down motorways had taken its toll. His interest in The Elevators was fading: he had moved in with a girl, bought a new car, and, understandably, was eager to build up his business as a self-employed decorator. But what made him start to distance himself from the band and miss out on a few gigs was Roger

Eagle's increased involvement with the band, and his off-hand treatment of Pete. Roger looked on Mick as his protégé and did not like anyone else getting too close. If Mick turned up to see him with Pete in tow, Roger would look at Pete and snap, 'What are you doing here?' to make him feel uncomfortable.

In his heart, Pete knew his days as The Elevators' manager were numbered, and that autumn he unwittingly took the first step that would lead to his sacking.

The band had secured their first London gig, supporting a major club group called The Skids at the legendary Hammersmith Palais. To Mick and the others, it was an exciting prospect and they set about scraping together the money needed to get them and their equipment to the capital.

But Pete refused to put any money into the trip and said he was not going. As far as Mick was concerned, that was not a good political move; he did not like it at all.

What angered him more, however, was what happened when Gary Livesey organized the transport. Gary was full of good intentions: he had taken a day off work so that he could pick up the band at 10 a.m. and take a leisurely drive south. But the van hire company discovered oil on his licence, and would not loan him a vehicle. In a panic, Gary called on all his friends, trying to borrow another van, but the only one who came up trumps was a builder, whose vehicle was normally used for transporting bricks and cement.

Mick was boiling mad when Gary turned up three hours late. But when he saw the back of the van covered in cement dust and building site mess, he blew his top. It was the closest the band had seen him come to actually hitting someone.

Sensing the danger, Kevin Williams went up to Gary as he pulled to a stop and warned him not to say anything; it would only make matters worse. The best thing, he said, was to get moving as quickly as possible, because it was 1 p.m. and they had to be in Hammersmith by 6 p.m. to start setting up.

They loaded up the van and Gary headed towards the motorway. Mick sat in the back, among the cement dust and builders' mess, too uptight to speak because he thought they were going to miss the gig. Once Gary started putting his foot down and it was clear they were going to make it, Mick cheered up. And by the time they were on the M6 he was entertaining the band with a brilliant impersonation of Elvis Presley.

The following month, The Elevators appeared at a musical festival called Futurama, in front of more than 6,000 people at an indoor arena in Leeds. The festival, on 14 September, was essentially a shop window for promising bands, but bigger names, such as Gary Glitter, Altered Images and Soft Cell, gave the twelve-hour show public appeal.

Being asked to appear was the highlight of The Elevators' three-year life. But, maddeningly, Gary Livesey's driving licence jinx struck again: he had sent off to Swansea DVLC for a duplicate, but it had not arrived by the time he was due to hire a van to take the band to Leeds.

Gary got on to his mates again – and this time he was luckier. He was offered not a builder's van for transporting bricks but one used for carrying bodies from hospital morgues to the chapel of rest! And the back – which had no fittings or boards – was so clean that it reeked of disinfectant. The back axle was falling apart, but after Gary's last experience it was nothing, and he gratefully accepted his funeral parlour friend's offer to borrow the van.

The band set off down the motorway to Leeds, gagging on the stench and hardly able to hear themselves speak above the grinding of the broken axle. They laughed at their discomforts because of the vehicle they were in. If the band had flopped, that van would have been appropriate for a group once nicknamed 'The Dying Band'.

As it was, they were given one of their liveliest-ever receptions and were cheered back on stage for an encore. A huge bonus of the gig was that highlights were being recorded for TV and each band got the chance to sing one song for the cameras, but The Elevators let themselves down by selecting 'Production Prevention', not one of their catchier numbers. Their logic was that it was long and would give them more air time. But the choice was a mistake: the song, written in their early punk days, had a monotonous, drill-like bass line and was a poor advertisement for what they had to offer. At that time, the band were high on their successful stage performance and did not realize their mistake.

That show was another gig Pete Dervin chose to miss. His absence was noted by the band, and when, two weeks later, he refused to chip in any money for a second London gig – supporting Wah! Heat at the 100 Club in Oxford Street – the writing was on the wall.

Pete did not miss much at that gig. Brian Turner was so drunk he could not plug in his guitar, and the band did not do themselves justice at what was a prestigious venue. But Pete's absence did achieve what, deep down, he really wanted – the boot.

Today, Pete recalls: 'I knew it annoyed them when I didn't turn up for a gig. They would say, "If you're our manager, you've got to come and see us play." But I knew I was manager in name only, and was not doing much of a job. After that London gig, I didn't speak to Mick for a couple of weeks, then one Saturday morning he came to my house while I was working on my car.

'I could see he was a bit nervous, because he didn't know how I was going to react to seeing him. There'd always been a bit of antagonism between us ever since he'd pissed me off by behaving like a prima donna.

'That morning, he looked at my car and said, "That's great." Then he said, "Can I have our scrapbook back?" The book had all the gig venues and reviews in it and it was obvious why he wanted them. It meant: "You're out." I wasn't bothered. I just said, "Fine," and went in to get the book. After I'd given it to him, there was an awkward moment, then we just said, "See ya," and he was gone. That was it. I wasn't hurt, because my life was going in a totally different direction. And anyway, I'd sort of instigated the split. I saw Mick a few months later and things were better between us. My one big regret is that I didn't tell them all in the first place that it was pointless having me as their manager, because I was just no good at it.'

For The Elevators, losing Pete as a manager was no great set-back. What bothered them was losing him as a friend, and it pleased everyone when they all reached an understanding and Pete started going to gigs whenever he had the time.

★

The band may not have had a manager, but, as that 1980 winter drew on, they did have a record in the shops. Roger Eagle's financial problems had eased, and in late December his company, Eric's Records, released the single The Elevators had recorded in Rochdale five months before. The songwriting cover credit said Neil Smith instead of Moss, because Moey was still worried about the DHSS questioning him – and, for some reason, Mick's name appeared second.

The title, 'You Know What You Told Me', would have been ironically comforting for Mick. He knew what he had been told by his pal Roger Eagle – and, unlike other small-time opportunists who had tried to cash in on his talent, Roger seemed to be keeping his word.

He had told him he could get gigs for The Elevators – and he had. He had told him he would produce their second record – and he had done that, too.

15

The single was another flop, but, as always, The Elevators refused to be discouraged. They had unshakeable belief in themselves and their music, and never seemed deflated by failure. There would always be another song, they told themselves; it was the next one that would break through, would be the hit they wanted.

Nor was Roger Eagle disheartened by the less than sensational response to 'You Know What You Told Me': at least the record had been reasonably well received by the music press – and the BBC's John Peel, who had once poked fun at the band's efforts, was so impressed with their improvements that he invited them to appear live on his late-night show. The record had not made money – either for Eagle or the band – but then, it had not lost any either; sales, small as they were, had covered production costs.

Most of those limited sales were in Liverpool, not Manchester. No matter how well the band played in their home town, the reception was always luke-warm – for some of the gigs, as few as six people turned up. In Liverpool, however, they had built up a considerable following. Not surprisingly, Mick felt they should concentrate on consolidating their position on the Liverpool music scene, particularly since Roger Eagle was confident of booking them gigs on a regular basis at £50 a time, and was prepared to invest in a third Elevators record.

With this and his general life pattern in mind, Mick was faced with a dilemma: whether or not to leave home and move somewhere more conveniently situated. He was now spending more time in the centre of Manchester: when he was not studying at the Medlock Centre, he was rehearsing at Little Peter Street, where the band met for their regular Liverpool trips; and when he had free time, he was drinking in pubs in Manchester city or going to gigs in the various clubs. Cycling to and from Denton was good for him; it kept him fit for his live performances. But it was a sixteen-mile round trip and it had become a pain. In his heart, Mick knew it made sense to move into the centre of Manchester, but he was worried what his dad would think. After so many years living on their own together, they had become extremely close, and Mick knew it would be a wrench for both of them if he left.

It was Pete Dervin who Mick turned to for advice. 'He didn't like the thought of leaving Reg on his own,' says Pete. 'With Mick always out doing things, they weren't seeing much of each other, but Mick thought the world of his dad and didn't want to hurt him. I made his decision easier by explaining that when I left home I actually got closer to my dad, because we weren't living on top of each other. Mick could see the logic in that, and decided to tell his dad what was in his mind.'

Reg reacted well. He had been called up for the RAF at the age of eighteen and was the type who believed that there was little wrong in a young man cutting his ties with home. He was not worried about Mick coping on his own; with no mother and a father working six days a week, the boy had been doing that for years anyway.

What might have worried Reg, however, was the area where Mick chose to set up home with Moey: a sprawling, run-down estate in Hulme, a notorious slum area on the fringe of central Manchester, with a massive crime rate. Neither Mick nor Moey relished the prospect of living there, but they had no choice; they had little money and, because of its notoriety, Hulme offered the cheapest rents.

They moved into a spacious two-level flat at the top of a four-storey block in Otterburn Close. One of the bedrooms was at the top of the stairs, leading from the hall, the other downstairs. The lounge was on the ground floor at the rear, and this is where Mick and Moey set about trying to write the songs they still believed would make The Frantic Elevators famous.

Weeks after moving in, Hulme and neighbouring Moss Side were engulfed in the terrifying riots of summer 1981, making both Mick and Moey even more aware of the volatile and dangerous nature of the area that was now their home – the place where they wanted to build on their dreams of becoming another Lennon and McCartney.

Despite the grim surroundings, they wrote a lively, catchy song, 'Searching For The Only One', which Roger Eagle said was their most commercial sound to date. To give it the best chance, Eagle and Pete Fulwell launched another label, Crackin' Up Records, designed to promote The Elevators. For the B-side, he chose a newer version of 'Hunchback Of Notre Dame', one of the band's earliest songs, originally recorded for TJM but never released.

★

In July Mick was awarded a 2ii BA Honours degree in fine art. Lecturers commended his attendance record, although no reference was made to the many mornings Mick arrived red-eyed through lack of sleep after travelling home from late-night gigs. He had 'natural talent', they said, but tended to 'jump from one piece of work to another'. His drawings, they also remarked, were better than his paintings.

The degree sounded grandiose, but Mick had no intention of capitalizing on it. After leaving the Polytechnic that summer, he put his signature not on the canvas of his latest painting but on a form claiming unemployment benefit. Despite all the disappointments, he still could look no farther than the record business for a career. Life on the dole in the roughest, toughest part of the city would not be easy, but it had an important benefit: it would give him all the time he needed to write music and listen to it. He had learned to live off very little money and, he consoled himself, he would be no worse off than when he had had his grant. And, anyway, the financial picture could improve suddenly: Roger Eagle was booking more and more £50-a-night gigs, and the new single was becoming a reality.

On the strength of this optimism, Pete Dervin suggested The Elevators should become more business-minded and open a bank account, to keep track of the money coming in and going out. It would mean they could write a cheque for their transport, for example, instead of having to scratch around for cash at the end of a gig. He even suggested the band could start saving up.

Mick laughed at the unrealistic idea of having spare money to put away, but he loved the thought of having a bank account. It suited his serious attitude, but, more importantly, it would be a sign of the others' commitment if they had to put money into the bank to open the account.

Comforted by Pete's assurance that they were legally allowed to earn a certain amount before their unemployment benefit was affected, the band contributed £15 each, and a business account under the name The Frantic Elevators was opened at the National Westminster Bank's branch at Crown Point, in the centre of Denton.

★

In such a crime-infested area as Hulme, it was only a matter of time before Mick and Moey were robbed. The burglars found the flat a soft touch: they simply kicked in the thin wooden panel beneath the glass of their front door and climbed through. It was pointless Mick or Moey asking the neighbours to keep an eye on the flat while they were out, because crime was so rife that nobody took any notice of the odd theft.

And, according to Pete Dervin, it was almost certainly the neighbours who were responsible for breaking into the flat.

He says: 'When either Mick or Moey went out, the curtains in other flats would move as neighbours checked to see if the flat was going to be empty. Once, some little kids knocked on the door, asking for some orange juice. But it was only a ploy to see if anyone was in the flat. If there was no answer, some older lads would turn the place over. After the first break-in, Mick rang the police, but it was hopeless – there was nothing they could do. He was really upset about it. Even though they were living in the worst part of the city, he couldn't believe it had happened to them.'

Moey, it seems, became so paranoid about being mugged that he bought a blue shirt, black trousers and a pair of Doc Marten boots to make himself look like an off-duty policeman.

★

That summer, Roger Eagle secured the band a resident Saturday night spot at Liverpool's popular Adams Club, while still planning the October release of 'Searching For The Only One'. The Adams residency was a wonderful break for the band, but it tested their passion and commitment to the limit. Every Saturday morning, they had to travel to Liverpool on a complicated and time-consuming network of buses and trains, rehearse all day in the grimy basement of a converted warehouse beneath Roger's offices, then go straight into the gig at night. Since it would be too late to travel home afterwards, they would go back to the warehouse and grab as much sleep as they could – either in chairs or on the floor – before starting the arduous journey home in the morning.

Often Mick would stay on in Liverpool to spend the day with Roger and spend the night at his home. The friendship between the two was growing all the time and, thanks to Roger's knowledge and influence, Mick's musical passion was intensifying and maturing. He was even more heavily into blues and soul music, especially James Brown – and when he was back in Manchester, he would borrow Ian Moss's record, *James Brown, Live at the Apollo, Volume 2*, so much that when he returned it, Ian felt he was borrowing it himself!

★

In October 'Searching For The Only One' was released, filling the band and Roger with hope. John Peel played the record a lot and invited the boys to London again to perform it live for his late-night programme.

The music press liked the record, too, and it began to move up the Independent Charts. Sadly, this did not add up to big sales; nor did it encourage a major record company to sign up the band.

The disappointment they must have felt did nothing to cool the band's passion or energy: they soldiered on, putting up with the arduous travelling and spartan sleeping arrangements, naively oblivious to the financial shortcomings of their set-up. That they were getting no tangible reward for their efforts did not seem to bother them. All that mattered was performing. They lived for it. And, as ever, they convinced themselves that it would all be worth it in the end. Maybe the next record would be the one...

They were being billed as 'Liverpool's finest', and when they made a return to Manchester to play The Gallery, it was a triumph.

What all the passion and energy could not hide, however, was poor performance – and Mick became increasingly unhappy with Brian Turner's playing on bass. Brian simply was not a proficient bassist and he knew it. Mick knew it, too. Brian had been on the receiving end of dozens of rollickings from Mick, but they had always seemed quickly forgotten. After all, Brian was a mate first and a musician second.

If Mick had had the courage to tell Brian face to face that he was not up to it and they wanted to try someone else, Brian would probably have gone quietly; in truth, he had expected the sack long ago. But Mick fought shy of being blunt. To save himself the embarrassment of telling Brian he was fired, Mick used a ploy he hoped would give his friend the message he was being edged out and, hopefully, persuade him to quit. Moey had confided in Pete Dervin what was going on and when a photographer was taking some photographs after one Liverpool gig, Mick asked Pete to get in the picture. He felt it might, in some subtle way, give Brian a hint that Pete was going to be his replacement. But Pete refused to play along.

'I didn't like the way it was being done,' he says. 'If they wanted Brian out, they should have told him direct, not used me. I told them I was happy to stay in the background.'

In the end, Mick could not bring himself to do the deed, and Brian remained in the band, still a poor player, still a happy drinker, but still a good bloke who made them all laugh.

The intrigue behind the whole affair, however, is highly significant. Mick unmasked a character trait that would have unpleasant consequences for others who came into his musical life in the future. He loved being considered down-to-earth and straightforward – someone who spoke his mind, and to hell with whoever he upset. In the band, as in art class, he delighted in cold, offensive put-downs, barbed to hit the target. But when it came to personal matters that could provoke confrontation, Mick showed an overwhelming weakness and lacked his normal bravado.

When it came to the crunch, he bottled it, choosing instead to play mind games to achieve what he wanted.

In these games, he would become a master.

★

That winter of 1981, Roger Eagle got a call from Elliot Rashman, the new entertainments manager of Manchester University, who wanted to know if Roger had any bands worth putting on at the University. Roger seized his chance: he gave Elliot a hard sell on The Frantic Elevators.

Elliot, a short, pale-faced, Jewish man with tight, curly black hair, was music-mad. At school, in the Jewish area of Higher Crumpsall in north Manchester, he always seemed to have a copy of *New Musical Express*, which he read intently between lessons. He became the first pupil to buy Joni Mitchell's *Songs To A Seagull* album, then available only on import.

As a teenager, Elliot longed to be in a band, but he was a hopeless musician. At fourteen, he tried to play bass guitar in a group performing at a youth club, but was so terrible he pulled the plug and mimed instead.

Abandoning all hope of being a performer, Elliot decided to aim for the next best thing – *managing* performers. While studying for an English Literature degree at Manchester Polytechnic, he fell in with a musically-orientated crowd in Didsbury, east of the city, and was captivated by their talent. He cooled his ties with the people he had grown up with, referring to them, somewhat disdainfully, as 'my north Manchester friends.'

Among the Didsbury set were some musicians in a rising group called Albertos Y Los Trios Paranoias, and Elliot happily joined them as a roadie. When some of the band broke away to form a new group called The Mothmen, Elliot left too and became their manager. Being on the dole, he had a lot of time to work for the band and did, in fact, achieve some success, notably a record deal that resulted in several single releases.

The band broke up in the early eighties and Elliot had to get a job. He became a joiner, but this did not work out and he signed on the dole again. Nearing thirty, he was depressed that he was having to be supported by his wife Lyndsay, a primary school teacher, and was getting nowhere in life.

And then Michele Fryman, the wife of an old school pal, David Fryman, told Elliot that UMIST – the University of Manchester and Institute of Science and Technology – wanted someone to organize gigs, parties and discos for the University. It was right up Elliot's street. When he applied for the job, he got it.

When Elliot heard Roger Eagle enthusing about The Frantic Elevators that winter of 1981, he was not surprised; he had heard the same enthusiasm from one of his Mothmen friends, Tony Bowers, who had seen them in Manchester. Elliot did not take too much convincing to book them for the University.

When he saw them a few weeks later, Elliot was more than impressed; he was excited. The band was good, but the singer with the red hair was special. He had a great voice, but he had charisma, too.

Elliot, still holding on to his dream to be a pop star manager, felt he was looking at a young man who could be a major star. And he believed, deep down, that he could be the one to make it happen.

16

Mick was sitting on a speaker cabinet beneath a single naked electric light in the dingy basement. Several feet away, Moey and Brian chatted over their cigarettes while checking the strings on their instruments. Kevin was setting up his drums. It was just before midday on a Saturday early in the New Year, and the band were rehearsing beneath Eagle's Liverpool offices prior to their regular spot at Adams Club. Mick started to strum his semi-acoustic guitar. Moving his head nearer the microphone, he started singing softly, 'Holding back the years . . .'

And Kevin, moved by the intensity on Mick's face, was enchanted by the beauty of the melody.

When Mick had finished, Kevin felt an urge to tell him how much he loved the song – but he knew better: Mick wanted hard graft and results, not flattery. So, all Kevin said was, 'That's a pretty ditty.'

Mick nodded. 'Yeah. Now, I want you to do this.' And he began to explain what drum beat he wanted to go with the song. Then he turned to Brian and told him what bass line he wanted, and the four of them began working on the song. They went through it at least half a dozen times that day, tightening the music to match the lyrics, and by the time it was complete they all loved it.

But, strangely, no one mentioned the significance of the emotional lyrics. Everyone in the band knew that Mick's mother had left him when he was a child; and it was obvious that the haunting song was about the mother he had never known. But that cold day in Liverpool they were all concerned with getting the music right, not examining what were highly personal words. So nobody said anything. Not even Moey, who had helped write the song in Mick's bedroom in Denton.

The Adams Club gigs were proving successful for The Elevators: they supported classic and popular acts, including Bo Diddley – one of Mick's heroes – and Junior Walker.

They were also booked by Elliot Rashman for a second gig at Manchester University. The band liked Elliot and felt he was a good contact, who might provide introductions to powerful and influential people in the music business. Elliot liked the band too, particularly Mick, and a friendship began to develop.

Mick's friendship with Moey, however, was fading. Since 'Searching For The Only One', Moey had changed and it was driving a wedge between them. As The Elevators matured, Mick became even more confident and gregarious, and began socializing with new friends in and out of the music business. Moey, on the other hand, was withdrawing into himself. While Mick would love going to lively clubs, particularly The Hacienda, drinking in the atmosphere and being part of the scene, Moey would stay in the flat, just drinking alone. If he did venture out, it was only to a rough pub, The Cyprus Tavern, with old friends. Like a married couple who had discovered different interests, Mick and Moey began to drift apart, and there was nothing either of them could do about it, even if they wanted to.

What upset Mick more than anything was that Moey seemed to delight in being a slob. He would sit in the flat for days on end, eating poorly but drinking constantly, and never giving a thought to cleaning the place: any guest who came and sat on a chair was covered in dust and dirt when they got up. He revelled in the reclusive life, and when Pete Dervin opened the lounge curtains one morning after staying the night, Moey got angry. 'Why the hell did you do that?' he demanded to know. 'We were seeing how long we could keep them closed!'

In June 1982 the World Cup was being played in Spain and Moey stayed in the flat, watching the games on TV, throughout the whole three weeks, never venturing out once.

Pete Dervin, who spent some of the time with him, recalls: 'We built a pyramid out of our used lager cans. By the end of the World Cup, it was virtually to the ceiling. Both of us were drunk during most of the matches.'

Despite having a slob for a flatmate, Mick enjoyed living in Hulme: the area was rough and the accommodation less than luxurious, but it had given him freedom and independence. He had never been wildly successful with girls and living at home had hardly helped his chances; but with a place of his own he could indulge in as many liaisons – one-night stands, or otherwise – as he wished. Moey was a constant embarrassment, but, perhaps for the sake of the band, if not himself, Mick was prepared to tolerate him.

The hopes that The Frantic Elevators had for a live album crashed that summer when Roger Eagle's Crackin' Up record company mirrored its name and fell apart. Releasing the album was out of the question. And Roger was sad to report that there would be no more singles, either.

For the band, it was another severe blow. But for Mick, it was a crushing disappointment. It was his motivation and enthusiastic bullying that had transformed the band into a tight, professional outfit. Now they had a song – 'Holding Back The Years' – which had 'HIT' written all over it, but no record company to produce it. Once they had recovered from the disappointment, the band decided there was only one thing to do: make the record and release it themselves.

It would cost money. It would need faith. And it would take bottle. Believing that 'Holding Back The Years' was *the* song that would be the breakthrough they wanted, the band decided they would make sure they had all three.

They did their sums and decided that they needed £1,000 to cover the costs of producing 2,000 singles. So Mick and Moey went to the National Westminster at Crown Point to ask for an overdraft. The meeting with an assistant manager was tense. On paper, their proposal made good business sense: they planned to sell the records for 90p each, giving them £800 profit after the bank loan was repaid. But, from the bank's point of view, it was hardly a non-risk investment. The fickle pop market was precarious enough for the most financially stable business-man, let alone four young men with barely a penny between them and a less than impressive track record in the music industry.

But Mick's smooth tongue, and persuasive way of using it, did the trick. The assistant manager allowed him to explain why the band should be given even such a modest overdraft, and Mick seized the opportunity: the 2,000 singles would just be the start, he said; 'Holding Back The Years' was so good, the £800 profit from the first pressing would be doubled – maybe trebled – when the record-buying public got to hear about it.

The assistant manager was impressed, particularly when Mick told him the band – and their photographer, Richard Watt, who was the 'fifth Elevator' – were putting their own money into the venture, and he okayed the overdraft. The band decided to name their company No Waiting, after a road sign Richard had acquired for the flat he was sharing with Brian Turner in Charles Barry Crescent, a short walk from Mick and Moey. In August they hired Hologram Studios in Stockport to record the song that carried so much of their faith and hopes.

For the record sleeve, Richard Watt took a picture of Mick in a striped woollen vest, with a toy gun in his mouth. It was an interesting photograph, but it had more to do with the flipside, 'Pistols In My Brain', than 'Holding Back The Years'. Compared to the massive mistakes that would follow, it was an insignificant error of judgement.

Mick turned to Steve Mardy for help in collecting the 2,000 records from Walthamstow, in north-east London, in September, prior to the release the following month. Steve, who had learned a lot from The Elevators and regarded his chauffeur role as part of the give and take of friendship, agreed to drive them to London, and hired a new red Ford Escort XR3. On Wednesday night, two weeks later, Steve went to Hulme and had a smoke and a couple of drinks with Mick and Moey before setting off for a leisurely drive to London. There was no need to hurry; the pressing plant did not open until 7.30 a.m. Mick and Moey slept through most of the journey.

Today, Steve recalls: 'The trip went really smoothly. We were outside the plant at 5 a.m., waiting for the first workers to arrive, and the eight boxes containing the 2,000 singles were waiting to be collected. Mick and Moey were as pleased as punch. It was their own thing and they had followed it all through themselves. For once, nobody had been able to put a spanner in the works.

'Before we set off home, they said they had to drop off some records to people on the music papers and the BBC, in the centre of London. I had no idea where we were half the time, but Mick and Moey seemed to know. By the time we got to Broadcasting House to leave a copy for John Peel, I was concerned about getting back to Manchester; I'd be in for an extra day's rental if I didn't get the car back by 6 p.m. But when I mentioned this to Mick and Moey, they said we weren't finished yet – we had to deliver some of the records to a shop in Liverpool! Don't ask me how, but we made it. The lads dropped off the records and I got the car back on time. Not that Mick and Moey knew much about the trip up the motorway. They snored most of the way up, as they had on the way down!'

The eight boxes containing The Elevators' dreams of stardom were stored in Charles Barry Crescent, while Mick and Moey considered the next two crucial stages of the enterprise: distribution and promotion. Sadly, both were disastrous. Mick and Moey managed to persuade a few Manchester shops to stock the record, but without a proper distributor operating in the customary way, most of the copies stayed in the flat. Even if shops had known about 'Holding Back The Years', it would never have taken off, because the promotion was virtually nil. Coverage of the band in the music press over the years had been modest, and interest outside Manchester and Liverpool had been minimal. The punk movement was over, but the band had a punk name and a record with a punk-style sleeve. To make promotion even more confusing, 'Holding Back The Years' was slow and rhythmic – definitely not punk. The odds were stacked against The Elevators. All they had in their favour was their admirable dedication and self-belief that had counted so much with their bank manager. But that would not clear their overdraft.

As the release date got nearer, Mick and Moey were hit by another setback: the flat was burgled yet again. The thieves got away with Mick's semi-acoustic guitar, and nearly fifty of his records and treasured James Brown tapes. Mick was devastated; the tapes would almost certainly mean nothing to the thieves, but Mick had spent years collecting them and listened to them all the time.

Steve Mardy has good reason to remember the burglary and the effect it had on Mick, because he had helped Mick find those cherished tapes in Yanks, one of Manchester's most popular record shops. 'Mick loved black American soul or blues singers and spent ages looking for particular records. He was passionate about collecting and he'd get very excited when he found what he was looking for. The stolen tapes and records were priceless to him – his pride and joy.'

Typically, Mick turned a sickening negative into a positive: he told himself he had been listening to music made before he was born so much that he was out of touch with what was happening in 1982. The theft might be good for him, he convinced himself; perhaps it would drag him out of his insular world and bring him up to date.

Pete remembers another occasion when Mick returned to the flat with a girl one night to find the front door kicked in again. Thinking the burglar might still be inside, he sneaked into the kitchen, grabbed a meat cleaver and waited for the intruder to come out. But Mick was too late: the thief had already fled.

But he refused to let it happen again. 'He and Moey devised a plan,' says Pete. 'They banged in a load of nails through the front door, so whoever kicked in the panel would spike their foot. They went to great lengths to make this effective. They became paranoid about leaving anything valuable in the flat. For a while, Moey would hide what money he had in a salmon paste jar in the kitchen, convinced no one would take the lid off. But, in the end, they didn't leave anything of value in the flat at all.

'Whenever there were a lot of us at the flat, we made sure we left in twos, rather than in a crowd, so that no one would know if the place was empty or not.'

The outlook brightened considerably when *Melody Maker* agreed to interview the band to publicize the single. They could not afford for everyone to go, so Mick went to London on his own, and impressed the paper enough for it to carry a half-page article on him and 'Holding Back The Years'. The band was excited but *Melody Maker*'s rival, *New Musical Express*, cancelled out what would have been superb publicity by reviewing the record cruelly: 'Like Led Zep on a bad day,' was one of the comments. Mick, Moey, Brian, Kevin and Watty were choked. They felt their endeavours had earned them a break, but they weren't getting one. The boxes of records stayed in Charles Barry Crescent. And The Frantic Elevators' bank account stayed in the red.

*

Elliot Rashman was doing such a good job as the University's entertainments manager that he was poached by the Polytechnic. He was on the way to becoming one of the hottest bookers in the North. He revelled in the power, taking immense pleasure in laying down his territory. He shouted at people when they failed to do things his way, examined any poster before it was put up in his part of the building and generally poked his nose into the tiniest detail affecting his little world. He was very image-conscious, and would wear a long, dark coat and a black trilby which he felt suited his showbiz job. But there was something that let down that influential image: Elliot suffered from asthma and had to use an inhaler.

Roger Eagle, beleaguered by creditors, urged Elliot to keep helping The Elevators while he sorted out his business problems. Elliot responded by booking the band to appear at the Poly, and by taking on Mick as a disc jockey one evening a week.

The more they saw of each other, the closer Mick and Elliot became. They shared a deep passion for music, but, more important, they both craved success in the record business. Mick may not have cared for Elliot's sycophantic praising of his 'wonderful talent', but it would not have done his confidence any harm after all the setbacks over the years.

Others in the band liked Elliot, too; Moey, particularly, was impressed by his enthusiasm and drive and even told his brother Ian that Elliot could be very good for them all.

What they did not know was that Elliot did not feel *they* could be good for *him* – or Mick. He appreciated they were a good band, but knew from his failure with The Mothmen that there was no room for passengers in the tough world of popular music. And some of the band *were* passengers, he felt; they even went on stage drunk. Slowly, Elliot began to talk to Mick about his future, skilfully sowing the seeds of doubt about the part The Elevators should play in it.

For the moment, though, Mick was still wrapped up in the band – still as enthusiastic, still demanding 100 per cent. One morning, for example, Kevin did not turn up for a rehearsal in a town ten miles outside Stockport. He had two reasons: (a) he was in bed with heavy flu; and (b) most of Manchester and surrounding areas were shrouded in fog and no buses were running.

Suddenly the phone rang at Kevin's home in Oldham. It was Mick.

'Where are you?' he demanded, somewhat unnecessarily.

'I can't make it,' Kevin told him. 'I feel terrible and the buses aren't running.'

'I've checked. The *trains* are running. Get a fuckin' train and get down here.'

And he put the phone down.

Kevin dragged himself out of bed and got ready. It was not an easy or comfortable journey, but he made it. When he arrived, Mick said, 'Yeah. You do look rough. Come on, let's get some work done.'

He could be unforgiving like that.

*

What the band had grandly called a release date for 'Holding Back The Years' came and went, barely noticed in the music business. It was as if the record had never been released at all, so, in December, Mick suggested sending it to the music press and disc jockeys again, as though it had not.

They called it a 'relaunch'. And Steve Mardy proved again what a loyal friend he was by persuading a girlfriend, who worked with BBC Radio Manchester, to interview Mick and Moey. She duly carried out the interview on a BBC radio tape machine, but did not do anything with it. Embarrassed, Steve set about cutting the interview himself.

'Someone had said we'd have a better chance of getting the tape broadcast if it was just three minutes, so I started editing out all the nonsense,' Steve remembers. 'I spent ages on it and even managed to work in a bit of 'Pistols In My Brain' in the middle, and 'Holding Back The Years' at the end. One night I sneaked into the BBC in the early hours and used a mixing machine. In the end, I got the whole thing down to three minutes fifteen seconds and was really pleased. To me, it was a really interesting interview, with Mick and Moey talking seriously about their music, and I couldn't wait for the band to hear it.'

Sadly, none of the band ever did hear that tape – or get to know of the efforts Steve had gone to on their behalf. His BBC friend finally persuaded a DJ to play 'Holding Back The Years', but without reporting any of the background, or anything about the group. Eventually, the tape was thrown away.

Steve was disappointed. 'From The Elevators' point of view, the air time was a hopeless waste of time. You would have thought that a local disc jockey would have been eager to give a Manchester band a boost, especially as they had put their own money on the line. What he said was very downbeat and hardly likely to make someone want to rush out and buy the record. But that was the way the lads' luck was going then.'

To Mick, however, it was not all about luck – good or bad. That depressing December, he was seeing signs that The Elevators looked like being defeated by their past failures and recent mistakes; that, in all honesty, they were unlikely to make the breakthrough they all craved.

On Christmas Eve, he decided to go to a pub in Hyde called The Whitegates, unaware that it was now being jointly run by Frank Ollerenshaw, his old Audenshaw pal and drummer mate. When Frank asked him how things were, Mick could not hide his feelings and told him that things weren't going well for the band.

For Mick, the beginning of the end of The Frantic Elevators came early in the New Year. He had always been the driving force behind the band, the one to encourage them to bounce back from their disappointments. But the disaster of 'Holding Back The Years' had hit him hardest: emotionally, he had put in far more than the rest, and he felt drained. He knew that if they were to try again, there would have to be changes. He had unshakeable loyalty to The Elevators: they were his friends first, fellow musicians second. At the same time, he knew that Brian and Kevin were not gifted enough, and would have to be replaced if the band was to get anywhere.

While making plans to go back into the studio, Mick and Moey were thinking of sacking Brian and Kevin. But then, during practice at Charles Barry Crescent, something happened that made Mick think that it was not only Brian and Kevin who threatened The Elevators' future . . . it was Moey, too.

The band were rehearsing a blues song Mick had written and Moey could not get the right note on his guitar. Every time he got it wrong, the band stopped and started again. But Moey kept hitting the wrong note, time and time again. Eventually, he forgot about the band, and what they were supposed to be playing, and kept his head down at the guitar, trying, again and again, to hit the note. He was in a world of his own, oblivious to anyone around him. Brian and Kevin looked at each other, both relieved that, for once, it was not one of them messing things up.

Then they looked at Mick. And his expression said it all: it was hopeless trying to carry on like this. He knew it was the beginning of the end; he knew in his heart that The Frantic Elevators were not going anywhere.

To his credit, Mick hid his fears and, with Elliot Rashman's support, hired Angel Grove studio, in Stockport, to record some new songs he had written. His belief was still there. Despite everything, he still felt The Elevators could bring out another single.

141

He was wrong. The band managed to get through the recording session – laying down the tracks of 'When I Go To See Her' and 'Haven't Got The Power' – but Mick's frustrations were there for all to see, and his new songs were doomed to be no more than yet another demo tape.

Steve Mardy, who went to the studio one evening when Mick and Moey were mixing one of the tracks, says: 'They were going through a split and it wasn't a healthy time to hang around them. Mick seemed to be cut off from the rest and was storming around the place. It didn't seem to be what he wanted. Brian was getting a bollocking for not doing something right. And Kev was just keeping his head down, reading a paper. I asked what was the matter, and they said it was Mick being his temperamental self, acting the "artist". But, to me, Mick was trying to make it work. And he was frustrated and angry that he couldn't. He must have thought: We've got a lot of grounding behind us. Why aren't people listening to us? What have I got to do to sell music?'

Things came to a head in February when The Elevators performed at the Band On The Wall. They had played there many times before and had always gone down well, but this night was a disaster that spelt the end for the band.

By now, they had become very 'bluesy' and would perform cover versions of James Brown and Bo Diddley numbers. But when Mick asked Moey to play a particular number that night, Moey admitted he could not manage it because he was too drunk.

Mick was beside himself with anger. Over a beer in the interval, he let out his frustration to Ian Moss. 'Fucking hell, Ian. What's the point of it all when we can't play the songs we want to play? We've rehearsed the song all fucking week and now he says he can't play 'cos he's too drunk.'

Ian calmed Mick down and, after the gig, they all went to The Hacienda, then back to Hulme for more drinks and a few joints. But, to Ian, the writing was on the wall – in big, bold letters. He had never heard Mick or Moey criticize the other. And he knew that, for Mick, there was no point in continuing the relationship, no matter how deep it had been, no matter how many dreams they had shared.

'It was inevitable,' Ian recalls, sadly. 'The friendship was like an old, wounded dog – somebody just had to put a bullet in it to end the suffering.'

*

A few days later, Mick confided in Brian that he was leaving the band and that he planned to tell the others when they met for rehearsal in Charles Barry Crescent that evening. It gave Brian a chance to warn

Moey and Kevin, and, shortly after 5 p.m., they were all sitting in the flat in a mild state of shock, waiting for Mick to arrive and break the news.

Mick arrived on his bike. He came in and sat in a chair, looking tense and troubled. He came straight to the point.

'I've taken this as far as I can,' he said. 'I'm leaving.'

Kevin was sitting at the drums. On the wall behind him were three huge plastic letters that Brian and Watty had bought in a junk shop to decorate the flat.

Moey, curled up like a ball as usual, his hands wrapped round his knees, looked into Mick's eyes.

'Is it Elliot?' he asked. 'Are you doing something with Elliot?'

'Yeah,' was all Mick said.

The atmosphere was sad, not hostile: Mick looked less tense now that he had told them; and the others respected his decision and did not question it. With no point in practising, they all sat around chatting for an hour or so. Then Mick walked out, leaving behind the hopefuls who had shared his life and dreams for so many exhausting years.

The big plastic letters on the wall behind the drums provided an ironic backdrop to a sad finale for The Frantic Elevators, spelling out the reality of Mick's farewell.

The letters were: END.

*

Shortly afterwards, Mick and Moey had a showdown. What was said has been kept private, between just the two of them; Moey has not even spoken about it to his brother. But what was said was serious and final enough for Mick to quit the flat, leaving Moey with £250 rent arrears.

For Mick, it was an emotionally shattering time: he had walked out on his home, his best friend, and the band that had consumed the bulk of his life for five and a half years. For Moey, it was terrifying. And one night, after Mick had left, he rang Pete Dervin in a panic, pleading for help.

'There had been a shooting and police had been coming and going,' says Pete. 'Moey was terrified. He said, "Can you help me? I've got to move out. Mick's gone and people are getting shot around here."

'I told him not to worry. I called Martin Kenyon and we went down to help Moey move out. I went into Mick's room. All that was left were his Doc Martens and a mattress on the floor and some of his paintings on the walls. From then on, The Elevators began to dissolve.'

143

Mick found a flat in the Withington area. Unwittingly, Moey moved into a tiny bedsit a few streets away. But neither knew. And even if they had, they would not have spoken.

Moey was devastated by Mick's decision to quit the band. He felt betrayed, and bitter about the part Elliot had played in it. Certainly Ian Moss is convinced that Mick and Moey could have struggled on for another year or so if Elliot had not been on the scene. 'Mick and Neil were like a married couple, but Elliot came along and sort of stole Mick away,' says Ian. 'Neil enthused about Elliot, about what a nice, very professional guy he was, and how he was going to do the band a lot of good. Much later, when I reminded Neil what he'd said, he just shrugged his shoulders and said, "Sometimes you're wrong."

'Mick leaving was a major trauma for my brother. They'd had amazing faith in each other's ability and had been through so many hard times together. I think they took a lot of pride in how hard it had been. They were so intense and took themselves so seriously. To them, having a hard time was their dues for success. They always believed in the next record making it for them.

'Even when "Holding Back The Years" failed, they never stopped believing in the quality of the song. They blamed the failure on the poor distribution and lack of publicity, not on the song itself. The longer it went on, though, it became harder and harder to sustain the belief. It was very hard to have sympathy, because they had got themselves into that hole and then would feel sorry for themselves that people didn't come and say, "We'll put your record in our shops." They never made any effort to deal with these people.

'I'm sure they had a collective chip on the shoulder. They saw themselves as a great band who were victims of fate. They didn't see any of it as being their fault.'

Moey and Kevin could not bear to give up the band. They changed the name to The Frantics and hired a saxophone player to help with the 'new look'. But the new man lasted only a few weeks; he left when he discovered it was not the band he had heard so much about.

Moey, it seemed to close friends, was keeping the band going because he felt it might make Mick come back. There was no real chance of that, although Mick did turn up to watch a few rehearsals. He was also there the night, early that summer, when the band played a gig above a gay bar near Manchester's bus station. It was just the three of them with Moey doing the vocals. To those who had followed the band over the years, it was a sad sight.

'It didn't seem right without Mick,' says Steve Mardy. 'The band was just a three-piece combo. After the gig, I helped them pack up their equipment and I remember Moey being drunk. For him, the split with Mick was like a divorce, and it brought him to his knees.'

Shortly after that gig, Brian Turner had had enough and quit. Moey tried to find someone to replace him, but his heart was no longer in the band and it fizzled out.

For Moey, it was as if a dear friend had finally died, and he needed to grieve. He shut the door of his bedsit, pulled the curtains and didn't open them, sinking deeper and deeper into a depression in which he drank heavily, took pills, ate junk food, and refused to see anyone.

He stayed behind those curtains for nearly six months.

Ian, whose band, The Hamsters, was still performing, remembers Neil's terrible time with sadness. 'His whole lifestyle had been bad and the end of the band was the final straw. He needed psychiatric treatment to bring him out of his depression. We have never been particularly close, and there's been a lot of bad blood between us, but, during his treatment, he came to a party and ended up apologizing to me for things he'd done to me in the past. He talked more honestly than he'd ever done before. That dark, depressing bedsit was doing him no good and I decided to get him out. I persuaded him to start rehearsing with my band and it seemed to sort out his problems.'

It did not solve his problem with his songwriting buddy, however. Mick tried to patch things up, but Moey was not interested. He retreated again into a reclusive lifestyle, preferring chess to the guitar, and studying for an Open University degree to socializing with old friends.

Those dreams of becoming another Lennon–McCartney with Mick were nothing more than a memory.

17

Elliot Rashman was a terrific salesman. And when Mick came to him for advice, he seized the opportunity: he said all that Mick needed was a band of good musicians – and he knew where to find them. From that moment, early in 1983, Elliot started dedicating all his time to telling all his musical friends in Didsbury just how good Mick was, and what a star he was going to be. He believed it. And he made sure everyone he told believed it too.

Three young musicians swept along on Elliot's hype were a drummer named Chris Joyce, a guitarist, Dave Rowbotham, and a bassist from Liverpool. They had formed part of the now disbanded The Mothmen, and were wondering what to do.

When they heard Mick's voice, they were as impressed as Elliot, and the four started jamming together at the Polytechnic. Another Mothman, Tony Bowers, had set up a recording studio on a government enterprise scheme, and after a couple of months' rehearsals, Elliot persuaded him to let the new band record some tracks for a demo tape.

For Mick, it was an exciting period, experimenting with new sounds and songs, and with new musicians. He was on the dole and was broke most of the time, but Elliot's enthusiasm kept him bubbling: at last he had someone as dedicated as himself; someone who treated the band and his ambition as a serious business, not a leisurely pursuit that merely filled in a few hours of the day.

The excitement of the New Year fuelled Mick with optimism, and when an actress friend offered to teach him how to get the best out of his voice, Mick accepted eagerly. Until then, he had not given voice technique a thought, singing instinctively in styles picked up from the thousands of records he had listened to over the years. But he was keen enough to cycle to Manchester College of Music several days a week to learn how to control his breathing and expand his range, and by March had noticeably improved. Coming up to his twenty-third birthday, he was professionally equipped to achieve all that Elliot had in mind.

Sadly, the far-reaching plans Elliot had for both of them were put on hold, as he battled with personal problems that would eventually destroy his marriage and the band. He and his wife Lyndsay had not been getting on, and that spring they decided to split. That in itself might not have affected the band, but, some time after the break-up, Lyndsay started seeing Dave Rowbotham, the guitarist. Elliot, it seems, was not too upset, because the marriage was more or less dead. But then Elliot got close to Rowbotham's girlfriend, Louise, and Rowbotham hated it. He and Elliot fell out. The band began to suffer from the tension.

One of the friends Elliot turned to for advice in his personal torment was his old school pal, Dave Fryman. The two had always enjoyed a deep friendship, but had drifted apart when Elliot started preferring the company of his Didsbury music cronies to that of his 'north Manchester friends'. Now, however, Elliot needed a strong, reliable mate – and Dave did not let him down: he invited him to stay at his home in Prestwich and listened sympathetically as Elliot poured his heart out.

Talk got round to Elliot's future and what he planned to do with his life. Elliot went on and on about Mick, about his exquisite voice, his dynamic star quality; and about how he could not fail to make it. 'His mum walked out when he was a kid – he was abandoned just like John Lennon,' Elliot said, excitedly. He seemed to think that was important, like a bit of mythology for his protégé.

Dave was stunned; he had never seen or heard his friend so enthusiastic about anything before. And when Elliot promised to bring the demo tape so that he could hear the incredible voice for himself, Dave was fascinated. He was a science schoolteacher now, not that interested in the music scene, but Elliot had sold Mick's talent so hard, he was intrigued. If only half of what Elliot said was true, the kid was Frank Sinatra and Mick Jagger rolled into one!

The next day, Dave listened to the demo tape on a Walkman. He was disappointed. 'Mick sounded like Noddy Holder out of Slade,' Dave recalls today. 'It was a piercing voice and, to be honest, I wasn't impressed.'

Unshaken and undeterred, Elliot pulled out a photograph of Mick. He thought it was wonderful, but Dave was horrified: he could not believe how ugly Mick was, and said so. With an ugly face and an unremarkable, piercing voice, how could he possibly get anywhere in the crowded, competitive world of pop music? Elliot, however, was deaf to any criticism, blind to Dave's look of disbelief.

And then, later that March, Dave met Mick. It was not the best of introductions. Dave's wife had thrown a surprise thirtieth birthday party for him at their home. The first Dave knew about it was when he arrived home around 8 p.m., having been working late, and heard the stereo blaring too noisily for his liking. Mick was the culprit; he had been invited by Elliot to act as disc jockey. The house was full of friends enjoying the surprise, but Dave had had a tough, tiring day at school and was not in the mood, and when he met Mick later in the evening, he reacted badly. Mick was now sitting on the central heating boiler in the kitchen, and had buckled the top with his weight.

'Do you mind not sitting on that,' Dave snapped, irritably.

Mick obliged. But neither was encouraged to pursue the conversation, and they did not see each other again until one Sunday afternoon, a few weeks later, when Elliot took Dave to the Poly to see the still-nameless band practising. Once again, Dave was less than impressed: the band spent most of the time fiddling with their instruments and Dave was bored. He failed to understand why Elliot was so enthusiastic.

Despite the tension between Elliot and Dave Rowbotham, the band persevered throughout the summer. But they still had not given thought to a name, or done anything other than the demo tape, and Mick started to worry. It had all promised so much in the beginning, but now he told Elliot he wanted to start again and work with new musicians; guys who would be better and more dedicated.

The first person Elliot approached was his pal, Dave Fryman, who had played guitar in several bands in the seventies. But Dave was committed to teaching science, not playing in a band, and said he was not interested. 'Can't you find anyone else in Didsbury?' he said.

Elliot would not be denied. He switched into salesman's mode, impressing on Dave, over and over again, how Mick was destined to make it; and that whoever was in his band would make it too. Feeling Dave wavering, Elliot talked about writing and publishing songs, which he knew was close to his heart. That's where the money is, Elliot said. Dave and Mick would write original songs together and become rich and famous; Dave would earn so much money, Elliot said, that he would not have to teach any more.

Finally Dave took the bait. 'Yeah, all right,' he said. And Elliot arranged for him to meet Mick at his latest flat in Hulme.

★

Dave was nervous the night he drove on to the estate, looking for William Kent Crescent, where Mick was now sharing a flat with another DJ from the Poly. He was not nervous at the prospect of meeting Mick, but of being mugged: he was well aware of Hulme's reputation for crime and, as he parked and started walking to Mick's flat, carrying his guitar, Dave kept looking fearfully over his shoulder.

'I was tense and on edge,' Dave admits today. 'Hulme was not an area

I wanted to hang about in. Certainly I didn't like walking in the dark with a guitar. As I knocked on Mick's door, I thought about my car. Would it be there when I got back, I wondered? If it was, would it still have its wheels?

'Mick was alone in the flat. It was a bit strained at first, because we barely knew each other, but then we sat down and he started playing me one of his songs on his guitar. He told me it was called "Wounded Animal" and proceeded to sing it, passionately and intensely, giving it everything. He wasn't embarrassed in the least, but I was; it was peculiar sitting in a room, listening to someone sing to me like that. I felt it was over the top, and what didn't help was that I didn't think much of the song. It was as if he'd heard the blues and then got it all wrong and missed the point. I could now appreciate that Mick did, indeed, have a great voice. But, in terms of musical ideas, I wasn't impressed. I didn't know where he was coming from.'

Dave did like the next song, however: it was one Mick had been inspired to write while spending lonely nights in the flat after breaking up with a girlfriend, and he called it 'Sad Old Red'. Mick sang a third song, 'Every Bit Of Me', which Dave liked too, and, over the next few weeks, they had three more sessions trying to perfect them. The reason, Mick explained, was that an eminent record company boss in New York, named Seymour Stein, was showing interest in him and wanted to hear a tape of his voice. They did make the tape and Elliot sent it to New York, but Dave was secretly amazed. Today, he says: 'When we played the tape, I thought: You can't send that off – it's awful! But neither Mick nor Elliot thought so, and it went anyway.'

Dave was the accompanying guitarist on the tape, but, in view of what happened later he would wonder whether anyone informed Seymour Stein of that fact.

*

Finding a drummer was Elliot's next challenge. It proved easy: Tony Bowers introduced Mick to Eddie Sherwood, who was well known on the Manchester music scene. Elliot knew Eddie well, too, and needed little convincing to meet him and sell him the idea of joining the band. Over a few cans of strong Tennents lager at Dave's home, he listened to Mick sing and Elliot and Dave tell him about the 'record company interest'. At the end, he could hardly wait to pick up his drumsticks.

The search for a suitable bass player proved more difficult. They tried a friend of Eddie's, but that did not work out. Then they found someone named Pete Hooker, who rehearsed with them in Mick's flat. But he was eventually rejected because Mick did not like him.

Shortly before Christmas, another bassist was mentioned: Ian Morris, who had played in Albertos Y Los Trios Paranoias, the band for whom Elliot had worked as a roadie, and a seventies band, The Smirks, before quitting to act in the Channel 4 soap, *Brookside*. Ian, known to everyone as Mog, had been in the series for three months and was planning a career in acting, but he changed his mind when he met Elliot and heard the sales pitch about Mick and the new band. What helped was that Mog had seen Mick three times before – and had been impressed. The first time was in 1979 when The Elevators were rehearsing in Little Peter Street; Mog was practising there too, and remembered Mick trying to arrange transport to get them to Liverpool. The second time was at the Grants Arms pub in Hulme: Mick was playing pool and Mog remembered how stylish he looked in his black brogue shoes. The third time, in February 1982, was at a Bo Diddley gig when The Elevators were under Roger Eagle's wing.

Mog had liked what he had seen. And when he met Mick for the fourth time, at one of Mick's Black Rhythms nights at the Poly, he liked him even more.

Today, Mog recalls: 'I sat in the DJ booth, chatting to him about all sorts of music and had such an affinity with him, I thought: This is the man for me. I was amazed at the extent of his record collection. His tastes were as wild as mine.'

On the afternoon of Christmas Eve, Mog went to Mick's flat for his audition and played on the various songs the band had been developing. Mick, Dave and Eddie liked him. And he liked them. A place in the new band was his if he wanted it.

For many, it would have been an agonizingly difficult decision: as a TV actor, Mog was earning £600 a week playing Mark Gossage in *Brookside*; as a member of the band, he would have to go on the dole to ensure he had the time to devote to rehearsing and gigging. Astonishingly, Mog did not hesitate. He shared the band's belief that they were going to be big. And he wanted to be part of it. He told Mick that afternoon to count him in.

Today, Mog says: 'I was slightly concerned that I had been off the music scene for over a year, but I was knocked out by Mick's voice, and thought: How can I not do this? I knew, that Christmas Eve, that he was going to be famous. It was a gamble, throwing away an acting career and all the money and fame that went with it, but I genuinely believed that the band was going to work and that there'd be something worthwhile at the end of it.'

Another New Year dawned. And Mog, like Dave Fryman and Eddie

Sherwood, greeted it enthusiastically, their faith in the new band, and commitment to it, generated as much by Elliot Rashman's irresistible hard sell as the potential of Mick's golden voice.

18

To Elliot, it was a business from the word go. Early in 1984, he arranged for the band to rehearse at the Poly on Tuesday nights and Sunday afternoons and would tell them which numbers he felt they should, or should not, perform. While making decisions, he rarely referred to them as the band; they were 'the project'. And it was clear which direction he wanted it to take.

It was important to get the band moving with a series of gigs. But it was also vital to choose the right venues. The Frantic Elevators had played hundreds of dingy pubs and clubs which had failed to pay dividends. With the new band, Elliot decided, it would be a case of quality, not quantity: he would try to put them in demand by keeping their early gigs scarce, hopefully creating a buzz. As an influential booker, Elliot could have had the pick of virtually any venue he wanted for that all-important first gig. But he chose the Poly. It was home ground; Mick was known and liked. The audience would be appreciative, but not so tough that it would discourage the band if they did not perform well.

He booked them in as a half-hour support, in early March, for a Cockney poet-cum-singer named Billy Bragg.

The problem was what numbers should they perform in those thirty minutes. In those early days, the rehearsals were so few and far between that the band were never together long enough to create fresh material. Mick had written lyrics to a handful of songs – 'Open Up The Red Box', 'Something's Burning', 'So Green', 'Tear The Valentine Up' and 'So Mean' – but these needed a lot of work. What time they did have together was spent polishing 'Sad Old Red', 'Wounded Animal' and 'Every Bit Of Me', but that was hardly enough to fill a thirty-minute set. In the end, they settled for adding cover versions, including a slow version of Talking Heads' 'Heaven'.

Almost as hard as deciding what to sing was deciding what to call the band. No one had any bright ideas, so they spent hours looking through film books, record sleeves, even the Bible, for some inspiration. One night either Mick or Elliot was listening to the BBC's World Service, so that was put forward. No one really liked World Service as a name, but, at the same time, no one came up with anything better. And with the gig getting nearer, it was agreed to put that name in the pre-date advertising.

For Dave Fryman, World Service's first gig got off to an inauspicious start: he embarrassed Elliot by not having a clue who they were supporting. He knew the name Billy Bragg because Elliot had mentioned it. But he had no idea who he was, or why he was topping the bill.

Today, Dave recalls: 'Elliot was so proud when he introduced Billy to me in his office. But I'd been so involved in teaching and out of touch with the music scene that I hadn't heard of Billy Bragg. So, when I was introduced, I said, "Who is it?" Elliot's face was a picture. He looked as if I'd really shown him up.'

The gig went well. The Poly was packed that night, and the audience liked World Service. Elliot liked the band's performance, too, but he had some criticism when he went to the dressing room after the show. He had arranged for all the musicians to leave the stage after the penultimate number, to allow Mick to close the show with a solo number, 'Every Bit Of Me', playing the guitar. None of the band had liked the idea, but they had, indeed, left the stage at the agreed moment. Elliot, however, felt they had let Mick down by making too much noise walking off. And he told them so.

For Messrs Fryman, Sherwood and Morris, it was their first taste of the manager's protectiveness towards his singer – and a warning of what was to come in terms of where they fitted into the band's image.

★

That image had been worrying Elliot for months. He knew the band needed something different, something special to set it apart from all the others, and he and Mick would often sit up all night discussing ways to achieve it. After one marathon session early in April, Mick went to a rehearsal and announced: 'From now on, my name is Red. I want you all to call me Red.'

The name may have been simply a way to create something positive out of his hair colouring, which, since grammar school, had been a negative feature of his life. Just possibly, however, there may have been a more profound reasoning behind it. At college, Mick's favourite painter was Matisse – and the French expressionist's favourite colour was red. It is the colour of blood, passion and life, and could be said to symbolize Mick's own exhibitionist and domineering personality. And, according to art experts, expressionism is the most musical of styles – it is the one most in sympathy with soul, funk and the blues.

153

Whatever the reasoning behind it, the others in the band felt it ridiculous, and ignored the instruction to call Mick 'Red'. But to Mick – and Elliot, too – the new name was important and they made sure local journalists knew about it when they interviewed Mick.

What the word 'Red' *did* do was concentrate the band's thoughts on the search for that much-needed name. World Service was dumped and a shortlist of titles containing the word 'Red' drawn up: Oh-Red, Just Red, All Red, Simply Red, and Red And The Dancing Dead were favourites. And for the band's second gig, when they would be supporting a promising Liverpool comedian named Alexei Sayle – at the Poly, again – they all plumped for Red And The Dancing Dead.

For that performance, Mick wanted to experiment with a brass section, and Mog – who was covering his outgoings by playing in a jazz band called The Oscar Bernhart Ensemble – enlisted the temporary services of an alto sax player, Neil Fitzpatrick, and a trumpeter, known only as Ojo.

If both men expected a light-hearted, casual atmosphere when they arrived at the Poly for a rehearsal shortly before the gig, they did not get it. The mood towards them, particularly by Mick and Elliot, was decidedly unfriendly and businesslike, and they were relieved to be told they could learn their parts off a tape, instead of attending more rehearsals.

'I don't think Elliot said more than a couple of words to me,' Neil remembers. 'Mick was dead businesslike, too, and I got the impression he was sort of in charge. It wasn't anything he said or did – it was the sense of control he conveyed. He was the band leader, and Elliot was fussing around, bending over backwards to ensure everything went the way Mick wanted. As far as I was concerned, I was just doing a bit of sax for a band to help them out. I wasn't aware that a new band was being built, or that it was a time to be nervous.'

On the night of the gig, on Saturday 31 March, however, Neil was left in no doubt that Red And The Dancing Dead *was* a business; that everyone connected with it took it very seriously indeed.

He recalls: 'They all seemed ridiculously uptight. They provided good stomping music with an appealing raw edge and the audience enjoyed it. But there was an air of disappointment in the dressing room afterwards. Everyone was sitting with his head down and Mick wasn't happy. I couldn't understand it. After I'd finished my part in the show I'd walked among the audience, getting a feel of how the band were coming over, and the reaction was great. I said, "Come on lads, what's the matter? It was fine." Because I was there on a temporary basis only, and hadn't gone through all the heartache, I could see they were being unreasonable.

I thought it was folly being so tough on themselves, because nobody really gave a toss. The audience had come to see a gig, they'd had a good time, and now they'd gone home. There was no point getting upset about anything.

'But Mick and the others didn't see it that way. They were a committed band and took the job seriously. They wanted to set the world on fire, and felt they'd done a crap gig.'

One person in the audience who *had* liked the performance was John Bradshaw, who had been sharing a flat with Mick in Didsbury since the New Year. He did not just like it – he was amazed. Mick had given him a couple of complimentary tickets without telling him what to expect; he had given no clue that he was such a professional singer.

Back at the flat, he told Mick he was impressed. 'You serious about this music business?' he asked. 'You going to stick with it?'

Mick nodded. 'Yeah. There are three things I want to do. I want to support James Brown. I want to perform at Old Trafford cricket ground. And I want to have a Number 1 in America.'

John has never forgotten those words. He says: 'Mick told me he was going to do all those things. And he said it very matter-of-factly, not like they were crazy ideas. I could see he totally believed he would do them – he was adamant.'

★

After that Poly gig, the buzz started going around Manchester, delighting Elliot that his softly-softly strategy seemed to be paying off. It was time to take them out of the relative safety of the Poly and put them in a more influential arena.

He wanted a gig where one had to be in the know, part of the local pop scene's inner circle, to get in; a small gig that the A&R men – talent spotters from record companies – would find too tempting to ignore. Elliot chose The Manhattan Club, a tiny cellar at 60 Spring Gardens, in the city's Bank district, which held just 100 people. He booked it for Thursday 31 May, and immediately started drip-feeding the A&R men with news of the gig. He deliberately did not tell certain key people, preferring to let hear about it on the music grapevine. If they felt they were missing out on something, so much the better, he reasoned; it would heighten their interest.

The name of the band was still a problem; now, no one liked Red And The Dancing Dead, so it was abandoned. The shortlist was shortening all the time and now it was down to three: All Red, Just Red and Simply

Red. For the Manhattan gig, they decided on Just Red. And by the time 31 May arrived, that was the name on everyone's lips. Elliot's plan seemed to be working. Now, all that was needed was for the band to do the business on stage.

As rehearsals continued, Mick became more and more the leader of the band. He was noticeable by his absence when it came to lugging the Poly's newly-acquired public address system in the lift and setting it up. And, when they got down to work, he began to irritate and frustrate the band with his inability to convey what he wanted. When he had a new song idea, he would sing a few bars, sweeping both arms about him like a gorilla, or thrusting his fists fiercely in the air like some mad conductor. Dave, Eddie and Mog would stare at him, confused. The more they did not understand, the more annoyed he got which, in turn, irritated the band. Tensions rose.

Dave Fryman recalls: 'Mick used to talk about James Brown as an influence. But I don't think he really knew what he wanted to sound like, other than broad. It was always difficult for us to work out what the hell he wanted. Mick admitted to me that he was very impatient. So we had this guy, walking around the room, waving his arms or punching the air, saying, "I want it like *this*!" And we'd all say, "What the fuck are you talking about?" He would do it again and we'd try to play what we thought he meant. When it wasn't like Mick's thrusting in the air, he'd get annoyed and we'd have the same performance all over again. It was a joke. Just ridiculous and daft.'

According to Dave, Mick lacked musical knowledge: 'Often I'd say, "You can't have that chord there because it doesn't work. It's in a different key and doesn't modulate." Mick would just say "Oh".'

By May 1984, Mick and Mog had become the hardcore of the band: they were both on the dole and had plenty of time to think about music, whereas Dave had a full-time teaching job and Eddie had a baby daughter to look after. Tired after a day at school, Dave would not generate much enthusiasm at rehearsal and, with ideas for new songs thin on the ground, he suggested they all spent more time on their own, developing tunes. Mick interpreted this as a lack of interest and at Mog's house one night he said he was going to sack Dave. Mog, who understood Dave's work situation and family commitments, talked him out of it.

Mick and Mog, particularly, shared a deep passion for music and the closer they became, the more time they spent together. They shared a passion for getting drunk, too, and would go off after rehearsals to a jazz disco at The Venue, to local band night at The Hacienda, or to any other club or pub that took their fancy. Afterwards, it was back to Mog's home, or wherever Mick was living, to listen to music and talk long into the night. Mog remembers regularly cycling home at four or five in the morning.

They both adored Indian food. And, not being able to afford to eat out often, Mick would buy the cheapest cuts of meat and other ingredients, and cook a meal for them at home for as little as 50p.

At that time, the miners were striking against proposed pit closures and, being working-class lads and staunch Labour supporters, Mick and Mog were in sympathy with them. Mog recorded a documentary about a famous Welsh pit, and they found it so emotional they both wept. 'Mick's the only bloke I've ever cried with,' says Mog. 'We were very good, close mates.' Most of their time together was spent laughing, however, and Mick would have Mog in stitches with brilliant impersonations of the miners' leader, Arthur Scargill. In contrast, Mick was often miserable at parties, and would criticize Mog for being friendly to comparative strangers. He did not like him being recognized everywhere he went – and even on stage – as 'that bloke from Brookside'.

Fame is what Mick coveted. And even at twenty-three, it seems, he did not approve of anyone close to him getting the limelight.

★

The gig at The Manhattan Club was a success. The band felt cramped on the tiny stage, but being close to the audience heightened the atmosphere and the energy they poured into every number earned wild applause. The set included several cover versions as well as original songs written by Mick and the band. One of the covers, 'Money's Too Tight (To Mention)', was suggested by Dave, who had used it in a school assembly to illustrate the problems of poverty. The song, which the others had heard on the club circuit, would later have a profound influence on Mick's career. It had been released by an American band, The Valentine Brothers, in 1981, but had never been a hit.

Despite the success, the alto sax player, Neil Fitzpatrick, left the band after that gig. There was no animosity: Neil always knew he would be paid for one or two performances; he had not expected to have a future with the band. Mick was keen to continue the brass section, however, and suggested taking on Tony Bowers, who ran the recording studio where Mick had made the first demo tape under Elliot's management.

After their Manhattan triumph, the word about the band – and the dynamic flame-haired singer with the great stage presence – spread around Manchester even faster.

Just Red were just that – red hot!

★

157

For Elliot the image problem was still a worry; he would always be discussing with Mick ways to get the band noticed. Often their observations concerned how the musicians behaved, or what they wore on stage, and the band would find them petty. One criticism that aggravated Mog concerned a CND sticker on his bass: he wanted as many people as possible to know that he was in favour of nuclear disarmament, but Elliot ordered him to remove it. The reason he gave, which astonished Mog, was that the band would never get a US tour if they were associated with banning the bomb.

Forward thinking indeed for a manager yet to pull off a record deal for the band in Britain!

To placate the socially-conscious Mog, Elliot and Mick promised to arrange a gig to raise funds for the striking miners. They never kept that promise.

Elliot felt it was good for the band's image to dress as though they had already made it; like pop stars, in fact. But that was precisely what Mog did not want. Already he was having to disguise himself because he was constantly being mobbed by Brookside fans; the last thing he wanted was to make himself *more* conspicuous.

'I told Elliot it was often a pain in the arse being recognized, and I was more likely to dress down than try to look like a famous pop star,' Mog recalls. 'But he wouldn't have it, and one day came up to me with a photograph of someone in *Vogue* magazine wearing a very expensive leather jacket. "That would be a good image for you, Mog," he said. "You should read *Vogue*, you know." I did start reading it, and then he'd say, "You should read old issues, Mog, not current ones." He had mad ideas.

'Me and Dave would say to him, "Look, we know how to dress. If we had money, we'd look great, but we haven't." I was on the dole, drawing £26 a week, and I didn't need being told to dress like someone out of *Vogue*. I told Elliot that if I had two hundred quid I'd have a decent hair cut and buy some bloody clothes.

'He was always fussing about the band's image. Before a gig, he was always saying to everyone, "What are you going to wear?" Once, he actually took Dave shopping and bought this atrocious grey jump suit. When Dave turned up at rehearsal, looking like someone out of Dire Straits, Mick and I looked at each other. "What's he fucking wearing?" we said. Mick had no idea the jump suit was Elliot's idea. Around this time, Mick would often appear in something new – such as a red jacket – and we felt sure Elliot was financing him.

'Image was Elliot's big worry. But if he wasn't worrying about that, he'd find something else to fret over – such as what the band were playing. One minute, everything would be great – then he'd complain to us that a song wasn't very good. He would boost our confidence, then knock it out of us. He was always putting spanners in the works, and we'd get so anxious we'd talk among ourselves about him. When he left a rehearsal, we'd think: Thank fuck he's gone. Don't come back.

'Elliot rarely criticized Mick, though. Often he would tell him how wonderful he was in front of people. We never did that. If we felt a song he'd written was a dog, we'd tell him. He took it okay.'

★

Having had a good feedback from the Manhattan gig, Elliot arranged for the band to play at another respected venue – Band On The Wall – on 12 June. The gig was hit by a problem before a note was played: during the sound check Ojo, the trumpet player, had a blazing row with Tony Bowers, who had accepted Mick's invitation to join the band to replace Neil Fitzpatrick on alto sax. After the gig, Ojo quit and Tony went back to his recording studio, saying he wanted nothing more to do with Just Red.

By that summer, Elliot had split with his wife and was renting a house with Mick in Northenden. He had also been managing a lesser band, Little Douglas, but was so convinced Just Red were going to make it that he dropped them. The temptation was there to fix more gigs, cash in on the success, but Elliot resisted it. He turned down requests for gigs, not only from club owners but from the band themselves. He still believed in his original policy of less exposure, more demand. And the band did little that summer except practise and record a demo tape.

They did, however, do one more gig at the Poly – at the end-of-year summer ball on 23 June. A few days before, Mick and Elliot decided that Just Red was not right: Simply Red had a better ring to it. The rest of the band went along with it.

★

The band were still keen on having a brass section and they hired three musicians from Manchester College of Music – Tim Kellett, a trumpet player who had been playing in a rising band called The Durutti Column, and two of his friends. One Sunday morning they arrived for rehearsal – and thanks to Mick's arrogance, all three were walking back out of the door even before they had taken out their instruments.

Mog, who had to apologize to them, explains: 'Mick was in a bad mood and had been his usual ignorant and arrogant self. The lads were on their way out when I called them back. I said, "It's okay, he'll be all right in a minute, once he's settled down." I don't know what Mick said, but the way he spoke had upset them. It was the sort of attitude of "All right, you bastards, I'm the star here – don't fuck me about." The three of them thought he was an absolute dickhead.'

Despite that early problem, the three new additions enhanced the band, and, as the summer wore on, Elliot started thinking they would soon be ready to make a major push for a record deal. The Manhattan and Band On The Wall appearances had attracted the talent spotters and created a buzz; the next stage of the plan would be to hold a spectacular 'show' gig to woo the men who held the record companies' purse strings. Firstly, however, there were a few problems that needed sorting out.

One was the lack of original songs, particularly a fast one to open their set. With schools still on holiday, Dave Fryman was able to devote more time and effort to the band, and one day he called on Mick and Elliot in Northenden with a song he felt could solve the problem. Mick loved it and they sat down and worked on the song together, Mick writing lyrics to go with the upbeat, catchy tune. They called it 'No Direction'.

Elliot suggested reviving 'Holding Back The Years', which Mick had never mentioned to the band. Mick was a bit awkward about performing it – possibly because it was co-written with someone he had not seen for some time – but finally agreed to start rehearsing it.

Another problem that was solved in September was the make-up of the band. The brass section had improved the sound considerably, but someone on keyboards was needed to give the band a new dimension. One of the bouncers at the Poly told Elliot and Mick he knew just the person: a black, unemployed son of a clergyman, with a name that sounded as if he was a Glasgow-born German.

The man was Fritz McIntyre. And he could not only play keyboards, he could play almost anything. Brilliantly.

*

For Fritz, the offer to join such a promising, much talked-about outfit was a spectacular break. He had been performing in bands all over Manchester, but had not made it. He had tried hard to get work as a session musician, but had not cracked that, either. He had been unemployed for five years and was thinking of going on tour with a band he did not like, just to escape his depression. He pulled out of the tour at the last minute, a sixth sense telling him he should stay in Manchester and battle on.

He was rewarded with a call from Mick that would change his life.

Fritz, who was twenty-five, added a wonderful, positive attitude and he was welcomed by everyone in the band. But, for Mog, he highlighted a worry that had been nagging him for months: Eddie's timing on the drums. When Fritz also started having problems blending in with Eddie's beat, Mog knew his fears were well-founded. He kept quiet, though, and so did Fritz, who did not want to rock the boat so soon after joining. But things only got worse. And it was clear that autumn that Eddie's days with the band were numbered.

At first, it seemed his problem was cannabis. After a brief smoking break during one rehearsal, he could not remember the beat he had been playing minutes before. Mog, who did not smoke, was furious and insisted on cannabis being banned from rehearsals.

Today, he recalls: 'I used to smoke, but I had stopped because I'd had enough of forgetting what I was supposed to be playing. We were rehearsing for only three hours and a lot of that time was eaten away by setting up the PA and rolling spliffs. I was getting really annoyed at wasting my life away. We'd work on Tuesday and by the time Sunday came around, what we'd done before was gone. I felt I'd still be at the Poly at fifty, trying to get 'Something's Burning' right! I was deadly serious about the band and had been working hard. I was really annoyed when Eddie's timing was slipping all over the show.'

*

Around this time, Mick was keen to improve his image, and the easiest way, he felt, was to change the hairstyle he had had for so many years. A girlfriend who worked in a hairdresser's in a fashionable shopping block in the centre of Manchester gave him a brutally close short back and sides, but did not touch the top at all.

Mick proudly told the band he was going to keep growing the top, while keeping the back and sides short. He thought the new style was great, but to the rest of the band it was a joke: all it did was accentuate his sticky-out ears, and they would laugh behind his back.

Dave Fryman says: 'Driving back in the van was never very enjoyable and we'd see the funny side of the smallest thing. Suddenly we noticed that each passing light silhouetted Mick, sitting in front of us, making his ears even more pronounced than ever. One of us whispered, "Holding back the ears" – and we fell about giggling like kids. It became a standing joke, but Mick never knew.'

For Elliot, however, it was all very serious indeed, and he was pleased that, after all the hard rehearsing, the band were a far tighter outfit, and ready for that crunch 'show' gig.

What he needed to do now was to put into action all he had been thinking and planning most of the summer. If he orchestrated the hype well enough, the gig would transform Simply Red from a band with a handful of gigs under their belt into a prized signing for a major record company.

19

The first call Elliot made was to Chris Paul of *City Life*. He had a proposition to make: he would share the profits of the 'show' gig with the magazine 50/50 in return for free advertising and promotional editorial. Chris listened as Elliot slipped into his hard but smooth sales patter: there would be powerful men from the music industry at the gig, he promised; it would be a high profile event that would make money on the night, he assured; the band were going to be big, so it was a shrewd move to be associated with them, he urged; all the magazine had to do was provide the space, not do the work, he stressed.

The magazine went for it; after all, the co-promotion was a limited financial risk, and anyway, the magazine had been supporting the band by reviewing their previous gigs. Chris Paul had even carried an interview with Mick and Mog a couple of months before.

With the promotion vehicle ready to run, Elliot and the band set about choosing a venue. They wanted something bigger than the Band On The Wall, but not so big they could have trouble filling it. They found the ideal place in Oxford Road, Manchester – a once-plush disco club whose only claim to fame was that Jimmy Savile was said to have done a gig there. The colourful carpets and deep red dralon furnishings had faded through years of neglect, but it hardly mattered. What was important was that the club, which held gigs usually once a week, was not sleazy and had a capacity of around 1,000 – perfect for what Elliot and the band had in mind. Just what the plastic palm trees at the back of the stage and nets on the ceiling had to do with a pop band, Elliot had no idea. But that did not matter either: people were coming to see the band perform, not admire the interior design.

The club where Simply Red would display their talents was called The Tropicana. The date for the most important gig of their brief professional life: Thursday 1 November.

The hype began in October. With only a shoestring budget, Elliot called in all the favours he had earned during his time as the Poly's Mr Entertainment. He got fly posters designed for free and printed at half price. He rented a top-quality PA system from Strawberry Studios in Stockport, at a knock-down price. And he arranged excellent but inexpensive lighting for the gig itself.

For their part, *City Life* carried punchy, full-page ads twice that month and helped put up the posters in their normal sites around town. The logo on the poster, designed by a Manchester artist, Chris Peake, had RED in Russian-type lettering, with a backward R and a line through the D. Neither Elliot, nor the band, were thought to have anything to do with Communism, but it did no harm. The word began to spread quickly: the hottest band were on again.

To attract the record bosses, Elliot used the same strategy that had worked so well with the A&R men at The Manhattan: he told a few key people, then let the music grapevine do the rest. He did the same with demo tapes, sending out a few to people he felt mattered and keeping the rest in the dark, to build the hype. Certain companies who might not otherwise turn up would do so, he reasoned, if only to see what their rivals were up to.

A few days before the gig, there was a hitch that Elliot could have done without: he was forced to drop the support band, The Rhythmaires, because of rumours that they were linked with a fascist movement. Fearing it could affect Simply Red, he hired a solo dance act from the Poly instead.

Around 500 people were at The Tropicana that Thursday. No one knows how many record companies were represented, but there was a long guest list, and the word afterwards was that just about everyone who counted was there. The band did a fifty-minute set of the songs they had polished during the summer – including a more upbeat, funkier version of 'Holding Back The Years'. And within weeks, Elektra UK – a new company formed as a subsidiary of the US giant WEA – emerged as favourites to sign Simply Red.

Everyone in the band was aware of the company's interest; they knew that one of Elektra's representatives, Simon Potts, had watched them in rehearsal and was talking with Elliot. What they did not know was that, by the time Potts came to talk figures, Elliot and Mick had worked out precisely what deal they wanted, and how it would work, without mentioning it to the band.

Dave recalls: 'One day, Elliot came to us and said, "This is how the deal is going to work. This project is called Simply Red. Mick and myself have formed a management company and you, the band, will effectively be sub-contracted."'

'At this point, Mog asked, "What do you mean? What about the songwriting royalties?"

'"Well, they're Mick's," said Elliot.

'Mog hit the roof,' says Dave. 'It was obvious we were subordinates to the two of them and it didn't go down well. Basically, it was only Mick's name that would be going on the recording contract. He and Elliot had obviously had it worked out for some time.'

Dave and Mog immediately demanded a meeting with Elliot to thrash it all out.

Mog says: 'What worried us was not being paid for work that had nothing to do with Mick – like our music being used as a TV theme tune, for instance. It was unfair for Mick to expect to coin in all the royalties for something like that. We told Elliot that there were two ways of working in a band: either with a genius, who tells you precisely what to play; or in the way that most bands operate, and that is by all sitting around and swapping ideas generally. With us, it had always been the second way: Mick would come in with the germ of an idea and other members of the band would develop it into a proper song. We had all worked for nothing, on the promise of money later, yet we were now expected to accept that when money *did* come in, the singer would receive 100 per cent of the royalties. It was bound to cause antagonism.

'Elliot explained that the record company was signing the management company – which he and Mick had formed – and that company would pay us. He said it made sense for various reasons, and that other bands were operating that way. But neither Dave nor I were happy. It gave Elliot and Mick the right to hire and fire who they wanted, when they wanted.'

The showdown ended with Elliot promising to think the matter over. A few days later, he told Mog and Dave that they would get what he described as 'arrangement royalties' for the work they did on Mick's songs. But they still were not happy.

'There was all this doublespeak,' Mog says. 'But, basically, we were not getting what we felt was fair. Elliot would say, "Everything is a band. It's not Mick – it's a band. We've got to get a couple of albums out, then Mick will want to do a solo album. And you can go off and do instrumental albums on your own."

'But it was all nonsense. It wasn't a band at all – it was Elliot and Mick. It was like a father and son relationship and they had the whole take.'

Nothing was finalized with Elektra UK at that point. But, unlike Dave and Mog, the three musicians in the newly-formed brass section were excited about the possibilities of a record deal, and – after a gig at the University of London Union – they confided to Mog that they were thinking of leaving college to work with Simply Red full-time.

Mog urged them to be cautious; to wait and see how things turned out. He was getting more and more wary about the way Elliot and Mick saw the band being run. The euphoria that had engulfed them after the success of The Tropicana had been replaced by a dark cloud of uncertainty and mistrust. Now, all that Elliot and Mick seemed to talk about was the image. The general mood of the band had changed. Mog began to wonder where it would all lead.

And then, later that November, his frustration over Eddie's erratic drumming became too much and he started a train of events that would prove to be his own downfall.

Mog and Mick were having a drink at a snooker club one Sunday when Mog turned the conversation round to Eddie. They had discussed his drumming before and, like Fritz McIntyre, Mog had been charitable and diplomatic. But Mog was fed up and not prepared to make excuses for Eddie any more. He decided to air his feelings, once and for all.

Today, Mog remembers: 'I was feeling bad about my own playing because Eddie was affecting my confidence. I told Mick I couldn't carry on playing with Eddie; I just couldn't do it any more. I wanted Eddie out.

'Mick thought it over for a moment or two, then said, "Okay. But we should act fairly as if we're in a trade union, and give him three warnings."

'I shook my head. "We can't," I said. "It's not like being late for work. We know he's not going to get any better. The band can't go anywhere with him as drummer."

'Mick had thought before about sacking people, but hadn't done it. I convinced him about Eddie and, basically, talked him into getting rid of him. In the process, I gave him the notion that it was all right to sack people.'

Mick decided that Eddie's last gig would be at the Sheffield Lead Mill later that month. What Mog did not suspect was that it would be his, too.

When the band arrived in Sheffield, everyone knew Eddie was getting the elbow – except Eddie himself. No one had the guts to tell him.

Dave was appalled at the way it was being done, but did not feel it was his place to say anything. 'I felt like shit that night,' he remembers. 'After The Tropicana, Elliot had called Eddie "a little gem" and kept saying how wonderful he was. Now he was going to be out, and I felt sorry for him. When I was told he was being kicked out, I thought: Fucking hell, that's a bit much. If someone's no good, he should be sacked after a week or so and not kept in for as long as Eddie was, then be told goodbye.

'Personally, I liked Eddie's drumming. There was no doubt he speeded things up, but it was not clockwork – it was full of character. There's no doubt that Fritz despaired of him. And Mog said the drumming was unrecordable.'

When Elliot told Dave that Mog had said Eddie's drumming was 'unrecordable', Dave made a comment he would have reason to regret. 'That's funny, coming from Mog,' he quipped.

Perhaps it gave Elliot the idea that, if he could get Mog out too, he could bring back Tony Bowers, who could play bass guitar as well as sax, and who was still a close friend. Maybe he could get his other Mothmen mate, Chris Joyce, to replace Eddie Sherwood on drums.

★

For most musicians, an exhilarating moment in any gig is when they get to stand at the front, singing backing vocals. It was the same for Mog, and his microphone was always at the front of the stage next to Mick's, with Dave's mike the other side. The minute Mog went on stage at the Sheffield Lead Mill for a sound check, however, he got a shock: Mick and Elliot told him to put his mike stand away from the front, nearer the back of the stage. Mog was mortified; so furious, in fact, that even today he cannot remember whether he played that gig at the front or the back of the stage. What he does know is that the decision was taken well before they arrived; and that he stormed off the stage and went for a pint in a nearby pub to calm down.

Today, Mog says: 'When I walked on the stage, either Mick or Elliot – I honestly can't remember who – said something like, "We've decided ... why don't you try with your mike back here ...." I noticed that Dave's mike stand was still at the front, next to Mick's. I was seething. I've got a pretty strong ego – you can't be a shrinking violet if you want to be an actor or play in a band – and I loved that moment when all three of us were at the front. It's pure rock and roll. To have that joy suddenly whipped away was horrible. I was well pissed off and stormed out of the building.'

When he returned, however, Mog walked into another humiliation. He had compromised over Elliot's request to 'dress like a pop star', and was planning to wear a jazzy, multi-coloured, shiny waistcoat his girlfriend had made specially for the gig. But when he put it on in the dressing room just before going on stage, Elliot and Mick were horrified. 'Take that off,' they ordered. 'You're not going on stage in that.'

'I thought: What the fuck!' A row started, made worse by Elliot and Mick comparing Mog to Fritz, who had become something of a favourite in recent weeks. 'Look at Fritz,' Elliot said. 'Fritz has had his hair cut. Look what Fritz is wearing.'

With only minutes to go before the band was due on stage, Mog had no choice. He took the waistcoat off.

'It was all so petty and annoying,' he says. 'Fritz was wearing some bland shit he'd got from the Army & Navy, but it was as if he'd made an effort and I hadn't. Whereas I knew damn well I *had*. The band's image thing was a constant topic and although the waistcoat was a bit garish, it would have looked great on stage.'

Still seething with hurt, Mog muddled through the performance. There was worse to come: after the show, Elliot and Mick were talking with some record company executives in the dressing room, but when Mog and other members of the band went in, Elliot told them to stay out. Mog, particularly, was upset, because it was yet another embarrassing and humiliating put-down, making him wonder what he could have done wrong; and whether, after all the months of dedicated slog and all he had given up, he had a long-term future with the band.

Meanwhile, Eddie was still in the dark that he had played his last drumbeat for Simply Red. Dave took him for a Chinese meal after the gig, but, no matter how much he wanted to break the news and make Eddie feel better, he could not bear to. 'It was so awkward, and I felt awful,' Dave admits today.

*

Mog's fears for his own future were eased a few days later when Mick phoned, asking him to go with him to sack Eddie. The deed took place in The Albert pub in Rusholme, and Eddie was devastated. 'Is it my image?' he asked. 'Do I look wrong?'

'No,' Mick and Mog had to say. And Mog was even more blunt: 'Your drumming's unrecordable.'

A week or so later, while the hunt was on for a new drummer, Mog bumped into Neil Fitzpatrick, the sax player, and told him about Eddie. 'Be careful,' Neil joked, 'you'll be next.'

Mog laughed.

*

On the first Sunday after Eddie's sacking, Dave thought: Great – no drummer, no rehearsal. He was wrong. At 2.30 p.m., half an hour after he was usually due at the Poly, the phone interrupted his afternoon relaxation. It was Mick, wondering what had happened to him, because the band was having a meeting to discuss who should replace Eddie.

When Dave said he did not know any drummers, Mick said, 'What? So, what do you want me to do? Give you a call once we've got one?'

'Yeah,' Dave replied, flippantly.

It was not a wise move. The level of paranoia, in the light of what had happened to Eddie, was escalating all the time, and the moment he put the phone down, Dave realized he had made a terrible political blunder. He had been resisting Elliot's pleas to give up teaching for the sake of the band, because he was unsure of its future. Now, not turning up for an important meeting would be construed as another sign of lack of interest and commitment.

He decided to abandon the idea of a restful Sunday afternoon, and drove to the Poly.

At the meeting, they voted to audition a drummer who had been in The Smirks, but he wasn't a 'soul drummer', which Mick wanted, so he was rejected. Mick and Elliot had moved out of Northenden, and Elliot was now living in Atwood Road, Didsbury, with drummer Chris Joyce. At a meeting in Whalley Range, where Mick was now living with Brian Turner, Elliot suggested that Chris join the band. But neither Mick nor Mog wanted to work with him. Mog was adamant: 'There's no way I'm working with Chris Joyce,' he said. Mog would appreciate the irony of that statement later, for, behind the scenes, Elliot was working on Mick, and managed to persuade him that Joyce was the ideal replacement. Mog would never work with him.

Elliot was usually on the phone to Mog several times a day, fretting over something or other. But after that meeting, he did not ring. Nor did Mick. The days turned into weeks. The silence was ominous. Mog was approaching the first anniversary of his joining the band, but the future was not looking so promising as it had a year before.

After three weeks' silence, there was a knock on Mog's door. He opened it to find Mick, Elliot and Dave standing there, looking sheepish. He invited them in, but knew by their expressions why they had come.

Mick and Elliot had taken Dave along because, it seems clear, they did not relish telling Mog themselves that he was being given the chop.

Dave remembers the episode well: 'Elliot rang me, saying they were sacking Mog that night and they wanted me with them. I asked why and was reminded I'd said that Mog was no better than Eddie, or something – making it look like I was somehow the instigator of sacking Mog. I had not said that. All I'd done was make a passing remark that it was funny coming from Mog. But it was picked up on.

'I was in no position not to go to Mog's home. I was constantly being nagged to give up my job, and people were being sacked all over the place. All I could think of was me, and who would be next. We all met at the Poly, then trooped round to see Mog. I was extremely nervous.'

It was an embarrassing and tense confrontation at Mog's home. Despite dragging Dave along, Elliot and Mick did the talking, claiming that Simon Potts of Elektra said the band needed to make 'a quantum leap in quality' to clinch the record deal – and they felt Mog's playing was not up to scratch.

Mog freaked out.

Today, he describes that awful December night: 'I said they were talking crap when they criticized my playing. I told them they were sacking me for not being a yes-man; that it was about politics, not performance. I had argued about clothes, the microphone, the percentages, and about it becoming more and more Mick and a backing group, not a proper band. And they hadn't liked it.

'I had started things with Eddie, I admit that. But I feel the sackings would have happened anyway. It was obvious what direction Elliot and Mick wanted the band to go. We were fed bullshit about it being a band. It was always Mick. Twelve months before, I had been the right person for the band. But I wasn't now, because my ideas of where I wanted the band to go were very different to Elliot's and Mick's.

'That night in my house was ugly and very uncomfortable. I was really angry that the sacking was being put down to my playing – which wasn't the case. When I argued the point, they didn't argue back. They just sat on the settee, all three of them, looking sheepish. Dave didn't say much. It was mainly the other two.'

For Dave, the scene was horrendous and he wondered why he had to be there. Today, he says: 'None of us was pleased with what had happened, and, driving back to the Poly, we were all very quiet. There's no doubt in my mind that Mog was sacked mainly for political reasons. What made me squirm was hearing Elliot have the gall to tell Mog his playing was unrecordable – the very thing Mog had said about Eddie. It sounded like Elliot had said it deliberately – some little management ploy he'd found in a textbook. It was incredible. I couldn't believe it.'

For Mog, the rest of that night was spent in a depression that would last many months. Closing the door on the three of them meant more than just the end of a musical dream – it meant the break-up of a friendship. He and Mick had been close pals, sharing many memorable experiences, and what Mick had done to him that night, and the way he did it, left a very sour taste.

Mog hurt like hell.

20

One night, just after Christmas, the phone rang at Dave Fryman's home. It was Tony Bowers.

Surprised, Dave asked, 'How did you get my number?'

'Er . . . um, Elliot gave it to me,' Tony replied.

'Oh! Why?'

'He told me Mog had been sacked,' said Tony. 'I was wondering if there was any chance I could get in the band.'

Dave decided he had to be straight with him. 'To be honest, Tony, Mick doesn't want you in the band.'

'Any chance of putting a good word in for me, Dave?' Tony asked.

Dave had got on well with Tony when they met through Elliot and thought he was a good musician; he felt he would be good for the band.

'Okay, Tony,' he said. 'I'll see what I can do.'

Shortly after he put the phone down, it rang again. It was Elliot.

'Has Tony called you, by any chance?' he asked. When Dave told him he had, Elliot said, 'Look, Mick doesn't want Tony in the band. But I know you rate Tony and get on well. Do you think you could try to talk Mick round?'

Dave agreed. And, a few days later, Elliot arranged for Chris Joyce to go out while Mick, Dave and Fritz came to Atwood Road, to talk about Tony joining the band.

Dave sang Tony's praises, particularly to Mick: he put forward a persuasive argument, saying his playing was good, he knew the stuff, he got on with everyone and, most important, if they took him on they would not have to audition someone they did not know.

After an hour, Mick said, 'Yeah. Okay.' And Elliot had another mate on the team.

A week or so later, Elliot owned up to Dave that he had told Tony to ring him at home. He seemed pleased with himself, almost proud of what he had done.

'Tony joining was all down to Elliot's wheeling and dealing,' Dave recalls. 'By using me to talk Mick round he was covering his tracks, so that he wouldn't be seen as the persuader. Looking back, I'm sure he wanted Chris and Tony in, and when the problems with Eddie started, he saw the opportunity. He was quite proud he'd duped me. I said, "Gosh, Elliot, you're so clever". But, really, I felt stupid. I can't understand why he wasn't straight with me. I would have played ball.

'After Chris and Tony started, they became the golden boys, and it was time for me and Fritz to get some stick. At one point, they were really having a go at Fritz, but he was prepared to put up with anything. He confided to me: "No matter what, I'm riding this train." '

★

As 1984 came to an end, Dave was in a dilemma that was tearing him apart.

Elliot was putting increasing pressure on him to give up teaching, and Mick was becoming more and more irritated at what he considered a lack of commitment. For many months, Dave had been tempted to throw in his lot with the band; he had been teaching the same subject at the same school for seven years, and the thought of leaving appealed to him. But something significant happened during the Christmas holiday that changed the whole picture: Dave was offered a better job at another school – and a higher salary.

He was in a dreadful predicament: did he turn the job down and devote himself to the band? Or did he take it and try to teach by day and play by night, as he had been doing for the past year? What made matters worse was that his wife, Michele, had given up her own job, making his own salary crucial. On top of these concerns, Dave had to consider the riskiness of his position in Simply Red. He had witnessed first-hand how a musician could be flavour of the month one minute, then out on his ear the next. Who was to say it would not happen to him? And if he had chucked in his teaching job, where would that leave him and his wife?

It was a risk Dave felt he could not take. He accepted the promotion – but he decided not to tell anyone in the band. He would ease Mick's worries about his lack of commitment by putting school out of his mind once he was with the band and throwing himself whole-heartedly into rehearsals.

Dave says: 'I felt I had to take the new job, just in case. I'd seen how things had gone in the band over the previous weeks, and I knew what Elliot was like. I thought: I've got to watch my back here. Once things with the record company were more certain and I knew where I stood with the band, quitting work would not be a problem.'

For the next three months, however, Dave would be caught up in the middle of a nightmare scenario from which there seemed no escape. By day, he coped with the extra pressures of teaching older children. By night, and at weekends, he was expected to perform as a 'pop star' and be a productive musician. And, all the time, the political forces of Elektra were coming into play, feeding his paranoia about his future with the band.

The recording contract had been drawn up, but Mick and Elliot were holding out on certain points. Both had been on the end of bad record deals, and were determined now to stick out for what they wanted. Both had the self-belief and iron nerve to see it through – or walk away.

In February, they *did* get what they wanted: a multi-album deal, with a £60,000 advance, against a lucrative royalty structure. Elliot and Mick recognized that both Dave and Fritz had contributed to some of the songs, and both were named in the contract. Neither was told at the time, however, and were not involved in signing the contract.

Dave remembers Elliot coming round to his house, with photocopies of Elektra's £60,000 cheque, saying, triumphantly: 'We've done it. We've done it. You *can* go to the ball!' He said the money was being paid into a bank and each member of the band – including Mick – would be paid £50 a week wages.

Elliot and Mick then decided to offer a payment to Eddie and Mog for the work they had put into the band. The figure they felt was fair was £1,000 each. It was hardly a magnanimous gesture, and certainly Mog felt his efforts were worth more, but neither he nor Eddie was in a position to refuse the offer.

Today, Mog says: 'How many people in 1984 would have worked all year for £1,000? I was earning £600 a week acting on television, but gave it up because I truly believed in the band and the recording future I felt it had. The work I put in over twelve months improved many of the songs that would appear on the band's first album, and, of course, we played the gigs that helped attract the record company's interest and eventually got the band signed. Although I felt I was worth more, I was hardly going to turn down £1,000, so I accepted it.

'But what happened to me with the band affected me badly. I more or less locked myself away because I was so depressed. My confidence in playing with other bands was shattered and sometimes I would play a gig and walk off stage half-way through the show.

'My friends wondered what the hell was happening to me. My experience with Elliot and Mick made me paranoid, and crushed my confidence. It took me the best part of a year to get over it.

'When I sorted myself out I told a friend who worked in medicine what I had been through and how I had been living. She told me I

should have seen a doctor for a depression that deep. Apparently it was
that bad I should have been on anti-depressants.'

Over the years, it has been suggested by certain people – including
Mick – that Eddie and Mog should be grateful for the pay-off, and not
moan about it. In their defence, it should be stressed that if either had
been anxious to cash in on their experiences with the band, they could
have done so easily. Both men have been offered money by newspapers
to 'reveal all' about Simply Red, but both have always said no.

★

With the record deal in the bag, Dave was now able to decide on his
teaching job. His £50 wages as a budding pop star was less than he
was earning at school, but the long-term financial prospects were far
greater. He had been at the new school only a matter of weeks and
it would be embarrassing to leave them in the lurch mid-term, but
Dave felt he had no choice. He had put in a lot of effort over the
past fourteen months and had given himself sleepless nights, and now
it was all paying off. He had the chance of a lifetime, the chance to
be rich and famous and lead an enviable lifestyle. Before the record
contract, it had all seemed so pie-in-the-sky, so risky. Now, it was
reality, not fantasy.

He chucked his job in and became a full-time Simply Red guitarist
on £50 a week.

Ideally, Dave would have preferred a gap between the two jobs – a
brief period of rehabilitation, in which he could have got acclimatized
to the dramatic difference in his day. As it was, things were moving too
fast for that: he had to forget about the blackboard and think about the
guitar instead. The record company were arranging for them to go to
Holland to record their first single, 'Money's Too Tight', and three
further tracks for their first album. And the band would have to rehearse
all the numbers in Manchester before they went.

★

Elliot and Mick were indebted and grateful to Simon Potts at Elektra
for signing the band, but certain things he said and did worried them:
having signed the contract and paid the advance, it seemed he looked
on Mick as his personal property and wanted to manipulate his talent
and the band's music generally. A few months later, Mick would put his
feelings about the unsavoury side of the record industry into a song

174

called 'Jericho', but early that year, he and Elliot settled for less sophisticated ways to irritate him and make him pander to them.

Once they turned up unannounced, with the rest of the band, at
Elektra's London offices, and embarrassed Potts into taking them all out
to lunch. For some reason, Elliot and Mick thought it would be amusing
and the sort of wind-up they felt Potts deserved. The whole episode,
however, was silly and immature, and merely proved awkward for the
musicians.

Dave remembers it with embarrassment: 'When we arrived at the
offices, Elliot and Mick disappeared to speak to Potts, while we were
left in a sort of waiting room with an underling, who didn't know
what to do with us. We all hated it. We couldn't understand why we'd
been brought there. We felt Elliot and Mick should have come on
their own.

'There was a cocktail cabinet in the room and one of us asked if we
could have a drink. Word came back from Potts that we couldn't. It was
all very awkward. Whether he wanted to take a handful of uninvited
guests to lunch at his company's expense, I don't know. But he did,
much to Elliot's and Mick's delight.'

Over that lunch, Potts asked Dave if he was still at school. For some
reason, Dave did not admit he had resigned; he just said he was supposed
to be teaching, but was never there. There was something odd in Potts's
manner, and, later, Dave started to wonder why he had asked that.

He could not put his finger on it, but sensed something was not quite
right.

Following that lunch, an American record producer, Stewart Levine,
who had been approached to produce Simply Red's first album, to be
called *Picture Book*, later that year, came to watch them perform at a
London gig. And the way he behaved afterwards made Dave start to feel
even more on edge.

'It was the beginning of a weird period, where I felt something sinister
was going on,' Dave recalls. 'Tony and Chris sat in the dressing room,
talking to Levine for a long time, but he didn't seem interested in talking
to me. I felt frozen out and started to feel uneasy. People were smiling
at me, but something didn't feel quite right. I told myself that it was just
me being paranoid, my usual suspicious self, and that I should think
nothing of it. But I couldn't help feeling edgy.'

Dave tried to force his worries out of his mind because there was a lot
of rehearsing to do before they left for Holland the following month.
But it was not easy.

Happily, things did not seem to have changed with Elliot. They went
back a long way, had even been on holiday together with their wives,

and he trusted him. He had told Elliot to keep him informed, not to mess him about; that if there were any problems, if things were not working out, to tell him. He had always been straight with Elliot, and he believed Elliot would be straight with him.

So it was reassuring, in the middle of all the weird uncertainty that was draining him, to come home and find Elliot chatting warmly to Michele, as normal.

Then Michele started acting strangely. When Dave came home from rehearsals, looking forward to seeing her and to talking about how he felt, she would make an excuse to go out. It went on, day after day, for a week.

Dave was too exhausted to notice that she seemed frightened to look him in the eye.

*

The rehearsals took place during the day in a nightclub called The Boardwalk. It was only a few yards from the converted cotton mill where Mick and The Frantic Elevators had slogged their hearts out night after night in that dank, depressing, windowless basement where the water ran down the walls. But for Mick, the distance was immeasurable in terms of how far he had come.

All those years ago, he was broke and naive, but full of dreams and thrilled at being signed by that little indie company, TJM. Now he had money in his pocket and the naivety had been replaced by a worldliness, if not ruthlessness, that would turn those long-ago dreams of recording success into reality.

Fittingly, that decaying mill was destined for demolition, and The Dying Band that had practised there were long since dead. Across the road, bursting with life, Mick poured all he had learned from those frantic yesterdays into what he hoped would be an exciting tomorrow.

*

Around that time, the band went to London on a shopping spree for clothes for their Holland trip in March. The musicians stayed in an hotel, but Mick stayed with a university student named Joanne he had fallen in love with over the past couple of months. The girl had been going out with Elliot's brother-in-law for several years; Mick had met her at the home of Elliot's in-laws in north London, where he and Elliot stayed while in the capital discussing the record contract. Joanne's relationship with Mick caused a bust-up between her and her boyfriend and a lot of bitterness within the family. Elliot was blamed, not only for introducing Mick to Joanne, but for taking his side. Despite the ill-feeling, Mick continued seeing her every time he was in London. Their relationship deepened.

*

The band were to fly to Holland on Sunday 3 March; they met up and travelled to Manchester Airport together. Excitedly, they checked in and went through into the departure lounge. While they were waiting to be told to board, Mick sat down next to Dave. 'Listen,' he said, 'we didn't tell you this before, but Simon Potts wants to get you out of the band . . .'

Dave felt as if someone had dropped a ten-ton weight on him.

21

Dave felt numb. He could not speak. And even if he could, he did not know what to say. He stared at Mick, his mind racing with a dozen thoughts all at the same time, and none of them making any sense.

Mick was going on about Potts wanting another guitarist. 'But we want you,' Mick said. And then Elliot and the others were chipping in, too: 'Yeah, Dave, *we* want *you*.'

'We weren't going to tell you 'till afterwards,' Mick was saying.

So why are you telling me now, was all Dave could think.

'We felt Potts might send this other guy out to Holland,' Mick said, reading his mind. 'We thought he might be there when we arrive.'

Dave sat there, listening to Mick, and the uneasiness and anxiety he had felt came flooding back; suddenly it all began to make sense, and he felt humiliated and silly. He had been dragged round to sack Mog because they did not have the guts to do it on their own. He had been manipulated to help get Tony in the band. And when it had been him that needed some help, some honesty, nobody had the decency to give it to him; nobody had the guts to tell him the truth about what was going on.

Mick and the others were still going on about how they wanted him in the band. But it didn't cut any ice. All he could think, in his numbness, was: I'm in the shit here. I gave up my job, laid myself on the line, and now I'm in the shit.

It was true. Dave had a mortgage and could barely exist on £50 a week. He felt as if he was going deeper into the red, just sitting there.

Today, remembering those terrible moments in that airport is difficult. Dave has always felt shaky about talking about it because he feels it might be meaningless to anybody but him.

'I cannot properly describe how bad I felt,' he admits. 'I was totally stunned, totally fucked, and I went through every emotion you can think of. Mick's tone was like he was talking to a five-year-old. I could not believe what I was hearing – it was as if I'd just entered a parallel universe.

'I didn't say anything, *couldn't* say anything. I just bottled the whole thing inside me. If I'd got up and screamed, or strangled Elliot, I might have felt a whole lot better. If I'd still had my teaching job, I'd probably have said, 'Look, guys, get who you want in – I'm off: shove it. I'll just catch my afternoon class. Take your fucking band and shove it up your arse – I've had enough.'

'But I was so numb, so hurt, I couldn't speak. I just did not know what to say. I was finished. I felt I'd gone.'

What seems clear is that Elliot, Mick and the band did not know what to do for the best. They felt they were strong enough to resist Potts's demands for a replacement for Dave, but became worried when he hinted the new man might be waiting for them in Holland. They did not want Dave to suffer the embarrassment and humiliation of coming face to face with his successor, having been told nothing about it. At the same time, they kept putting off telling Dave about the behind-the-scenes intrigue because they feared he might not make the all-important trip.

As the band's manager, Elliot could have been expected to tell Dave the full story; after all, they had been friends since school. But, for reasons known only to himself, Elliot chose not to – even though he had told Michele that her husband was going to be sacked. Instead, it fell to Mick to break the shattering news. It must have been a dreadful task.

A few minutes after Mick's bombshell, the Amsterdam flight was called. Dave was, as he says, 'between a rock and a hard place': with no job to fall back on, he had no choice but to get on the plane and go through with the trip.

'I felt absolutely diabolical,' he recalls. 'It was down to me to forget it and just do the stuff, because the others still wanted me in the band. I was expected to go, "Hey, man, let's groove. Let's get in that studio and really get it on." Happy, happy, happy, keen as mustard. But, in truth, I just felt stunned and, as a result, felt less than enthusiastic or dynamic.'

Dave boarded the plane, fearing what lay ahead and wondering how he would cope with it all.

*

From the moment Dave arrived, to see a look of surprise on Stewart Levine's face, to the moment he left two weeks later, it was a nightmare. Never in his life did making music bring him so little pleasure. He could not believe how something he had wanted so much could be so awful. No one actually told him he was going to be out, but the trust in people he had thought were his friends had been shattered, and he felt an outsider. He did not want to be there, but he had nowhere else to go.

Understandably, he was paranoid, suspicious of everyone. He did not take kindly to being told what to do, even by Mick. And when Stewart

Levine said something which ordinarily would not have bothered him, Dave would think: Patronizing bastard. Soon, Dave was seen as difficult and uncooperative.

He admits he was so confused about what was required from him that he ended up doing the minimum. 'At first, I thought: Christ, they must want me to play something absolutely brilliant to be in this band, so I'd try to come up with something amazing for a track. But brilliance was not required. All they really wanted was a little bit of very boring rhythmic guitar for the background, but nobody came out and told me that. I'd think: What the hell do I have to do – play it standing on my head? You don't want too much ... you don't want too little! Not too loud ... not too quiet! What do you want, for Christ's sake?

'Really, what was wanted was much less than what I imagined they wanted. But I often had trouble because Mick wrote songs around only two chords and there is only so much one can do with that.'

Dave found himself resenting Tony and Chris for stepping in and performing the songs that he, Mog and Eddie had spent over a year rehearsing at the Poly and playing at gigs. But even harder for Dave to stomach was overhearing Levine talking on the phone to Potts about the replacement guitarist.

The musical differences Dave had with Levine only made the atmosphere worse. When he made an 'editorial' decision not to play guitar on the song, 'Picture Book', because he felt it did not need it, eyebrows were raised; everyone, particularly Levine, accused him of being awkward. When that song was later re-recorded for the album, however, it was clear Dave had been right, because there was no guitar on the record.

As if his psychological trauma was not enough, Dave's eyes started causing him agony. He had agreed to wear contact lenses to help the band's image strategy, but he developed an allergy to the cleaning fluids and his eyes started to sting and go bright red. He had taken a pair of plain National Health specs for using late at night. And, much as he hated the thought, he was forced to wear them all the time in the studio. It did not go down well with Mick and the band. 'Wearing the lenses, my eyes were bright red and I looked like Christopher Lee in Dracula, but with the specs I ended up walking round the studio looking like a cross between Morrissey and Groucho Marx.'

Moments of humour were few and far between, but Mick's insistence on being called 'Red' by the Dutch studio staff did give Dave and the others a laugh. The engineers, particularly, would poke their heads round the door and say, in heavy accents, 'Hello, Red, how's it going?'

or 'Where is Red?' and the band found it 'preposterously funny', because they never thought of calling Mick anything but Mick.

During those two weeks, the band recorded four tracks – 'Money's Too Tight (To Mention)', 'Picture Book', 'No Direction' and 'Open Up The Red Box'. For 'Picture Book', the three-man brass section was flown out from England, but Levine hated their contribution and told Elliot and Mick it was not good enough.

The band flew back to Manchester, the brass section's future uncertain. But that was insignificant when compared to the torment Dave suffered when he got home to Prestwich.

Unable to bear the strain of keeping the secret of Dave's impending sacking from him, Michele confessed what Elliot had told her before Dave had left for Holland. Embarrassed and guilty, she tried to explain why she had kept it to herself. Dave listened to her in disbelief. He was shell-shocked. And disgusted.

Dave's marriage went downhill after that. Fast.

'When I came back from Holland I had an ugly row with my wife,' says Dave. 'I was so screwed up by what had happened that I went off the handle. It was an awful scene.

'I was furious with Michele and felt she had betrayed me. She had known Elliot for years and should have realized that he was the last person in the world to play games with, especially if they involved me.

'She told me she felt terrible and that she hadn't known what to do for the best. Maybe her intentions were good but her loyalty should have been with me, not him.

'I thought she was stupid to try and play along behind my back and I felt very resentful. We had been together since I was eighteen and had been married for nine years, but it went downhill from there.

'We hadn't been getting on too well before the Holland incident but that made things so much worse. It accelerated the decline of our marriage because I felt she should have been honest and shouldn't have treated me like an idiot.

'Once the rot set in, it never really got any better. We split up two years later and that was the end of our marriage. I always resented the way she had behaved.'

Shortly after arriving back in Manchester, Elliot arranged a meeting in a pub, when it was decided that the brass section would have to go. A couple of weeks later, however, Mick decided he wanted a 'soul trumpet', so Tim Kellett was rehired. In the meantime, Dave was battling to come to terms with his own precarious position. Still no one was saying anything to him; instead, Elliot seemed more concerned about the band's image, and told Dave he looked thin and 'a bit short'. Eager to do something right, Dave went into the city centre and bought a pair of suede boots with two-inch heels and a leather jacket.

Later, he walked up to Elliot. 'I really feel like a pop star now,' he said. It was an ironic joke, but Elliot did not laugh. 'It's all going to be Mick, you know,' he said. 'He'll be doing all the interviews.' It was as if he was warning Dave not to get any big ideas.

Today, Dave says: 'I was amazed when Elliot said I could do with being a bit taller. What do you say to something like that? I did try to sort it out, but the boots crippled me and only added to my general discomfort. At one meeting, Mick warned me I'd have to go if I didn't pull my socks up – and this really annoyed me. After all that had gone on, he still expected me to be inspired.

'I wanted to tell him to fuck off, but I couldn't because I was out on a limb and didn't have a leg to stand on. I hated feeling like that. I hated losing my independence, hated being so broke that I had to ask Elliot for a fiver for something to eat. It wasn't me.'

What was becoming increasingly hard to take, not only for Dave, but for others in the band, was Mick's self-interest. Since the record deal had been clinched, there had been signs that he saw himself as the star, the one everything revolved around. Elliot would talk about 'the band', but Mick left people in no doubt that it was becoming 'him' and 'them'.

Shortly after recording the single 'Money's Too Tight' in March, the band returned to Holland to record an interview for the BBC's *Old Grey Whistle Test*. Mick arrived at the studio on time, but the rest of the band were late because they had been waiting for Elliot, who had taken a long time to get ready. Furious, Mick snapped, 'Who said you could be late?'

'Ask the manager!' they all said, with pleasure.

During the interview, Mick was asked his musical ambition. 'I want to be one of the greats – like Aretha Franklin,' he said immodestly.

That spring the pressure was on. Not only were the band due to complete the album, they were facing a hectic three-week period – from late May to mid-June – when they had two crucially important gigs. One was arguably the pinnacle of their career so far; the other was a showcase designed to launch the next stage of it.

Mick was excited about both, but particularly the first, for the band had been chosen to support his musical hero, James Brown, at Hammersmith Odeon for three days, starting on 25 May. And it would be the realization of one of the three ambitions he had confided to his old Didsbury flatmate, John Bradshaw, after the band's second performance at the Poly all those years before.

Dressing like pop stars, but there are early signs
that Mick is separate from the band.

The first Simply Red line-up who were sacked. From right to left: Mick, bass player Mog, saxophonist
Ojo, drummer Eddie Sherwood and guitarist Dave Fryman.

With guitarist Dave Fryman.

Mick and Dave Fryman at one
of the first Simply Red gigs
in 1984.

The Simply Red line-up soon after the release of *Men and Women* in 1987. Right to left: Fritz McIntyre, Tony Bowers, Tim Vellett, Sylvan Richardson, Chris Joyce and Mick.

Mick's face is etched wih pain as his golden voice captivates the audience.

Mick with a friend's baby.

With his surrogate mum, June Shaw, and her daughter, Gaynor,
shortly after making it with *Picture Book*.

Mick backstage in 1987. A primary school mum once said that
long fingers meant Mick was talented.

Dee, the beautiful Texan model
who inspired *A New Flame*.

Mick's modest house near Old Trafford in Manchester.
The shutters stay down even when he is at home.

Caught while changing backstage on tour in 1987.

Aziz Ibrahim, right, and Sylvan Richardson. Neither one made it as Simply Red guitarists but remain good friends.

Mick lets his wild dreadlocks loose on the *Stars* world tour in 1992.

The second important gig was a showcase, organized by Elektra, at The International in Manchester's Victoria Park, where Simply Red would perform in front of a carefully-invited audience of VIPs and music journalists.

The tension began to show when the band started rehearsing at The Boardwalk in Little Peter Street. Mick thought Dave was not up to scratch and flew into a rage. 'I've got an album to do,' he fumed. 'I've got my career to think of.'

Tony Bowers looked at Dave sympathetically. '*His* career,' he muttered. All Dave could think was that he was losing his home, and possibly his mind, to launch Mick on his 'career'.

Signing a major record deal and being obsessed with his career did not mean that Mick had forgotten old habits, or principles, as Dave discovered at the pool table during a break in rehearsing.

'Do you want a game?' Mick asked.

'All right,' Dave replied.

'Got 20p for the table?' Mick said.

Dave did, and paid for the game. Mick won. 'You having another?' he asked.

'Yeah,' Dave said. 'But you'll have to pay. I haven't got a 20p.'

Mick shook his head. 'I'm not paying. I just won.'

And he refused to give in. Instead, he put a 20p coin in for himself and had a game on his own.

Today, Dave is still amazed at Mick's attitude. 'This was the man who had just signed a massive record deal,' he says. 'But it wasn't about money – it was a principle. Mick was used to the "winner-stays-on" rule and honestly felt he shouldn't have to pay to play me again. I did find it pathetic, though – quite unbelievable. But then, Mick always wanted to be a winner. I don't think he is a good loser at anything.'

★

The band were booked in for an all-night, 9 p.m.-to-9 a.m., session at Stockport's Strawberry Studios to record 'Something's Burning' for a flexi-disc to be given away with *Jamming* magazine. And the emotional roller-coaster that had been turning Dave's insides took another agonizing twist.

The problem, it seems, was that Mick's musical knowledge was limited. Everything he wrote revolved around just two chords, and it put Dave and Fritz McIntyre in a trap: they were skilful enough in their own right to produce virtually anything, but those two chords restricted them. Everything they did had to be within a certain range. And that early summer night in Stockport, Mick got more and more frustrated at not getting what he wanted.

Fritz coped with the pressure well, calmly going through every sound imaginable on his computer keyboard, trying to find the sound Mick was looking for. When he could not get it right, he would say, patiently, 'Okay. Let's try Number 91.' When that didn't work either, he would say, 'Right, we'll try Number 92.' And if Mick thought that was wrong too, Fritz would sit there, calmly, and try something else. Finally, after five mentally-exhausting hours, his patience paid off and Mick got what he wanted. But it had been a long, strained night, and he was far from happy. Although Dave did not feel he was responsible, he was sure Mick would blame him, and later that morning, driving Fritz home, he said, 'That's it for me, I think. I'll be getting the elbow after this one. It's all going to be my fault.'

The following Sunday, Dave went out for a few hours. When he got back, Michele told him Mick had rung.

'He says you're sacked,' she said. 'But he wants you to call him.'

Mick wanted Dave to ring because the James Brown gigs were only two weeks away. And he had intimated to Michele that if Dave 'brought the house down' he would be reprieved; he could stay in the band.

Today, Dave laughs at the memory: 'I was never going to be in that situation. There was only one person in the band who was going to bring the house down and that was Mick.'

But he rang Mick anyway.

'Obviously, you've been told what's going on?' Mick said.

'Yeah,' Dave replied.

'No hard feelings?'

'No.'

'But will you do the James Brown gigs?'

'Yes,' said Dave. 'I suppose so.'

Amazingly, perhaps stupidly, he was still clinging on to a forlorn hope that maybe, just maybe, all was not lost. It was a short, wafer-thin straw. And Dave was reaching out, trying desperately to clutch it.

Being so keyed up at supporting his musical hero, Mick was in an even more dominating mood when the band began more rehearsals – in a converted mill in Oldham. He did not want anything messed up, he warned; he wanted perfection.

For Dave, it was always going to be a no-win situation: even though he was sacked, and not a welcomed band member, he was still expected to perform well. Everything he did, however, seemed to be wrong.

He came up with some guitar ideas, which he felt enhanced 'Holding Back The Years'. A musician from another band, who had been brought in to bolster the band's sound, thought the piece was good, but Mick shrugged it off cruelly: 'We don't want any of that wallying bullshit,' he snapped. 'Wallying' was his favourite put-down for Dave's extended guitar-playing. He did not like 'wallying'; he wanted Dave's guitar in the background – quietly in the background.

Mick had not been speaking much to Dave. Mostly, he kept his back to him, and once, when he made lemon tea for the band during a break, Mick missed him out. 'Sorry, Dave,' he said, when he was reminded, 'I forgot about you. Forgot you were there.'

'It was an impossible situation,' Dave says. 'Emotionally, Mick is very hard, and things were very unpleasant. He seemed to add more insult to injury as every second went by. If I tried to add something to a song, he would shout it down. I never said anything when he was having a dig – I just thought: You fucking bastard.'

Shortly before the James Brown gig, the band shot a video for 'Money's Too Tight' at a snooker club in Kilburn, in north London. There was some doubt as to whether Dave should take part, but it was finally decided he should. While in London, the band did a live broadcast for Capital Radio, and he was included in that, too. He began to feel better, more like the person he had been before the torment.

★

On Saturday 25 May, the band travelled down to the Hammersmith Odeon for the James Brown gig. And, around 5 p.m., the band witnessed a rare moment when all Mick's self-confidence and assertiveness, which dictated their lives, vanished in front of them.

For years Mick had worshipped Brown, traipsed around town hunting for rare recordings, played them over and over again, and had even modelled his stage performance on Brown's own style. Mick had longed for the day he could play the same venue as the great man – he had even confessed to a pal that it was one of three lifetime ambitions. And yet, when the hero of his musical dreams was only a matter of feet away, he bottled a perfect opportunity to speak to him, perhaps shake his hand and tell him what a fan he was.

The band were setting up their equipment on the stage when Dave Fryman spotted a portly man wearing a brown pin-striped suit and glasses, standing alone about ten yards away, by an organ.

The man looked like an accountant, but Dave recognized him as James Brown. So did others in the band.

They looked at Mick, and motioned towards the lone figure staring up at the stage. 'Hey, that's James Brown,' one of them whispered.

Mick said nothing.

'Aren't you going to say hello?' Dave asked.

Mick said nothing. He stared at Brown thoughtfully, as if weighing up what to do.

'Mick,' Dave said, 'it's James Brown. Aren't you going to say anything?'

Mick shook his head. 'No.'

'Go on. Surely you're going to introduce yourself.'

Mick looked awkward, inhibited, perhaps over-awed. 'No,' he said, more firmly. 'I'm not going to do it.'

And he turned his back and got on with setting something up on stage.

Who knows why Mick did not seize the chance. Maybe he had adored James Brown for so long that he did not want to risk shattering the illusion. Perhaps he was simply too proud and did not want to appear a sycophant. More likely, it was fear of running into the notorious James Brown temper – and a snub that would humiliate him in front of the others.

Mick preferred to do his talking on stage. And over those three days, supporting Brown, his performance spoke volumes for Simply Red's growing appeal. The success filled Dave Fryman with renewed confidence; he might have done enough, he felt, to change Mick's mind. He dared to hope that he might survive; that he had done enough to weather the storm and stay aboard.

Back in Manchester a few days later, he knew he had not. Elliot and Mick started talking about the 'Money's Too Tight' video and the big launch of Simply Red at The International on 14 June. And Dave knew he was not part of their plans.

'We were having a meeting,' Dave recalls. 'We discussed several things, then Elliot said to Mick, "What about personnel?' And Mick said, "I'm going to have to get a band together, aren't I?" In other words, I was still sacked.

'I said, "So, there's no change, then?" Nobody said a word. The atmosphere was awful, terrible. I just said, "Right, let's have a look at the video, then . . ." '

Strangely, even that was not the end of Dave Fryman and Simply Red. Despite that meeting, someone had the gall to ask if he would record a BBC Radio One spot the following morning. Surprisingly, Dave agreed.

He says: 'We did a couple of songs in this old BBC theatre in Hulme. The atmosphere, again, was appalling. I was out to lunch! I couldn't believe what was happening. After the recording, I put my guitar in its case and walked out. That morning was the last time I had contact with the band. My relationship with Mick had deteriorated and soured to the point where I couldn't stand the sight of him. I would think: God, go away.

'Mick would say we used to be so close, but we never were. Being close to him is a contradiction in terms. He has learned to be hard, and, as the record deal arrived and things took off, I found him more and more obnoxious.

'In the end I hated him.'

22

Sylvan Richardson was excited. He did not know much about Simply Red, but he was aware they were a hot new band: their name had been buzzing around Manchester for several months; everyone in the know had heard they were cutting their first album. When Elliot's partner, Andy Dodd, asked if he would like to audition for the band, Sylvan said yes eagerly. For a twenty-year-old guitarist with no regular job, it was the chance of a lifetime.

It was not so much an audition as a personality check. Mick and Elliot knew Sylvan was a good enough guitarist; it was just a question of what he was like on stage and whether they felt he fitted in with the band.

The audition was the hour-long launch gig at The International in Manchester's Victoria Park, and rehearsals for it were held over two five-day weeks in a massive old building in Oldham. For Sylvan, that period was a strange and new experience. For the first time in his life, he was working with musicians who were not his friends, in an intense atmosphere where everything was taken very seriously. It was far from a casual musical interlude. It was business.

'Those ten days were tense and positive,' Sylvan remembers. 'I was quickly aware that I was dealing with a very serious band who were very set in their goals and had very high standards. Mick was such a powerful visionary, who knew where he and the band were going. The management was of the same mind, so it was like a machine we were preparing – a slick, smoothly-run machine ready to take on the world. The rehearsals had that kind of intensity.

'There was no honeymoon period. After a couple of days, I arrived late, and I had my girlfriend with me. Mick quickly took me to one side and said, very directly, "I don't want you to be late. And I don't want you to bring anyone to rehearsal again." I thought that was a bit tough, but I understood him. The thing about Mick is that he will tell you what his requirements are, and you can't misunderstand him. He was right. It was his band and he wanted to run it in a certain way, so it was up to us to respect that.

'With the music, it wasn't hard to know what he wanted, because there was no bullshit. He didn't bother to be diplomatic. It was a question of "do this, do this, do this". And when he didn't get what he wanted, he'd let you know immediately.'

For Sylvan, being part of Simply Red full-time became all-important; he knew it could be the turning point of his life. Not once during those rehearsals, however, did anyone give him any clue he would be taken on. Musically, he knew he was faultless. He also knew that his suggestions for some of the songs were good, because Mick would say, 'That's great. That really works well.' But whether The International would be Sylvan's first and last Simply Red performance, no one was saying.

In the second week, he could stand it no longer. After one rehearsal, he got Fritz on his own and asked, 'What's happening? Have I got the job? I really want the job. What's happening?'

Fritz tried to calm him. 'Don't worry. If you're meant to get it, you will.'

There was nothing Sylvan could do, except keep working, keep doing his best. He just wished someone would tell him how he was doing.

At the end of the second week, when the rehearsing was coming together as a set, Elliot and Andy arrived to check everything. Sylvan seized his chance. 'By the way, Elliot,' he said. 'How do I fit into all this?'

'Wait till after the weekend, after the gig,' was all Elliot said.

The show at The International was a challenging event. It was the launch of the new Simply Red, and a critical, discerning audience, including influential journalists, would be there to see if the band were as good as the word on the grapevine. One of the people there that night was Mick's songwriting partner from The Frantic Elevators, Neil (Moey) Moss. They had patched up their differences after the bitter split and Mick was keen to tell Moey that he was going to earn royalties from Simply Red: as a token for all the songs they had written together, Mick had credited him jointly on 'Holding Back The Years'. Moey was touched. It was a gesture that would earn him around £50,000.

At the end of a seventy-minute performance, in which Simply Red played every track on *Picture Book*, everyone knew they *were* hot. The gig was a resounding success. And afterwards, the band, the management and close followers were elated. Sylvan, looking good in a blue silk shirt and white trousers designed by Chris Joyce's girlfriend, had played the best he could, only a little nervous that his future with the band depended on that one performance.

Amid the quiet celebrations, Mick said, 'Well done.' Then Elliot came up and, abrupt as ever, said, 'You've got the job.'

Delighted, Sylvan went out front, where his parents were waiting. 'I'm in,' he said. And they glowed with pride.

Two summers later, that pride would be replaced with deep concern when it all went sour and their son wrestled with the anguish of a shattered dream.

*

Shortly after the International performance, 'Money's Too Tight (To Mention)', the song recorded with Dave Fryman in Holland two months before, was released as a single. It got massive airplay and Dave Fryman would wake up to his alarm-clock radio, hearing himself playing. It was bizarre. He felt he was living in the Twilight Zone, seemingly involved in something, but knowing he really was not. Worse was to come, however. With 'Money's Too Tight' climbing the charts, Simply Red were invited on to Wogan, and Dave found himself staring at his replacement, Sylvan, miming to a guitar accompaniment he had played himself. Then he watched *Top Of The Pops* and saw himself actually performing in the band's promotional video.

It was an agonizing experience that plunged him into a deep depression that cost him his sanity for a long time.

'I don't really want to admit that to the world, but I went through shit,' Dave says today. 'I was deeply depressed and had lost my job and a lot of brain cells. I was a shambles.

'I had to watch Wogan because I wanted to see what my replacement was like. When I saw him, it all made sense. He had a low-profile image and it undoubtedly helped being black. I felt the same numbness as when I'd been woken by the clock radio.

'After *Top Of The Pops*, people said, "Saw you on telly." I'd tell them I wasn't in the band any more. They just said, "Oh". Then *The Old Grey Whistle Test* programme was shown and it started all over again. People I'd known from work were all saying, "Great, Dave – really glad you made it." I had to say, "Actually I'm not in it any more." And they'd look bewildered: "What?"

'Later, when I started temporary teaching, the cousins of some of my former pupils would say, "Eh, sir, didn't you used to be in Simply Red?" I would say yes. Then it was: "Why aren't you in it now, sir?" And, of course, it would bring it all back.

'They were not the greatest of times. I did not end up in a mental hospital, but the depression was a good black one. And it lasted a long time. Like Mog, my confidence was shattered and I couldn't play my guitar.

'The way the airport deal happened blew me away. It was Elliot playing games. But I was out on a limb, because it was important to me to be in a band. Looking back, I feel I would have liked to have been on that first album, so that I could say to somebody, "Listen to this. This is me. Good that bit, isn't it?" But in all honesty, I never felt that was going to happen. Even if I was still in the band, I'd be saying, "If you listen *very hard*, you can hear that little thing there. That's me!"

'I didn't get any satisfaction out of it. I felt I'd let myself down, really. I came away from it thinking that it was all my fault; that, obviously, I was a crap guitarist. I felt I'd made a fool of myself.

'But the sequence of events and the mind games Elliot played made me sick. I'd said, "If there's a problem, let me know, and I'll bow out." But Elliot said nothing – even though he knew. With him, things can change very quickly. Yellow socks can be in today, but tomorrow it could be blue and, if you're still wearing the yellow ones, well, it's really not on. But then, I have to ask, what did the others say or do to deserve the chop?

'I read that Mick said people had to be sacked because they weren't good enough. There's no way we couldn't play what was expected. To turn round now and say we weren't good enough is rubbish.'

★

At the end of July 1985, Sylvan Richardson went with the rest of the band to RAK Studios in the St John's Wood area of London to record the first album, *Picture Book*. From day one, Elektra gave the band star treatment; for two weeks, they were put up in sumptuous rented flats with all mod cons, while in the studio, where they started early and finished late, a catering company was hired to serve lunch and dinner in an elegant dining room.

For Sylvan, it was an eye-opener that endorsed his feelings that Simply Red were being taken very seriously indeed and destined for some sort of stardom.

Today, he recalls: 'When I saw where we were going to stay, I thought: Wow – yeah, we're making it. I mean, I thought I might have had to sleep on my auntie's floor in Balham, but we were in the middle of town, in beautiful self-contained flats. It was obvious Simply Red was a very serious set-up.

'Boy George came into the studio one day and sat with his feet up, listening to one of the tracks. He stayed a few hours and he and Mick got on really well.'

Sylvan may have been a little in awe of what was going on around him, but to Mick and, particularly, Elliot, it was no more than they expected: it was the beginning of their five-album plan to conquer the world. The plan was no secret: Sylvan had heard Mick talk openly about producing five 'killer' albums, then growing a beard and retiring to a Caribbean island to paint.

'He and Elliot were totally convinced they could take the world by storm and get out after five albums,' says Sylvan. 'They inspired me, but frightened me, too, because I thought: These people are ruthless and quite capable of hiring and firing without a thought for the human element.'

★

During the recording of *Picture Book* and afterwards, Elliot talked a lot about the image of Simply Red; how it was a band, not a solo vocal act backed by musicians. But when prints of the album cover arrived at the management's offices in Didsbury, Sylvan and his colleagues got a shock: staring back at them was a huge, close-up photograph of Mick, wearing a brown, thirties-style cloth cap. Pictures of the band were conspicuous by their absence. There was an awkward silence as each member wondered what to say. Finally, someone found the courage to inquire, 'How come we're not all on the cover?'

'Oh, it was easier to profile one person than six,' was Elliot's reply.

Another embarrassed silence. The band stared at the unfolded colour prints, all wondering: What's going on here?

'It didn't smell very good,' Sylvan recalls. 'The management would have known about the photo. So would Mick. But nobody told the band. None of us said anything. Nothing could be said. We couldn't change the cover. In a sense, Elliot was right that it was easier to profile one person than six, but that's not what he'd talked about. He had gone on so much about the band image; then, as soon as the product came out, it was the reverse. It didn't go down well with any of us.

'The record company had wanted to sign Mick as a solo act, but he said, "No. This is my band. We're all in it together." Obviously, between then and the printing of the album cover, something changed. It was a weird feeling in the management offices. Everyone had expected six faces of the band or nothing – and, looking at Mick's photograph on its own, it was evident to all that Simply Red wasn't a band as we'd all been led to believe – it was The Mick Hucknall Show.

'I didn't discuss it a lot with the others, but there were a few passing comments that made me realize there was some resentment. No one said anything to Mick, though. It was very much a case of "Let's keep Mick happy and agree with him on everything." If he suggested going out somewhere, they'd pander to him, making sure they never put a foot wrong. But there was no way I was going to be part of that. I hated pandering to him. Which didn't do me any good in the long run.'

It is significant that, although Mick was in the So What offices when the band saw the album prints, he left it to Elliot to explain why their photographs were not on the cover. He seems to have been more comfortable making sure he got his own way musically than risking challenging confrontations over personal matters he might find difficult to justify.

★

The band were popular in Italy long before they were big in Britain. Soon after recording *Picture Book*, they appeared live on TV from a massive amphitheatre and the Italian girls fell in love with them. Sales of 'Money's Too Tight' soared, and when the band went back to perform at a pop festival or on TV, they were besieged by screaming fans, swept along on a wave of Simply Red mania. It was the beginning of a love affair that continues today.

The more popular they became, the more star treatment they received: soon they were being ferried around in gleaming limousines to the best hotels, and eating the finest foods. TV and radio stations begged them to appear. Newspapers and magazines pestered them for interviews. In Italy, if nowhere else, Simply Red were hot. And the band were flattered by the adulation.

Mick, understandably, was the one most affected by the attention; it was him, after all, the media wanted to interview. At first, the management plan was for Mick not to be available for all interviews and for the five other members of the band to share the load. But it did not work out that way. TV producers and journalists were not really interested in having anyone else on their programmes, and even when another band member went along, Mick was always the one they wanted to question. The more interviews he did, the more he seemed to enjoy them and the more he wanted to do. From being flattered by the adulation, he was now revelling in it. And the band began to sense that he really did believe it was The Mick Hucknall Show.

According to Sylvan, Mick began to take himself more seriously. 'It was a subtle change. He wasn't flash – just more arrogant and egotistical, more aloof. He'd always have to be the centre of attention, not just on the road but all the time, regardless of what situation we were in. It was as if he was thinking: I'm a star now. He'd always thought a lot of himself, but suddenly he stepped up a gear. We were all flattered by the attention in Italy, but Mick began to absorb the adulation for himself. The band image that had been talked about so much was gone. It was Mick doing all the interviews, Mick's face in the newspapers and magazines. It was becoming him – and the rest of us. Personally, I became a bit resentful, because it wasn't supposed to be like that.

'What made it worse was that Mick started having tantrums if something wasn't to his liking; he'd rant and rave over the least little thing. Once, he had a blazing row with a coach driver taking us from one venue to another, and I thought it was going to end up with punches being thrown. It was all over the music tapes Mick wanted to play. He never cared what other people might want to hear – he always had to have on what he wanted. And he'd play it loud. On this particular trip, the driver couldn't stand it and turned his tape off. Mick went berserk, screaming, "How dare you turn my music off!" The driver wouldn't put the tape back on and Mick, bright red with anger, started swearing at him. The driver stopped the coach and they sat there, shouting at each other. To the rest of us, it had started off as a bit of a giggle, but the longer it went on, with neither giving way, it became very serious and I felt sure they were going to come to blows. Mick took the view that the band had hired the coach and because they were paying, he could have what he liked on. All the driver was saying was, "Show some respect, please. I'm trying to drive. Your music is too loud." But, with the language problem, there was a communication breakdown. Mick made sure he had the last word, though.

'Another time, in a dressing room before a show, something like cheese was missing from a salad buffet spread, and Mick flipped again, shouting and screaming as though it was the end of the world. He'd rant and rave at members of the band or backing singers too, and they would just sit there and take it until it was all over. He had a quick, fiery temper and would throw a tantrum at the drop of a hat.'

★

When *Picture Book* was released in October 1985, it was received icily by the critics. Some accused Mick, the working-class boy with tough, punky ideals, of selling out to musical blandness. Others complained that the production obscured much of the band's hard playing, and translated little of their live potential: the raw edge their energy gave the music was missing, they said. It was as if something was in the way, as though the production had a gossamer sheen on it.

But Mick and Elliot were happy. They had put their faith in Stewart Levine, and he had produced what they wanted.

That summer, Mick's relationship with Joanne – the former girlfriend of Elliot's brother-in-law – blossomed and they went on a cycling holiday to Clonakilty, County Cork, in Southern Ireland. Mick was serious about Joanne and was falling in love, but the relationship was doomed. Soon Mick was back on the relentless trail of stardom and she became another casualty of his unshakeable ambition.

The outlook for the band, however, was not bright. For a debut single, 'Money's Too Tight' had done well, but their second release, 'Come To My Aid', flopped dismally, peaking at Number 66 in September. The following month, *Picture Book* hit the shops and went straight into the charts at Number 34. But all the early signs of a runaway success stopped when it peaked at Number 33, then started dropping dramatically.

In November, 'Holding Back The Years' was released – a far slower, more mournful version than the one The Frantic Elevators had cut in 1982. Mick had added the chorus, 'I'll keep holding on . . .', which wasn't in the original, and he was confident the new version would succeed. He was wrong. Despite the promotional muscle of a big record company, the record reached only Number 51, then drifted to Number 67, and finally out of the Top 100.

In contrast, Simply Red were red hot in Europe, especially Holland. In January, *Picture Book* topped the album charts, giving the band their first gold disc. Mick gave the disc to his dad, who proudly put it on the wall in his front room. 'Holding Back The Years' went to Number 3 in Holland, and from mid-February the band's mega-status there was confirmed when the album began a run of nine consecutive weeks in the Number 1 spot.

Sadly, that success was not mirrored in Britain. 'Jericho' – the number inspired by Mick's early experiences in the big time – stalled at Number 53 and, to make matters worse, *Picture Book* dipped to Number 96.

Elektra had not lost faith, however, and in May re-released 'Holding Back The Years'. For some reason, Britain was now ready for Simply Red: the record went in at Number 55, soared to Number 19, then to Number 6 in three weeks.

On the strength of that single, *Picture Book* sales rocketed, and on 7 June, the day before Mick's twenty-sixth birthday, both records were at Number 2 in their respective charts. When the chart positions came through, the drinks flowed, and the hangover was sweet indeed.

But then Mick went on BBC TV's *Top Of The Pops* programme to promote the record – and he provoked an upsetting train of events, forcing him to agonize over one of the most emotionally difficult decisions of his life. For it was that brief appearance that brought his mother back into his life after twenty-two years.

On the Thursday the show was due to go out, Florence Gibbons was sitting at home in Croft, reading the *Sun* newspaper, when she noticed a story about the new release and that night's TV appearance. The story mentioned Mick Hucknall by name, and Florence began to wonder. There might be more than one Michael Hucknall, of course, but it was not a common name. She thought she'd ring her daughter Marlene, just in case.

'I told her about the story and asked her to watch the programme,' Florence recalls. 'When *Top Of The Pops* came on, I sat on the floor on my knees, close to the screen, and stared at Michael as he held the microphone.

'To me, he looked like he did when he was a baby. His red hair, chubby cheeks and face had hardly changed. He was the little baby grandson I had lost all those years before.

'And then he started to sing, and I broke my heart crying. I couldn't stop the tears streaming down my face. It was very moving watching him, because it was as though he had come back into my life. And when I heard the words of the song, and about hoping for the arms of mater, I cried even more, because it was all about Maureen.

'Immediately Michael finished singing, I decided to go to Marlene to talk to her about him. I reached the front gate, my eyes still red from crying. My next-door neighbour, Jim, was getting into his car with his wife, Shirley. When he saw me, he turned to Shirley and told her I was upset. When Shirley asked me what was wrong, I just said, "It's all right. I've just seen the face of a grandson I haven't seen for twenty-two years." '

The next day Florence went to see Maureen, who was divorced from her third husband – a Danish sea captain – and living in Warrington with two children she had had since leaving Imre with Ricky and Lyndsay.

'Maureen was shocked when I told her,' says Florence. 'She really couldn't take it in. But when it sunk in, she said she was very proud that her son had made a name for himself.

'I told her about the lyrics – and the reference to mother's arms and meeting sooner or later – and she said she must get in touch with him. If he'd written words like that, she thought he must need her.'

Maureen found out the address of Simply Red's management company and rang, asking to speak to Mick's manager. Elliot took the call and when Maureen explained who she was and what she wanted, he said he would pass on her message to Mick.

Mick would have rung his father first, naturally. But he was not on the phone. So Mick phoned June Shaw, who – like Nellie Spike – had been like a mother to him.

Gaynor Shaw remembers that day well: 'Mick said, "My mum's been in touch 'cos she saw me on the telly. What shall I do?" My own mother wasn't the type to tell anyone what to do and she didn't want to be nasty about Mick's mum. She went about it in a different way and what she said has always stuck in my mind. She said that if she had ever had reason to leave home, she would have taken Gary and me with her. She said she could not understand how a mother could ever leave her kids.

'In a gentle way, she was trying to tell him not to bother – that his mum was trying to get in touch only because he was famous. Why hadn't she bothered all the years he was growing up? she asked.

'Mick always had a lot of respect for my mum and for everything she had done for him and I'm sure he was glad of the advice, particularly as my mum had known Maureen.'

Reg was not so calm when Mick told him. He hit the roof and said Maureen had a 'bloody cheek' getting in touch. But he said he was not going to interfere: Mick had to make up his own mind whether he wanted any contact.

Mick thought long and hard, and finally decided he would speak to his mother – but only on the phone. It was not a long conversation. But it was a blunt one; Mick felt bitter about being abandoned and let it show.

'He was really hard and terrible to Maureen,' Florence says. 'He asked her, "What do you want? Why are you contacting me after all this time?" He made it clear he didn't want anything to do with her. And he certainly didn't want to see her.

'He was so hard with her that the first thing Maureen thought was how much like her he was! She's not the type to cry – she blew her top instead, because she was so angry with him. And then she slammed the phone down.

'Mick's manager rang back, saying she should not have put the phone down. I took over and told him the full story of what happened all those years before, and how I had taken Michael back to his father. Maureen was standing next to me, going mad – it was the first time she had heard the whole story from my point of view. The manager listened, then said, "I'm not saying anything about this to Mick – it would crucify him."

'After a while, Maureen wasn't bothered about meeting Mick. She took the attitude: if you're not bothered, neither am I. And since that day, there has been no contact from either side.'

While Mick tours the world, revelling in his superstardom, his mother, now fifty-two, is living in Texas with her fourth husband, a fan of her son and his music, but resigned to being out of his life forever. For Florence, it is very sad. 'Michael will always be the little boy I lost,' she says. 'But, no matter what he feels about Maureen or our family generally, he can never escape the fact that he's our flesh and blood. He's shown he has a fiery streak. And this obviously comes from Maureen's side, not his father's.'

For his appearance on *Top Of The Pops* that June night, Mick made an unprecedented request to the BBC producers to sing 'Holding Back The Years' live. Many other performers mime their hits to soundtracks recorded earlier in the day, but Mick did not want to do that; he felt he could get more feeling across singing live and he knew he had the confidence and ability to pull it off.

Mick has generally taken the credit for 'Holding Back The Years', but it is a fact that other members of the band have always helped him shape his songs. Mick would have an idea for a lyric but, not being as musically gifted as his musicians, would need help making it work. Fritz McIntyre, particularly, has played a big part in transforming Mick's ideas into the finished product. Even 'Holding Back The Years' needed some work by Simply Red musicians to develop it. Sylvan says: 'One day, he brought the song in and strummed the guitar. "There are the chords," he said. And we started jamming. We developed it into a band sound.'

That summer, Simply Red's success in America had been simmering for four months since 'Holding Back The Years' entered the charts at Number 88 on 5 April. By early June it had captured the public's imagination and was at Number 16. For the next five weeks, the record kept climbing until, on 12 July it hit Number 1 – realizing another of Mick's ambitions.

By the end of the US tour that summer, Mick *was* Simply Red. The much-talked-about band image had gone for ever. The general sound was good, but Mick was the driving force, the one with the voice and charisma. And it was him the fans in their thousands flocked to see.

Fame bred curiosity, and Mick became the target of tabloid gossip, prompting Elektra to do some research to find out just how much people in Britain knew about its hot property. Much to Mick's amusement, the three main findings were: (a) he didn't like Margaret Thatcher; (b) he had stolen Andrew Ridgeley's girlfriend; and (c) that Simply Red were like another band, called The Communards. Mick took pleasure in pointing out to inquiring journalists that only one – the first – was true.

In little more than a year in the spotlight, Mick had earned a reputation as sullen, brash and prickly – an arrogant upstart who saw himself as the wilful boy genius, impetuous and imperious. Outside the confines of his own band, he would play the star, and in one magazine photo session made one demand after another, and generally kept everyone flapping around him until the whole studio staff were a bag of frayed nerves. This behaviour conflicted with his eagerness to convince other media people what an earthy, unaffected, unspoilt working-class boy he still was.

There is no doubt he loathed the phoneyness of certain people in the music business. Having struck an agreement to work on Simply Red's second album with Lamont Dozier, an architect of the Tamla Motown sound and one of his heroes, Mick was asked if he had been intimidated by him. He hadn't been. 'Why should I be?' he asked his questioner. 'He's a musician. And musicians don't fuck around with all the bullshit. They judge people by what they can do, not by who they are. It was *easy* working with him.'

At the same time, Mick would walk around in a big black hat carrying a walking stick – rather like his favourite movie star, Orson Welles. And, like the great Hollywood legend, he seemed preoccupied with creating a larger-than-life persona and myth out of his own personality.

The UK success of 'Holding Back The Years' and the heavy sales of *Picture Book* ought to have ensured that future records would jump into the charts. But the band had no new recordings and were forced to release a remix of 'Open Up The Red Box' in August, which got no higher than Number 61.

The new songs, written on the road during the *Picture Book* tour, were not ready until early 1987. A single, 'The Right Thing', was released in February and the band went on the road as the album *Men and Women* hit the shops two weeks later, going straight to Number 2. The new album reflected Mick's life over the past eighteen months: his feelings and emotions in relationships he had been unable to fulfil because of his work pattern.

While admitting a liking for sex, Mick denied he was anything like the sex maniac a *New Musical Express* article made him out to be. Sylvan, who saw him at close quarters over two years, says Mick was obsessed with women and seemed insatiable in his pursuit of them. Not that it was difficult for Mick: there were always young women around him, either backstage during gigs, or at parties afterwards. 'If he saw someone he liked, he simply made a beeline for them,' says Sylvan. 'His sexual drive was well known. When we got to a hotel, we'd say, "Oh, who's next to Mick?" Whoever it was would be in for a noisy night. Mick never failed to score. He could have had a girl every night. They threw themselves at him. He was powerful, but he was charming too. He knew how to turn on the charm to get a girl into bed. And they didn't need much coaxing.'

Outside the bedroom, Mick was revelling in another sort of power – the power to hire and fire people. 'One minute the guy was with us, the next, he was gone,' Sylvan remembers. 'Mick showed no remorse, no sentimentality. It was a case of: swish, you no longer exist – next one, please. I found the lack of feeling very distasteful.'

Mick was becoming a megalomaniac, seemingly obsessed with being able to do anything he wanted, when he wanted, and it made Sylvan retreat into his shell, unable to relate to him any more.

And then in May, as the band arrived in Scandinavia at the start of their world tour, Sylvan could stand it no longer. He did not want to go to restaurants and spend four hours over dinner. He did not want to go to parties and speak to people he'd never see again. And he did not want to listen any more to Mick ranting any more. He began to distance himself more and more from the band, particularly Mick. By the time the band reached Rotterdam, he and Mick were barely speaking and Sylvan would phone his mother in England, upset and depressed, saying he could not handle it any more and wanted to leave the band. Concerned and worried for his financial security, she told him to hang on and earn a lot of money before he broke away. But for Sylvan, it had become too much. Mick's prima donna behaviour and all the phoneyness peculiar to showbusiness, and the record industry in particular, had swamped him. He felt he was drowning.

What made Sylvan so sure he had to get out was that he had heard rumours that Mick and Elliot were thinking of getting rid of him anyway; that they wanted one of his friends, Aziz Ibrahim, to replace him. Nothing had been said to his face, but then, nothing would: neither Mick nor Elliot would risk telling him in the middle of the tour that he was being fired, in case he stormed off, leaving them in the lurch.

Today, Sylvan recalls: 'I was making £50,000 a year – a fortune for a 21-year-old. But I was prepared to give it up so that I wouldn't have to deal with Mick or his managers any more. All I wanted to do was play music, not be involved in all the bullshit. By the end of that 1987 tour I was pissed off, utterly frustrated with the whole set-up. It just got to a point where it wasn't a very good atmosphere at all. There were times I was so upset, I'd sit at a table and not say a word, ostracizing myself from the rest. It was a mixture of not knowing how to voice my feelings and being immature. It was Mick who really got to me. I'd had enough of having to deal with a prima donna.

'I wish I'd been able to handle it all better, and to deal with everybody, maybe share my problems and say I was having difficulties with this or that. But I just bottled it all up for two years. When I finally did confront

Mick, I got it off my chest. I told him I was sick of him playing mind games and exercising his power all the time. He just said, "Everyone else plays mind games – why can't you?" I said, "I don't see the point. Why can't you be straight?" He didn't really have an answer.

'When I look back, and think how I felt at the time, I know there was no way it was going to end any differently. If it happened now, it would be a different kettle of fish and I'd be able to handle it. But then I was too young.'

Sylvan was right that Mick and Elliot had decided to get rid of him towards the end of the first leg of that European tour. He had been an integral part of the band – from his talented contributions on both albums, to his live performances – but his isolation and seeming lack of interest had got too much. The band generally, and Mick and Elliot in particular, felt there was a hole on the stage where Sylvan was meant to be. And, for the long-term future of Simply Red, it was best if he left. If it bothered Elliot and Mick that Aziz Ibrahim was a friend of the young man they were about to sack, they did not show it. Early in June, shortly before the band were due to fly home to Manchester, Elliot told his secretary, Lindy, to get the 24-year-old Pakistani guitarist on the phone.

Aziz was alone in his bedroom at his parent's home on an estate in the notorious Long Site area of Manchester, where he had lived all his life, when the call came through. Elliot explained who he was, then said, 'We're returning home for a week or so, then going back to Italy on the 24th. We've heard you're the best around. Would you like to come? Are you available to join Simply Red?'

Aziz thought it was a wind-up.

Not wanting to sound too eager, too available, he played for time. 'Can you hold on a minute, Elliot, while I check?' He pretended to go through a diary for a few seconds, then said, as matter-of-factly as he could, 'Yes. I've nothing fixed. I can do that.'

A meeting was arranged and Aziz put the phone down. Then he ran around the bedroom, jumping up and down. 'Yes, yes, yes,' he shouted. 'Thank you God.' Even as a God-fearing Muslim, Aziz felt this was too good to be true.

In a way, he was right.

*

Sylvan was sacked the day the band returned from Europe – the day of the Lord Mayor's parade through the centre of Manchester. As sackings go, it was quite amicable: Mick and Elliot said they felt it better if Sylvan left because he was not happy. The decision had nothing to do with his ability, they stressed; they knew he could play their music in his sleep.

For his part, Sylvan got everything off his chest – how he was sick of all Mick's mind games and the way he exercised his power all the time.

While Elliot finalized the split, Mick heard the sound of a jazz band and wandered over to a window of the first-floor office. Looking down onto Princess Street, at the crowds cheering the Lord Mayor's procession, he saw a familiar face playing double bass on the colourful float carrying the jazz band. It was Mog.

The coincidence made Mick shudder: another casualty of Simply Red, another musician he had sacked. He knew that getting rid of Sylvan was best for the band, as it had been with Mog. And, no doubt, there would be others along the way if the band was to achieve the perfection he desired. But watching his old friend getting the most out of that happy, if humble, stage that afternoon spooked Mick nonetheless. It hit home just how tough he had learned to be since those carefree days when he and The Elevators had been happy to play for fun, or for a bit of beer money if they were lucky.

23

The call from Elliot was the biggest break of Aziz Ibrahim's life. And he had earned it. He had been brought up on one of Manchester's toughest housing estates, enduring a school life of bullying and racial abuse, and had dedicated himself to learning the guitar while his pals drifted into a life of crime and, ultimately, jail. He had built a strong reputation as one of the most gifted guitarists on the music scene, playing in a number of highly-respected jazz and rock bands and, more significantly, in reggae groups in the Hulme and Moss Side areas which Mick knew so well.

All the hard work seemed to have paid off in that brief conversation with Elliot: excited and optimistic, he went to the So What offices to pick up tapes of Simply Red's records and live performances. He had one week to listen to what they wanted him to play, while the band went back to Italy. When they came home, he would join them for two days of rehearsal the following weekend to see if he fitted into the band.

Despite his desire to quit the band, Sylvan was still bruised by his sacking and planned to go to America to visit friends and contemplate his future. But when Aziz phoned him, asking his advice, Sylvan did not hesitate. A religious young man, he was pleased for his friend's good fortune and agreed to tell him all he should know about Simply Red: who to trust and who to avoid; the protocol and general do's and don'ts. Unselfishly, Sylvan went to Aziz's home, keen to do all he could to ensure that his friend's relationship with the band was happier than his.

Aziz was surprised that Mick did not turn up the following Saturday. But the rehearsal went ahead, giving Aziz the chance to get re-acquainted with Fritz McIntyre – with whom he had jammed in reggae groups in the past – and meet the others in the band. He hit it off with them all, particularly Ian Kirkham, a highly-talented Liverpool-born sax player who joined the band in 1986. And it seemed to go well with Mick, too, when he strolled in halfway through rehearsal the next day.

Strangely, one of Mick's first questions had nothing to do with music.
'Do ya like curries?' he asked, quite abruptly.
'Of course I do,' Aziz laughed. 'I'm Pakistani.'
'And reggae?'

Aziz nodded.

After they had run through a few songs, Mick looked pleased: a lover of reggae and Indian food, and a great guitarist, with all the enthusiasm and energy Sylvan had lost.

'You're in,' he said. Then he looked disapprovingly at Aziz's metallic pink guitar. 'But you won't be playing that!'

Aziz thought: Uh-oh, the start of a problem. But then he said, 'Fine. But I can't afford to buy another one.'

'Okay,' Mick said. 'We'll buy you another one.'

A few days later, Elliot took Aziz shopping, not only for the guitar, but also for something to wear on stage: they agreed on a black designer suit costing £850.

The likeable, God-fearing Muslim, who had been so grateful for this chance, had to pinch himself that he was not dreaming. Little more than a week before, he had been scraping a living in uninspiring rough-and-tumble clubs in dreary areas. Now he was being kitted out, seemingly with no expense spared, to tour the world with one of the hottest bands around.

The following week, on 24 June, Aziz took the stage in Milan in front of 15,000 screaming fans, and witnessed first-hand the extent and passion of Mick's popularity among Italian girls. Many were crying in ecstasy – even before Mick had opened his mouth!

Mick wallowed in the adulation, but, the same day, Aziz realized he was nobody's fool where girls were concerned. If he felt he was being used, he was not afraid to deal with it.

Backstage after the concert, a glamorous young girl enticed him downstairs, where a paparazzi photographer was waiting. Suddenly aware he was being set up, Mick grabbed the photographer's camera and tried to take out the film. Police were called as a struggle broke out. They started shoving Mick around, but he pushed them back. When they were told who he was, they threw the girl and the photographer out.

'It was an early lesson for me that if Mick feels he's in the right, he doesn't take any shit from anyone – even the police,' says Aziz.

After Italy, Simply Red began what they called The End Of World Tour, a six-month trip to territories they had not visited before – Japan, Australia, New Zealand, Canada and South America – to promote *Men and Women*.

In Japan, sales of *Picture Book* had gone well, but nothing could have prepared the band for the hysteria that greeted them. Since it was their first visit, the band did nothing but promotional interviews and photo sessions, followed by dinner and live TV appearances which often did not go out until 1 a.m. It was a hard slog, but one interviewer provided some light relief when she asked the band to dress in traditional Japanese costume – kimonos and wooden shoes. The band's co-operation was rewarded when they were given the clothes as gifts. Such generosity, they discovered, was typical of the Japanese, particularly, their girl fans. All the band were given numerous silk shirts, and one admiring girl gave Mick a hand-sewn wedding kimono he later discovered cost £700.

Japanese hospitality did not stop at material goods, however; Mick quickly discovered that his superstar status was the key to sexual favours, too.

The red-haired kid those girls in Denton had found too ugly to kiss now had the pick of some of the world's most beautiful young women. They fell over themselves to meet him at gigs and parties and clubs, and all the time Mick would enjoy them and their bodies, never getting, or wanting, more out of the liaison than a night's passion.

But then he met Dee. Soon everything would change.

Dee was from Dallas, Texas. She was a model in her early twenties, slim and pretty with a stunning smile, and when Mick met her in Tokyo, she had such an effect on him that he promised to get in touch when the Simply Red tour arrived in Texas later in the year. If Dee thought it was the empty promise of a pop star known for his womanizing, she was wrong. Her warm smile and engaging personality lit something in Mick that would inspire not only a meaningful relationship, but also the title and some of the lyrics of Simply Red's next album.

For the next four months, however, Mick would continue to lead the off-stage life he had been living since he had hit the road promoting *Picture Book* and, now, *Men and Women*: another town, another hotel, another woman. Soon after meeting Dee, the band rolled into the Japanese city of Osaka, and not one but two gorgeous young girls wasted no time charming their way into Mick's hotel bedroom.

Fritz and Aziz were chatting in one of the rooms on the same floor when they heard a girl moaning. It got so loud they went into the corridor to investigate; the moaning was coming from Mick's room, and it got so loud that Chris Joyce came out of his room, too, wondering what was going on. They all stood outside the room, giggling, listening to the moaning getting louder and louder. Suddenly they heard the voice of a second girl shouting, as if giving orders, and Mick saying: 'For fuck's sake, shut up making all that noise,' and Fritz, Aziz and Chris stood outside, aching with laughter.

★

After Japan, the band toured New Zealand, where, again, it was a hectic round of promotion, photo shoots and concerts. It was the same in Australia, but it was made worse by the huge distances between cities. In Melbourne, Mick was the target of yet another amorous duo, but this one did not turn out successfully for either Mick or the girls.

Aziz agreed to take care of one of the girls while Mick took the other to his bedroom. But she ended up walking out on Mick, cursing him in most unladylike language. According to Aziz, they were involved in some sexual activity and Mick asked her to go down on him. When she refused, Mick asked her to leave. She did – and later told Aziz what a horrible person she thought Mick was.

Aziz says: 'Most of the band preferred to stay in the hotel after gigs, but Mick always seemed to want to go out to clubs. I was single and wanted to sample the nightlife of every city we visited, so Mick knew he could rely on me to go with him. Before Simply Red, I'd always been on the other side of the fence – not allowed into parties or clubs. But with Mick it was all different. The girls wanted to speak to us. We wouldn't have to do a thing, just sit at the bar and wait for them to come up and talk to us. He could not get enough of women – that's why the band started calling him "Dick Fuck All".'

Mick had always resisted the temptation to have a minder when mixing with the public: he felt confident dealing with any situation, whether it was fans wanting autographs or photographs, or young men looking for trouble. Normally he was charming and cooperative, but he could be blunt, and downright rude, if not in the right frame of mind.

One night in a club in Canada – which Simply Red played after Australia – a young woman came up to him and told him how much she liked him and Simply Red's music. Mick thanked her, then turned away, thinking that was the end of the matter. But the girl took offence. She went back to her boyfriend, complaining, 'I say all that and he ignores me!'

Aziz, who heard the exchange, says that Mick turned round and said, 'Look, I *didn't* ignore you. I said thanks. And that's it. I don't want to talk. All right?'

The girl's boyfriend thought Mick's attitude boorish and arrogant and intervened, threatening to teach him a lesson in manners. Fortunately, another clubber stepped in and defused the situation.

That young admirer would seem to have escaped lightly; Mick is known to have been far ruder to others unlucky enough to catch him in the wrong mood.

Aziz describes him as one of the rudest people he has ever met. 'He has little consideration for people's feelings. I've actually heard him say to fans who have complimented him, "Yeah, all right. I haven't got time at the moment. Will you fuck off." '

This surliness is not always saved for fans; members of his band are known to have suffered, too.

'Most of the time it is difficult to talk to Mick,' says Aziz. 'You'll be chatting to him and he'll pretend you're not there and totally ignore you. You'd say, "Mick, are you listening?", and he'd say, "Yeah, wait a minute, I'm busy." Then he'd not say anything, cut you dead.'

This rough, abrasive side of Mick's nature, inherited from his mother, not his placid, easy-going father, has always been there; he was never the most diplomatic person in the world, and frequently upset people. But the pressure of being the driving force behind Simply Red appears to have made Mick more tetchy, more demanding, and less likely to suffer fools gladly. It is, after all, his voice, his performance, that fills stadia and concert halls all over the world, night after night. It is he, after all, who will be castigated by the press if the show is less than 100 per cent.

Throughout the years of struggle, watching other bands closely, Mick learned that the difference between success and failure often had as much to do with attitude as talent: if the commitment was not there, the chances of success would probably be missing too. Hadn't he witnessed that, so painfully, with The Frantic Elevators? To get where he was, Mick had played it tough, letting his band know who was boss, and he was not the type to let other people's hurt feelings bother him. He had a loving, caring dad, who had taught him to work hard and be prepared to make sacrifices to achieve what he wanted. Mick had worked long and hard to become a major singing star, and one of the sacrifices he had made to ensure he stayed there was his personal popularity. With Simply Red, everybody did what he said; and if they did not like it, or the way they were told, tough shit. If they didn't like it being The Mick Hucknall Show, too bad . . . it was.

According to Aziz, Mick modelled himself on James Brown, off stage as well as on. 'Brown rules his band with an iron fist and so did Mick,' says Aziz. 'He was strict on everything, especially timekeeping. He would fly off the handle if any of the band or crew were late for anything. Everyone was well versed in his tastes and moods, so much so that some of the band went along with what he said, or wanted to do, just for a quiet life. If Mick changed his mind about something, they would change, too. Some of them even began to sound like Mick.

'If I was late for a sound check, for example, the others would say, "You're fucking late – what's your problem?" And I'd think: That's not you talking – it's Mick.

'Once, in Washington, some of the guys and I were due to go to a club to see a highly-respected band, noted for its brilliant brass section. But when Mick said he had gone off the band, one by one the others all came up with reasons why they didn't want to go either.

'Everyone was allowed to like James Brown, Miles Davis, The Rolling Stones and several other artists, but you weren't expected to listen to anyone else. I was in the back of a coach in the States, listening to a well-established guitarist called Larry Carlton, when Mick came up to me. "What's that shit you're listening to?" he said, and turned the tape off. I swallowed it. It wasn't worth causing a problem over. But it was ridiculous not being able to listen to the music I enjoyed.

'I liked rock stuff, but Mick hated it. He even ordered a motif on some speakers to be removed because it was associated with heavy rock bands.

'Musically, he always had the last word, whether he knew what he was talking about or not. That isn't a bad thing, though. A band needs to be organized and somebody has to make decisions. Working with Mick was never easy. You always had the feeling he was looking at how you were playing. You always felt on edge. There were times when he'd have a go at me after a gig for playing too much. He would tell me to stick to the parts I'd been told to play – and nothing else. He told Ian Kirkham that too.

'At one gig Ian and I were enjoying ourselves so much on our solos, we played more than we normally did. It wasn't a case of "Hey, look at us, we're brilliant" – it was a great audience and it was in the spirit of the moment. We were having a great time.

'Afterwards, Mick went mad and shouted at us, "Who said you could do all that? It's not your fucking show – it's *my* show. If I want all that shit, I'll tell you!"

'I just took it, but Ian was so pissed off he walked out of the dressing room, slamming the door. Mick shouted, "Don't fucking slam the door on me," and went out after Ian. I hate to think what he said to him when he caught up with him.

'When Elliot flew out for certain gigs, he would also chip in that I was playing too much – or that my legs were too far apart when I played the guitar solo. You had to remember there was only one guy who could have the limelight – Mick.'

That limelight provided an open-sesame to anything – literally any-thing – Mick wanted. Eager-to-please tour organizers lavished star treat-ment on him, and when something he considered important was not laid on, Mick would go spare. After all, he was the one paying the bills.

His mountain bike, for example, was dear to his heart and he arranged for it to be flown out to every location he visited with the rest of the band's equipment. Sometimes, however, it would go missing – and Mick would explode. 'Where's my fucking bike?' he would scream. Intimidated staff would rush off to look for it.

Mick loved his bike; having not yet passed his driving test, he was still riding it when he went home to Denton. On that tour, Aziz says Mick was known to have ridden his bike around a stadium car park, while hundreds of fans looked on in amazement.

Whether it was the tension a tour generates or just Mick's general bad temper and impatience, Aziz is not sure, but he found that tantrums were never far away. Waiting in transit for a flight from Canada to the United States, for example, Mick wanted to play a machine with a fighter helicopter game, but could not start it.

'Aziz,' he called out. 'Where's the start button on this?'

Aziz went over. 'There it is,' he said, pressing the button.

Caught by surprise, Mick grappled with the joystick, desperately trying to defend the helicopters as they came under fire. But he was hopeless. One helicopter after another was blown up and the game ended with Mick hardly scoring a point.

He chose to attack Aziz instead: 'You fucking idiot,' he shouted. 'Why the fuck did you do that – you've messed everything up. I wasn't ready. I wanted to read the fucking instructions before I played the fucking game, you twat!'

Aziz just stood there, astounded. 'Mick went absolutely mad and bright red in the face,' he says. 'He was over-reacting so much it was ridiculous. I took another coin out of my pocket and handed it to him. "Have another bloody game if it's that important to you," I said. It was the first time I had ever answered him back.'

When Simply Red began the American leg of the tour, Mick got in touch with Dee, the blonde model he had met in Tokyo, and their relationship began to take off. Dee would travel on the tour bus and stay in hotels with Mick; if she was working, she would fly to the band's concert venues between dates.

It was rare for Mick to be spending so much time with one girl. She would be there in the hotels, at concerts, at after-show parties, and during the day they would swim together in the hotel pools. They became increasingly 'lovey-dovey' and would often walk around holding hands and kissing – a stark contrast, the band noted, to the endless stream of one-night stands Mick had had in the past. There was no question about it: Mick was in love.

When Simply Red's world tour finished in New York, Dee was there again; she had become a regular feature of the tour.

Shortly afterwards, Mick flew home to Manchester to prepare for the band's British tour. But it was jinxed from the moment someone cocked up the design of the metal beams holding the light display above the stage at Brixton Academy, the band's first date. Technicians had built the beams too long and the curtains could not be closed on the stage. Mick was furious and flew into one of his worst rages. 'I have never seen anyone so angry in all my life,' says Aziz. 'He went mad and said they were throwing his money away. He was determined to get someone's scalp for messing things up.'

The problems were overcome and the Brixton gigs were a great success, with Mick beginning each show with a stunning solo set of four songs, including 'Holding Back The Years' and 'Lady Godiva's Room', accompanying himself on acoustic guitar. But then Mick went down with flu and had to cancel his Wembley dates, rearranging them for March.

Dee flew over from America to spend Christmas with him and he revelled in the rare opportunity to enjoy a simple, normal relationship on home ground. He took her to Denton to meet his dad and Auntie Nellie, and to the pubs where he had spent so much time while at school and while trying to make it with The Frantic Elevators. He even took her to Barrow-in-Furness to meet Auntie Barbara and other relatives from Reg's side of the family.

Mick could not see enough of Dee. And when the band went back on the road in mid-January – to Brazil – she went, too. Again, the band would see them walking hand-in-hand, shopping together, and sharing intimate dinners. She was even caught in the background in the video for 'I Won't Feel Bad', the single off *Men and Women*, filmed before the Rio gig.

In Rio, Simply Red appeared in the Hollywood Rock Festival, alongside supergroups such as Duran Duran, Simple Minds, The Pretenders and Supertramp, and stole the show despite a tropical rainstorm. They performed in front of 60,000 at Rio's Morumbi Stadium, and nearer 100,000 in Sao Paulo. All the time, Mick and Dee went everywhere together, so very much in love.

*

At the beginning of 1988, Mick was under pressure to plan the next album. *Men and Women* had become Britain's nineteenth best-selling album of the year, and that success had pushed *Picture Book* back into the album charts. Now the record company wanted the next album lined up to maintain the momentum.

Mick had never had difficulty writing lyrics and melodies. He had always got his ideas from what was happening in his life: *Picture Book* depicted those frugal days in Hulme, and the struggle of breaking into the music business; *Men and Women* drew from experiences on the road as a rising pop star.

Now, pondering on a new album, Mick was in love – and it was his love for Dee that inspired the song that gave its title to the third album, *A New Flame*.

From Brazil, Simply Red returned home for a rest before performing the rearranged Wembley concerts. Afterwards the band had a short holiday, then left for Italy, where they would spend most of the rest of the year as tax exiles. They chose Italy because Tony Bowers's Italian wife, Antonella, had recently had a baby and he wanted to be with them both. It was impossible to prepare for an album without him, so it made sense to stay there.

By now, Mick was spending so much time in Italy he decided to buy a home there. He settled not on the archetypal pop star's mansion, but a modest apartment about fifteen miles outside Milan.

*

Being merely a session musician engaged for the concert tour, Aziz was not invited to Italy. He was put on a retainer wage and told to 'stay on ice' until further notice. Knowing the band were writing for a new album, he sat back and waited for the call to be asked to record his guitar sections.

Mick and the band were happy with Stewart Levine's work on *Picture Book* and asked him to produce *A New Flame*. He flew to the studios in Gallarate, near Milan, and spent two weeks discussing the songs planned for the album. It was clear from the lyrics what Mick was experiencing: 'Love Lays Its Tune', 'To Be With You' and 'More', apart from 'A New Flame' itself, all seemed to suggest his love for Dee. It was all so romantic, so much in contrast to the crudeness of some of the songs on *Men and Women*.

*

Aziz continued to wait for the phone to ring. But the decision not to use him again had been made. He was a supremely talented musician, but Mick and his management felt he wasn't right for the band; he didn't fit in with the others, and his guitar playing was a touch too prominent. No one told Aziz. When he called the office, the answer was always the same: 'Just hang on. We'll let you know when you're needed.'

But Aziz would never be needed by Simply Red again.

Stewart Levine, who felt part of his job as record producer was to match musicians with groups, rather like a casting director, had already found someone he felt was the perfect full-time replacement – a good-looking Brazilian named Heitor TP.

Levine had worked with Heitor on an album by one of Brazil's top artists, Ivan Lins, and had been impressed by his warm, enthusiastic personality and his dedication and energy.

In July, Heitor joined Mick and the band on the tiny Caribbean island of Montserrat to work on the third album at Air Studios. The island was chosen by Levine because the tranquillity and lack of distractions were conducive to work and inspiration, but no sooner had they arrived than the band found the heat and humidity conducive to skin rashes, too. The band's personal chef, George Henry Morgan, was told to put them on a strict diet of chicken and fish and lots of vegetables, and no red meat.

Mick had written another two songs with Lamont Dozier – 'You've Got It' and 'Turn It Up' – and one, called 'Enough', with a jazz musician friend of Levine's, Joe Sample. The songs were part of an album Mick felt was good enough to increase his following but not powerful or innovative enough to give him the megastar status he longed for.

Back in England, Aziz was getting impatient. His weekly retainer had been stopped, he was told, because the band were living in Italy to avoid tax. Thinking the band were still there, he would ring So What and ask, 'What's happening? When do I go out?'

He would be told, 'Not yet. We'll let you know.'

Throughout that July, Aziz called several times. The answer was always the same. Then he spoke to his closest friend from the band, Ian Kirkham, who told him the band had been recording the new album in the Caribbean.

Aziz hit the roof.

He stormed into the So What offices and confronted Andy Dodd. 'Look, let's not mess around,' he said. 'Just tell me – I'm not working with the band now, am I?'

Today, he says: 'Andy started a little speech, and said, "Yeah, well, basically, they don't think you get on with the band. And, musically, there are differences."

'That was it. But then he said, "We think you could have a great career as a session musician. We want to manage you."'

Aziz turned down the offer. He felt he could get work on his own. He did not need their help, did not want to split any percentage with them.

He walked out into Princess Street, his eight-month spell with the band over.

In talking about what happened, Aziz is quick to admit it is 'sour grapes' because he lost a well-paid job he feels would have taken him on to a higher level. But he is a straightforward person, who says he had every right to expect to be treated as fairly as he treats people himself.

He says: 'Working with them was weird. It was like the movie business where you have to lick people's shoes to get on to a different level. You have to hang out with the right people, say the right things. You had to learn when to keep your mouth shut, know when to stay out of the way, when not to talk to Mick.

'Mick is a bizarre contradiction. One minute he is very authoritative, making important decisions about the tour and big gigs. The next, he's a vain and spoilt child throwing a tantrum.

'He is very talented. He's a great singer and songwriter, and very professional. He works incredibly hard and gives everything to each performance. All that makes him as good as he is. They are the positive things.

'But, as a person, I think his character stinks. Friends of mine say they love him and I think: You don't know anything about him. You wouldn't think that if you met him. Basically, people get their fingers burned, and if you work in the furnace, like I did, that's what happens.'

★

In August, while in Los Angeles mixing *A New Flame*, Mick revealed to a dentist friend how fascinated he had been, as a fifteen-year-old, by the guitarist Buddy Guy's diamond-studded tooth. When the dentist offered to do the same for him – for free – Mick could not resist. But he did not choose a diamond, he bought a ruby. Far more fitting for the star of Simply Red, he thought.

Mick sat in that dentist's chair for six hours while a small, twisted eye-tooth on his left side was drilled out and replaced by a perfect-fitting false tooth with the gleaming red stone.

The ruby cost him £1,000. That and the time under the dentist's drill was a small price to pay for making a childhood dream come true.

Back in Manchester a few weeks later, Mick bumped into his old pal Gary Hulston's father, Brian. Noticing the ruby, Mr Hulston said, 'What the bloody hell is that in your mouth for?'

Mick laughed. 'When you're a rich bastard like me, Brian, you can afford daft things like that.'

That winter, after doing all the promotional work for the album,

Simply Red toured nine cities in Spain and Portugal and tried out their new material on audiences who had never seen the band live. The reaction was phenomenal; Simply Red had cracked a notoriously tough territory.

Exhausted, Mick went home to Denton for Christmas, happy to catch up with what his dad had been doing and to have a few drinks with Auntie Nellie and the few friends he was still in touch with. He was talking to a crowd of girls in The Britannia Hotel, in the centre of Manchester, one night when a blonde-haired woman nudged him on the shoulder. 'Hi, Michael,' she said.

Not recognizing her, Mick turned away.

'Eh, Michael,' the woman said, nudging him again.

Mick looked again. His look of irritation vanished as he recognized Freda Gagey, one of Auntie Nellie's oldest friends, whose mother had run The Gardener's Arms in Denton. He flung his arms round her.

Today, Freda says: 'I was with a group of girlfriends from a keep-fit class that night, and Michael brought us over a bottle of champagne and sat down for a chat. He said, "It doesn't surprise you where I am, does it, Freda?"

'My mind flashed back to the little boy who stood on my mum's bar, singing to us all so confidently. "No, love, it doesn't," I said. "Not in the least." '

*

Before Mick had time to enjoy the three-bedroom, detached house he had bought near Manchester United's Old Trafford ground, he was back on the road for an eighteen-month world tour. By the time the tour began in Ireland, *A New Flame* was Number 2 in the album charts.

Sadly, the love that had lit Mick's musical fire to write the title song had died. But the talent, singleminded dedication and tireless energy that had driven him from Manchester's backstreets on to the world stage was burning more brightly than ever.

24

It hit home at the end of the *New Flame* tour. Sales of the band's three albums and hit singles, particularly 'Holding Back The Years', totalled more than twenty million worldwide, making Mick a multi-millionaire. But he had paid a heavy price for that enviable status. The whole point of making money was to have the freedom to do what one wanted, but for four years now Mick had been on a gruelling merry-go-round, writing and producing albums and touring the world, with little time for anything except what made that revenue – and it had taken its toll.

He loved making music and performing all over the world. But at the same time, he did not want to fall victim to the superstar syndrome and live a goldfish existence, seeing life only from limousines and luxurious hotel suites. He began worrying not only about how life on the road was affecting him as a person, but also about its effect on him as a songwriter. How could he write fresh, new songs living the same stale life? How could his lyrics mean anything to anyone if he was losing touch with everyday life and everyday people?

In fifteen exhausting months he had been to Eastern Europe, the Far East and India. But now he found himself longing for the home comforts of Manchester and began to realize how much he had missed sleeping in his own bed, popping into one of his favourite local pubs for a pint of good old Northern ale, and strolling around the supermarket. Above all, he wanted to cook his own meals. Everywhere he had been he had lived like a king, fawned over by flunkies anxious to satisfy his every wish in first-class style, and he was fed up with it. He wanted to be on his own, in his own kitchen, cooking for himself, and mopping up his own floor.

After that world tour, Mick's hair mirrored the mess he was in. It had not been cut properly for months and was growing out of control. The hectic on-the-road lifestyle had reduced it to a mass of knots and tangles which took forty minutes to comb, and Mick never seemed to have the time to deal with it.

The hair-style he had had for so long – short at the back and extra long on top – was gone: now it was long all over. But the neglect had left it in such appalling condition that Mick faced having to have it all cut off. He couldn't bear the thought of losing his flowing red trademark, so he asked a friend who worked in one of America's top hair salons to treat it for him. The woman – a top executive – spent hours combing through the knots and repairing the damage, then wove false hair-extensions onto the ends to keep Mick's hair separated and let it grow without knotting.

That was the beginning of the wild Hucknall dreadlocks that are his image today. Since then he has been growing it, much to the amusement of his former-barber dad, who says he would like to give him a decent haircut!

When the tour finally ended in March 1990, Mick decided to take a whole year off, catching up with old friends in Manchester, spending time at his apartment in Milan, going on away-from-it-all holidays he had always dreamed about and could now afford, and generally getting his breath back and enjoying as near a normal life as he could.

He became a familiar figure in the shops and stores around his Manchester home, particularly Safeways, and once more music began blaring out from behind the heavy security shutters on his windows which are kept down all the time, whether he is home or not.

The neighbours have accepted him as a person first, pop star second. Munaver Rasul and his wife, who live next door, often swap spicy foods with Mick, and the millionaire singer is plain Uncle Mick to their six-year-old son Omar. Mick likes the little boy: he has given him Simply Red T-shirts and some of his home-made pizzas, and does not bat an eyelid when Omar slips through a hole in the fence to play in his garden.

'He is a good man and we treat him like a normal person,' says Mr Rasul. 'We get on very well, because we are not the type of people to stare at him through the window or take photographs, even though we can see him cooking in his kitchen, often until 11 o'clock at night.

'The fans have started to come more and more, but generally he has hardly any visitors. When he goes out, he always makes sure his face is covered.'

Enjoying the quiet, reclusive life, Mick went to Milan, happy to stay in his modest but smart two-bedroom apartment, cooking or watching TV and catching up on all the world news he had not been able to absorb in detail while he was on tour; for example the fall of Communism and the Berlin Wall and the idea of Euro-unity.

It was in Milan that Mick learned to drive and, when he passed his test in Britain, finally swapped his much-loved mountain bike for a red Mazda MX5. He bought a similar car in blue for driving in Britain and took great delight in driving to his dad's home in West Park Avenue, along the streets where he had cycled as a schoolboy and student.

The people of Denton who had watched him grow up and had seen the colourful, oddball weirdo turn punk then pop star welcomed him back warmly, although it was their children, of course, who revelled at being bit players in the exciting real-life story of Local Boy Makes Good.

Mick discovered that most of his former mates – mainly from Poly days, not Audenshaw or Tameside Tech – had married and settled down. While he was carving out a stunning career, they were coming to terms with middle-of-the-night feeding times for their children. It was the stark contrast of their lives with his that struck a chord with Mick and inspired him to write the song 'For Your Babies'.

As 1990 drew to a close, Elliot Rashman began negotiating a new record deal for Simply Red. In the industry, his volatile temper and bullying have earned him the nickname 'The Shouter', but for all his political games, paranoia and often petty behaviour, he has accomplished all he has set out to achieve for Mick, the band and his company.

In 1985 he had jubilantly photocopied Elektra's cheque for £60,000 and showed it off to all and sundry, boasting, 'We've done it, we've done it.' Five years later, he concluded the deal for Simply Red's fourth album, *Stars*, and felt less need to shout about the advance. It was for precisely one million pounds.

Elliot had so much wanted to be a big wheel in pop management that Dave Rowbotham, the mickey-taking guitarist in the embryonic Simply Red, dubbed him 'Harry Paranoid, Top Rock Manager'.

Dave was later murdered in a drugs-related axe attack, but if he were alive today he would appreciate the irony of his joke. For the pale-faced, curly-haired Jewish wheeler-dealer is indeed a Top Rock Manager, if not one of the biggest and most powerful people in the music business. Whether the money, fame and prestige have made him less paranoid is questionable.

Certainly, like Mick, he has a cold, calculating streak and lacks sentiment when it comes to deciding what is best for the band. After the *New Flame* tour, Tony Bowers, his old pal from The Mothmen, was dumped from Simply Red amid bitter acrimony, and went home to his Italian wife in Milan, seething.

And when the band got together in April 1991 to begin recording *Stars*, drummer Chris Joyce got the elbow in typically cruel and cowardly style. No one had the guts, much less the courtesy, to tell Chris that his services were no longer required. Elliot chose to let his former flatmate fly to Paris to begin recording, before discovering that a Japanese drum programmer named Gota had been brought in as his replacement behind his back. Chris was in an impossible situation, and a few weeks later was out of Simply Red.

In May 1991, ten of the songs Mick had written during his year off were recorded at a beautiful sixteenth-century villa with a studio on the outskirts of Venice. Mick knew the album was his best work to date. So did Elliot: after listening to the demo tape, he described it as 'the greatest moment of my life'.

Nothing, however, could have prepared either of them for the sensational response later that year. Firstly, on 9 September 'Something Got Me Started' was released, and two weeks later burst into the charts at Number 16. Then, on 30 September the album shot straight to Number 1, selling an average of 100,000 copies a week in the build-up to Christmas. *Stars* was in the shops for just thirteen weeks, but it was the best-selling album of 1991, outstripping even Michael Jackson's *Dangerous*.

The critical acclaim followed. Simply Red won several Brits awards, notably joint best band with KLF, and, in the spring of 1992, Mick won the Ivor Novello Award for Songwriter Of The Year – a music industry tribute Mick considered the most important accolade of his life, and one he truly valued.

Then came another world tour of 150 venues, including two triumphant gigs at Wembley Stadium in the summer, and the realization of the third ambition Mick had revealed to flatmate John Bradshaw eight years before – a performance in front of 50,000 at Lancashire Cricket Club's ground at Old Trafford.

By the time the *Stars* tour ended in Birmingham in February 1993 – and Mick and the band had won two more BRIT awards – the album had sold more than seven million worldwide. It was Britain's biggest-selling CD ever, with sales of more than three million. Combined sales of the first three albums top twelve million.

The six-year-old with the curly red hair who sang to his friends on a garden wall had performed on every major stage in the world.

The schoolboy who stole lead to pay for his illegal pints of ale had enough money to buy all the pubs he once drank in.

The shy teenager the girls thought too ugly to kiss was now bedding some of the world's most glamorous women.

The penniless student who went into debt because he believed in a song was hiring his own musicians and recording in the Caribbean.

And the punk who once took the bus to gigs was now travelling in limousines and staying in five-star hotels.

By any stretch of the imagination, it is a stunning success story of determination, driving ambition and unshakeable self-belief, made all the more poignant by Mick's one-parent upbringing. He battled to make something of himself without a mother's influence – which many would consider a crippling handicap. But it is also possible that Maureen's early exit from his life is precisely – and ironically – *why* Mick made it.

Certainly, grammar school seems to be the key. Having settled into a cosy routine with his dad, being fussed over by Nellie Spike's family and later by June Shaw, Mick was shaken not only by Audenshaw's strict routine, but also by being so out of his depth academically. Rebelling more from misery and disenchantment than idle waywardness, he was lost, unhappy and, more importantly, unsure what to do with his life. He turned to the one attribute that gave him confidence and made him less of a misfit – his voice.

If his mother had been around throughout his childhood, it is likely Mick's life would have been different. A forceful, dominant and materialistic personality, she would probably have pressurized her son into getting his head down and studying for a job guaranteed to pay well.

As it was, Mick chose to chase a career in the notoriously rough and tough music industry, and the ambition and singleminded determination he inherited from his mother drove him to the top. His strength of character, dedication and tireless energy pulled him through the difficult days and made him a winner in a world of also-rans.

Most people who make it to the top in any profession have a ruthless streak, and Mick is no exception. The cold, tough and unemotional side to his personality, illustrated in his insensitivity to people no longer useful to him, has made him enemies in the business. This seems to be born out of a blinkered pursuit of excellence, rather than out of malice, although that is no consolation to the casualties who have fallen by the wayside on Mick's route to the top – the musicians discarded because they did not fit in with the blueprint for the success of The Mick Hucknall Show.

One of these musicians says that Mick 'has no appreciation of the people who have helped to make him famous'. But Mick has not forgotten some of the people who were close to him when he was a nobody. For Alf and Nellie Spike's golden wedding, for example, he laid on a surprise 'This Is Your Life'-style champagne party for them at a Manchester restaurant. And after Alf died, Mick introduced 'Holding Back The Years' at a gig in the city's G-Mex centre by looking up and saying, 'This one's for you, Alf.'

Unfortunately Mick has earned a reputation as one of the rudest men in the music industry. But that has nothing to do with his rise to megastar status, his bank balance, or a sudden belief in his own publicity. Mick has *always* been arrogant; he has always been Joe Blunt, and to hell with whoever he upsets.

What is refreshing is that, thanks to his father's down-to-earth approach to life and steadying influence when it mattered, Mick is handling his fame and riches well. Reg, who knows about poverty, brought him up to have a healthy respect for money, and Mick has responded well. With millions to spend on any hedonistic lifestyle he might care to choose, he has resisted all the archetypal pop star extravagances, preferring to invest in two modest homes and two relatively inexpensive cars. Typically, he was more concerned about his dad, whom he adores, but Reg turned down the offer of money to move out of his two-bedroomed semi in Denton, and when it comes to holidays, is happier with a cut-price deal in Tenerife than five-star luxury in the tropics.

Music has always been Mick's motivation, not money. What he does on stage is what matters to him, not what people think of him off it: you take him for what he is, or you don't take him at all.

People may find the insensitivity and arrogance hard to swallow. But it is impossible not to respect the man for what he has achieved, and admire the talent and drive that have helped him do so.

Index

2) Aspects of life and personality
appearance: as a child, 8, 17; as a
schoolboy, 24, 37, 38–9, 41–2, 54,
66; as a student, 77, 91, 92, 115;
later references, 147, 158, 161, 199,
215–16
art, 49–50, 65, 66, 97–8, 105, 153–4
audiences, hostile, 100, 101, 102–3,
111–12
burgled, 129–30, 137–8
Butlin's holiday camp, 63–4
cadet force, 50–1
car, 216–17
diet, 120
drinking, 41, 42, 45, 54–6, 61–2, 68–9
drugs, 86, 87
economics, 65–6
football, 44
girlfriends, and disappointments, 23–
4, 35, 42–3, 44–5, 45–7, 62–4, 68,
69, 78, 120–1, 135, 176, 195, 199,
204, 205, 206, 209–11
does impressions, 43–4, 69–70
intelligent, 8, 24, 25, 48, 54
and his mother, 19–20, 27, 31, 33, 99,
134, 195–8, 219
mountain bike, 208–9, 216
his name: abbreviated to Mick, 10, 37;
in capitals, 23; Red, 153–4, 180–1
newspaper round, 40, 53–4
personal hygiene, 120
personality: as a child, 17, 19–20, 21;
as a schoolboy, 23, 24–5, 26, 29–
31, 41, 43, 45, 49, 54, 66; as a
student, 77, 93, 94, 98, 103, 114–
15, 122; later references, 159–60,
176, 183, 185, 187, 193–4, 198–9,
200, 206–7, 208–9, 213, 214, 219–
20
pool-playing, 68
ruby in his tooth, 213
run over, 28
smoking, 42, 44, 52–3, 56, 64
stealing lead, 57–9
tattoo, 60–1
voice, 14, 21, 34, 40, 64, 98, 112, 117,
120, 146, 147, 150–1
waiting at table, 71–2, 85, 86, 102
Hucknall, Reg (Mick's father), 1–2, 15,
220

meets Maureen Gibbons, their
marriage, 1–2, 3–13
brings up Michael, with help, 15, 17,
18–20, 22, 23, 26–7, 36
divorces Maureen, 32
life with Mick in West Park Avenue,
54, 61, 61–2, 64, 70, 71, 92, 99, 120
Mick leaves home, 127–8
proud of Mick's achievement, 195
and the reappearance of Maureen,
196–7, 197
mentioned, 210, 216
Hucknall, Ronald (Reg's brother), 15
Hucknall family, 4, 15, 31, 210
Hulme, 128, 129
Hulston, Brian, 213
Hulston, Gary, 37, 51–3, 66, 73, 74–5,
76, 79–80, 82, 83
Hulston, Jenny, 82
'Hunchback Of Notre Dame', 115–16,
128

'I See Nothing And Everything', 116
'I Want To Hold Your Hand', 22
'I Won't Feel Bad', 210
Ibrahim, Aziz, 200, 201, 203–4, 205,
206, 206–7, 207–8, 209, 210, 211,
211–13
Inman, Billy, 59, 60–1
International, The, 183, 188–9
Ireland, 214
Italy, 193–4, 204, 211
Ivor Novello Award for Songwriter Of
The Year, 218

Jackson, Michael, 218
Jamming magazine, 183
Japan, 204–5
Jaundrell, Keith, 53–4
Jaundrell, Sylvia, 53, 54
'Jericho', 174, 195
Joanne (girlfriend), 176, 195
Joe Stalin's Red Star Band, 84–5, 86,
87–9, 90
John the Postman, 101
Jolly Hatters, The, 95
Jones, Barbara, 34
Jones, Derek and Audrey, 40
Jones, Gwynn, 119
Joyce, Chris, 146, 169, 171, 172, 175,
205, 217–18